BROKEN CODE

The Exploitation of DNA

Marc Lappé, Ph.D.

Sierra Club Books SAN FRANCISCO

To my mother and father,
JEANNETTE and PAUL LAPPÉ

The Sierra Club, founded in 1892 by John Muir, has devoted itself to the study and protection of the earth's scenic and ecological resources—mountains, wetlands, woodlands, wild shores and rivers, deserts and plains. The publishing program of the Sierra Club offers books to the public as a nonprofit educational service in the hope that they may enlarge the public's understanding of the Club's basic concerns. The point of view expressed in each book, however, does not necessarily represent that of the Club. The Sierra Club has some fifty chapters coast to coast, in Canada, Hawaii, and Alaska. For information about how you may participate in its programs to preserve wilderness and the quality of life, please address inquiries to Sierra Club, 530 Bush Street, San Francisco, CA 94108.

Library of Congress Cataloging in Publication Data

Lappé, Marc.
  Broken code.

  Bibliography: p.
  Includes index.
  1. Genetic engineering—Social aspects.   2. Recombinant DNA—Social aspects.   3. Genetic engineering.
  4. Recombinant DNA.   I. Title.
  QH442.L38   1985   303.4'83   84-22190
  ISBN 0-87156-835-7

Research for this book was supported in part by NEH/NSF grant number 1SP-8114338. The views expressed are those of the author.

Jacket design by **Paul Bacon**
Book design by **Rodelinde Albrecht**

Printed in the United States of America
10 9 8 7 6 5 4 3 2 1

Contents

APPENDICES

List of Figures and Tables

Preface

My interest in the social implications of science dates back to the days of unrest in 1969 and 1970 on the Berkeley campus of the University of California when the Vietnam War forced many basic science and postdoctoral students to question the ultimate uses of the science we were learning to do. In 1971, this interest and growing concern led me to leave my work in basic science and join the Institute of Society, Ethics and Life Sciences to study the link between ethics and science more closely.

The group I directed considered genetic engineering a good model for exploring the ethical dilemmas posed by pure science, but we were put off by the popular notion of "cloning a human being" and creating "superhumans" through genetic engineering. These futuristic eventualities appeared to be more journalistic sensationalism than the focus of serious debate. The question of how science would be used seemed more pressing than what scientific data or techniques would be uncovered.

We decided instead to look at the more imminent problems inherent in mass genetic screening and genetic counseling. We were fascinated by the issues of compulsion and privacy—e.g., could the state legitimately conscript adults or newborns into screening programs for genetic disease or carrier-detection tests for which no therapeutic alternatives existed? We would also consider the probity of having genetic counselors act as agents of the state in advising couples at risk for genetic disease. But most of us doubted that genetic engineering was on the near horizon.

Our educated guess at where the action would be was flat wrong. And all bets were off in 1972, when a group of Stanford scientists discovered how to transfer genes directly from one organism to another, making science fact out of science fiction. The images that had lived only in the collective imagination of the public were now on the laboratory bench. The newly acquired capacity to restructure life and harvest genetically determined commodities produced by virtually any genome on earth posed awesome problems of priorities and risks.

For me, our group's discussions of the issues involved with genetic screening and counseling prepared the soil for the more intense debates to follow about applied genetic engineering. It was clear by the mid-1970s that recombinant DNA would provide the genetic markers for mass genetic screening, prenatal diagnosis, and genetic counseling. It was therefore a surprise when the first issue to be joined was a purely pragmatic one: Could any of this research be done safely?

This concern was taken seriously by all involved. To the enduring credit of the scientific community, the most avid recombinant-DNA researchers themselves issued guidelines for their own work and proscribed whole categories of potentially risk-laden research. The most pressing issue of the day (circa 1974) became whether or not the technique of transferring genetic material posed a hazard to life on earth. It is now fairly clear that a genetic apocalypse is not upon us. In fact, the issue of biohazards dissipated over the last decade, until now, in 1984, an entire recombinant-DNA industry is thriving in the Western world.

The ethical issues scoped out by the earliest critics of the field—myself included—have paled with time and experience. The biohazards of recombinant DNA perceived as most immediate—those in the laboratory—have largely gone the way of anxiety over adverse reactions to polio shots. Now we must be concerned with the much more complex ecological problems posed by the intentional release of laboratory-generated genetic variants and the priorities being chosen by ever more powerful biotechnology conglomerates.

The still valid concerns of a few academic scientists that the purity of their endeavor might be trammeled by the commercialization of their techniques have been all but lost in the helter-skelter jockeying for capital. In the first three years of the 1980s, industrial corporations plied literally dozens of the best universities in the Western world for exclusive patents and the most lucrative research arrangements. Even where these liaisons involved nothing more than "first-look" rights at new university research data, many took it as a sign that innocence in the biological sciences was being irretrievably lost, just as it had been in physics forty years ago.

The rights and wrongs of these choices may never be fully parsed out. It is extraordinarily difficult to argue dispassionately about an issue that touches the very cornerstone of life. On the one hand, the field of recombinant DNA appears no different from that of any budding technological innovation. Money is to be made and patents received, and universities and industry alike are to share in the wealth and wisdom. However, the fundamental power of this particular scientific breakthrough is so immense and relates so directly to the public weal that a failure to recognize the public's right to some say in its application is short-sighted at best—and dangerously monopolistic at worst. Within a few years we will have to cope with a new genetic–industrial complex that will make decisions affecting the entire world community.

We have an awesome new tool in our hands that can be used for good or ill—or merely wasted on frills and trivia. It can provide a lens for looking at the basic makeup of our genetic heritage in ways previously unimagined just ten years ago. If we wish, we can resurrect whole genetic sequences of extinct species. Or we can use recombinant DNA to make a better potato chip. But the choices go deeper than that between the sublime and the ridiculous.

Recombinant techniques allow the most inquisitive of scientists to probe the innermost secrets of our personal heredity. These discoveries can help us or harm us. If our employers want to hedge their bets on our capacity to work long and hard at stressful jobs, the recombinant-DNA scientist could provide probes or monoclonal antibodies to reveal evidence of cracks in our genetic resilience. If society wants to predicate Medicaid or other forms of health benefits on our likelihood of costing the system X dollars in thirty years, the new genetics could enable us to anticipate the most crippling or disabling diseases virtually from birth. Cancer and many dreaded diseases of old age are likewise subject to a wholly new assault, with immunotoxin magic bullets that even Paul Ehrlich, the father of the antibiotic era, could not have imagined. And if nuclear war should ever really become unthinkable (God willing), then recombinant DNA offers some startling and equally repugnant alternatives in the guise of biological-warfare agents of astonishing toxicity. A still greater impact can be expected from the role of the genetic revolution in agriculture.

An immediate question of special interest to me as an expert in public health policy is not, How might the new genetics be hazardous to our health? but, *Whose* health will the new genetics serve? Will only the chronic diseases of the developed world—our heart disease/cancer/stroke triad—be seen as the exclusive financial targets for a health care industry based on recombinant DNA? What about the 300 million people with malaria or the almost equal number with trypanosomiasis in the Third World?

What about the priorities that are now being set? Will we continue to develop vaccines for crowded and poorly husbanded animal populations in high-tech feedlots, or can mechanisms be found to make it attractive to do the same for the masses of humanity in the *favelas* and ghettos of the world? And when we do make the dramatic breakthroughs in customizing new plants, will they be sold on an ability-to-pay basis, or allowed to be released through multinational agencies and philanthropic organizations? Who is to say? And will we have any say once plant crop DNA becomes a commercial commodity, to be bought and sold on the open market much as cocoa or coffee futures?

Today the major issue of recombinant DNA is *not* whether we will produce a new Frankenstein or create ecological monstrosities, but how we will use this technique most wisely. Any wisdom to be had is fast being obscured by the lure of the dollar sign.

Recombinant DNA really is the millennium in biology, just as the discovery of nuclear fission was the millennium in physics. The power to do good or ill from both techniques is virtually limitless. We need not exaggerate our concern about what a few mad scientists may inadvertently create in a laboratory or release into the environment, but we must hold accountable what whole industries or governments will choose to create with this newfound power.

The precept of *Broken Code* is that DNA is not merely a commercial curiosity, but something much more fundamental. Some of these arguments were put forward in the debate over whether or not we should allow patenting of this essential molecule. But since the first round of that debate was lost, the methods for producing DNA and its variants, as well as any of the novel rearrangements of the material itself, are now fair game at the Patent Office. Therefore we must now ask how we should encourage the best—and discourage the worst—uses of this material.

Acknowledgments

I want to thank those in the biotechnology industry who gave of their time and consented to be interviewed for this book, notably J. Leslie Glick of Genex Corporation; Ron Cape of Cetus Corporation; David Martin, Jr., of Genentech, Inc.; Tony Allison of Syntex Corporation; and Peter Carlson of Zoecon Corporation.

I also want to acknowledge my appreciation for my friends and colleagues who encouraged this effort and reviewed parts of the manuscript. In particular I am grateful to Sheldon Krimsky of Tufts University for a careful and detailed reading and critique of a draft of the book, and to Burke Zimmerman and Charles Weiner for providing research materials and offering valuable suggestions and critiques of its content.

I am especially appreciative of the confidence and commitment of Sierra Club Books and my editor, Danny Moses. The especially careful copy editing of Ms. Suzanne Lipsett was an inestimable aid to the production of the book. The secretarial assistance of Alice Murata is also gratefully acknowledged.

During the writing of this book I was supported in part by a Sustained Development Award from the National Science Foundation and the National Endowment for the Humanities. The views expressed in *Broken Code* are not necessarily those of the funding agencies.

Finally, I am extremely grateful—and fortunate—to have had the loving support and encouragement of my wife, Nichol Lovera, who painstakingly and unstintingly gave of her time and editorial skills to critique the entire book, and offered invaluable suggestions for improvements to the text.

While all of these persons contributed to the effort of writing the book, I, of course, take the responsibility for its technical accuracy, content, and viewpoint.

INTRODUCTION

The Quest for Genetic Control

We are on the crest of the first scientific revolution since Einstein reset the rules of nuclear physics. Biologists have decoded the secret language of the gene and are fast learning to control it. In breaking the code of life, we have opened up a previously closed system. We can now add genetic information to the flow of life on earth—or we can subtract it. We can plumb the most secret depths of that information. And we can use our new knowledge to shape our own destiny in unprecedented ways.

The new science of recombinant DNA promises humankind the ability to control what genetic information is carried into the future. Scientists are capitalizing on this newfound power by selectively culling desirable genes, harvesting their products, and reshaping whole species that have particular commercial interest. If we are lucky, there will be at least as many astounding successes as pitfalls in this new revolution. But no one can doubt that we are on the cusp of the most risky and adventurous quest since our species began to cultivate crops and domesticate animals.

Subduing the Earth

From the beginning, our dominion over the planet has depended on an implicit understanding of the heritable qualities of domesticated plants and animals. Human beings have controlled these qualities by manipulating genetic characteristics—whether they were aware of the existence of such characteristics or not. In so doing, people created the sciences of agriculture and animal husbandry.

We know that much of the variation we see in the natural world is due to genetic factors, and that much of this variation is threatened by human efforts to shape the natural world to human needs. The *Endangered Species Handbook* lists 194 animal species that have become extinct since A.D. 1600—most of them since the Industrial Revolution.[1] Another 617 species of mammals, birds, reptiles, and amphibians are currently threatened with extinction. "Monocultures" of single, genetically homogeneous crops and highly inbred livestock threaten to reduce the repository of genetic variation that is the mainstay of evolutionary survival for still other groups of plants and animals.

Ironically, it was a desire to further the understanding of the origins of this seemingly unlimited variation that first stimulated Gregor Mendel's floral studies in his monastery garden. Now, just 150 years later, recombinant-DNA genetics has been used to reshape those self-same peas and petunias through controlled manipulation of their genetic makeup and the addition of foreign genetic material.

From Mendel's time through the work of Thomas Hunt Morgan, who, at the turn of the century, first intuited the chromosomal location of genetic information, we have acquired a remarkable understanding of the material basis for heredity. At each turn in the evolution of our knowledge of our genetic past, we have increased our ability to control our genetic future. With Mendel's work on the common garden pea, we learned how to systematically cross-pollinate plants with aesthetic or commercial value. With Morgan's work, we learned how to predict where certain characteristics would appear from generation to generation.

Today's venture is different from these past interventions in both kind and degree. For the first time since we selected plants or livestock for qualities we only darkly suspected would be faithfully transmitted, we have the power to systematically select genetic properties without waiting for the laborious and time-consuming propagation of the species in question. Within this decade we will begin to modify the genetic makeup of plants and animals at will. We will be able to select, design, and mass produce almost any biologically defined substance in commercial quantities. And we will know enough about the genetic basis of inherited diseases or susceptibilities to disease to anticipate and perhaps thwart biological destiny itself. We will be able to engineer human cells and return them to the body and thereby arrest or cure previously fatal genetic diseases.

The advent of these developments raises the most basic questions of science. Who will control the fruits of this new scientific knowledge? Who will direct the ends to which new techniques will be applied? Where will we draw the line between the rights of individuals to control newly constructed life forms and those of the public to have access to them? Who will bear the cost of developing the most essential technologies, and who will reap the benefits? Finally, how will we apportion the risks and burdens of the first failures that will undoubtedly dog the heels of progress?

These are just some of the most pressing questions posed by the new science of recombinant DNA. Of even greater concern for some is the almost godlike power that this knowledge seems to confer on the scientific community. It is an index of the truly humbling power of these new technologies that they have inspired both awe and dread in the public mind. And it is no accident that organized religion sees more of a threat than a promise in this newly acquired power. In one sense, scientists have indeed taken on the biblical power to shape and control life on earth.

The purposes of this book are to put this power into a new perspective, to defuse fears where they appear unwarranted, to highlight previously unrecognized perils, and to investigate the promise and potential of genetic engineering to generate good. In all this the book takes a new tack, critiquing not so much the development of the basic science of recombinant DNA as its applications. For it will be our choices as to how we use this unprecedented biological tool on which we will be judged.

Deoxyribonucleic Acid—DNA

The vehicles for our new dominion are deoxyribonucleic acid, or DNA, and more recently its congener ribonucleic acid, or RNA. These are the two cornerstones of the genetic material of every living organism on earth. It is through the faithful replication of DNA molecules that hereditary information is transferred from generation to generation, and through the incorporation of chance errors in this replication that new variation is created.

By successfully recombining the DNA of organisms widely separated in evolutionary time, we now know that the instructions carried in the DNA molecule are essentially interchangeable among all the planet's species. We can fuse the protoplasts of plants of diverse origin, creating in a few minutes new genetic combinations that plant breeders previously needed years to do. Or we can insert portions of the genetic material of higher organisms into simple bacterial cells, in which the new "recombined" DNA will produce previously inaccessible biological products. In the words of scientist and historian George Pontecorvo, "We [have] come to the concept that the whole biosphere on Earth shares a common gene pool. A new view of the unity of life on Earth becomes imperative."[2] For Pontecorvo, this realization led to a renewed sense of reverence and awe. But for many others in the newly emerging biotechnology industry based on recombinant DNA, expansion of our power over genetic systems is a tantalizing invitation for blind exploitation.[3]

The temptation is understandable. Manipulations that used to be cumbersome, uncertain, and not much more than educated guesswork are in principle routine. The possibilities for genetic manipulation are protean—for example:

- Controlling the genetic basis for photosynthesis and nitrogen fixation, the critical step in converting atmospheric nitrogen into usable plant food

- Developing new and safe vaccines against previously uncontrollable parasitic viral and bacterial infections

- Breaking the genetic code of rare or endangered species

- Re-creating the genetic makeup of portions of the genome of extinct species

- Synthesizing medically valuable human hormones and blood proteins

- Developing diagnostic probes and antibodies for important human diseases

Some of these achievements appear imminent and readily achievable—and seem to be virtually unmitigated blessings. Others pose hidden traps for the unwary and overambitious. One development that appears eminently reasonable is the use of new microbial species to digest our sewage or detoxify our wastes. But even here, some outside the commercial sector are beginning to question the environmental ramifications that might accompany the widespread release of these or related organisms into the environment.[4]

Others believe that we are on the verge of being able to clone (make genetically identical) highly valuable livestock.[5] But how far should we extend this technique, which by its nature may further reduce the genetic diversity of our herds? (One major artificial insemination program faltered when it was discovered that a heavily utilized prize bull carried a previously unappreciated recessive deleterious mutation!)

It is the fate of many of the most important and fundamental discoveries of science that when they open new avenues of research, they simultaneously open new avenues for generating great societal good or evil. We saw this dichotomous evolution in the progress of nuclear energy. Now we have the opportunity to shape a new revolution— the biotechnology revolution—before it takes a wrong turn.

The last decade has seen an astounding growth of so-called genetic-engineering firms. More than a hundred of the Fortune 500 companies have already committed substantial amounts of investment capital into these fledgling companies, heralding a major new area of exploitation. Worldwide, nearly 2,500 companies are exploring genetic-engineering techniques to produce feedstuffs,[6] energy products, fragrances, pharmaceuticals, diagnostic reagents—and almost any imaginable biological substance with sufficient economic value to warrant commercialization.

According to a major historian of this new science, Tufts University Professor Sheldon Krimsky, this explosive new growth should be viewed cautiously because it is occurring without direct regulation. Krimsky is concerned about its likely impact on human affairs, predicting that "to judge from past experiences with similarly transforming technologies . . . the developments in biotechnology will have mixed outcomes."[7]

Other academicians have been concerned about the lack of public involvement in setting priorities for the biotechnology industry.[8] Indeed, this is one of the focuses of this book. Unlike other major technologies, such as nuclear energy or hydroelectricity, neither the public nor its representatives have been given meaningful regulatory authority or input into biotechnological decisions—many of which will have long-lasting impacts. Although Congress is considering the establishment of an oversight committee, the existing structure for regulating biotechnology research and development in the industrial sector is entirely voluntary.[9] And the Environmental Protection Agency, to which we might look for leadership in controlling the environmental impact of new substances, must share its oversight with numerous other agencies, including the Food and Drug Administration, the Department of Food and Agriculture, and the National Institutes of Health.

Presently, it is unclear how and if the public is to have any say in the development of this industry, except perhaps in exercising the downstream power of the purse. This is unfortunate, and perhaps will prove to be tragic, as many of the industry's short-term objectives may be inconsistent with the public good over the long term. Whatever is done with recombinant-DNA-based biotechnologies, the choices made now by various firms and their boards of directors will undoubtedly carry unforeseen "opportunity costs." What the recombinant-DNA industry selects to study or produce now necessarily limits what it may choose to develop later. Without public involvement or a means to map out the broad picture, hundreds of economically based decisions in the microcosm of each competing company may stifle the grand plans to which some biotechnologies lend themselves so admirably. Vaccines to combat the major scourges of the developing world, new energy sources, and novel conversion schemes for the by-products of development may all go wanting for lack of the broad view.

In an ideal world, those who ultimately benefit or suffer from a new technology would have some say in its evolution. With the present system of proprietary secrets and patentable inventions, it is the venture capitalists and their corporate partners who control a technology's evolution. As University of California, Berkeley, professor Leon Wofsy has observed, "The actual shaping of the 'biofuture' seems to be the exclusive province of the marketplace."[10] And why, you may properly inquire, should this industry be different from any other?

We will see that response to this question must be conditioned on two realities. The first is that recombinant-DNA techniques have enjoyed almost unprecedented support from the public. Most of the fundamental techniques were developed with public funds. Basic discoveries, and in some cases key cell cultures, were taken directly from public to private institutions.[11] Second, some progenitors of the basic techniques justified the freedom of their inquiry on the promise of public benefits that were to accrue to humanity as a whole from their application. In a sense, the biotechnology companies which were the immediate beneficiaries of rDNA science have a covenant with the public to use this knowledge well. The fact that nonessential or even nefarious uses of recombinant DNA have become more rather than less plentiful (a point discussed in Chapters 8 and 9) suggests that this promise may not be kept.

The words *broken code* thus carry a double meaning for the biotechnology revolution: breaking the genetic code made the flowering of that revolution possible, but the moral code of scientific inquiry may be in jeopardy. I believe that basic scientists have an implicit contract with society to use their freedom to advance knowledge—and, where appropriate, to use that knowledge to do good.

To evaluate the ethical argument for scientific responsibility, we must understand the social function of science. Conversely, to evaluate the claim that biotechnology has some special obligation to serve the public good, we must understand both its origins and its capabilities. It makes no sense to hope that biotechnology can solve the world's parasite burden, for example, if there is no possibility that it can be applied in immunization or other eradication schemes. To clarify these matters in this book, I both review the capabilities and limitations of biotechnology and weigh the reasonableness of corporate objectives and priorities. I explore how current and future developments are likely to affect the biosphere generally and humankind particularly. Finally, I examine the case for these enterprises serving broader societal goals.

This book addresses the complexities of making wise and judicious choices about a technology with a panoply of potential uses. Its timeliness is underscored by the realization that the two previous concerns about recombinant-DNA have been almost fully aired: (1) the hazards of the research per se are now recognized not to be as great as previously thought, and (2) the possible distortion of academic values by the wholesale departure of many skilled faculty—and many of the most gifted graduate students—to the corporate world, once predicted, is now a fait accompli.

The cat is out of the bag. Biotechnology is operating at full bore. We are in a time when initial warnings about potential risks must be considered history. Whatever risks may be carried by full-scale research and development will be seen in the real world rather than the small-scale pilot models some of us had initially hoped would precede wide-scale development. The wholesale collaboration of entrepreneur and research scientists has been officially sanctioned, and the line between pure research (and researcher) and applied research is forever blurred.

This book, then, is about the urgent need to frame priorities for the burgeoning recombinant-DNA industry and to anticipate where its developments are most likely to help—or hurt—us.

Notes

1. G. Nilsson, *The Endangered Species Handbook* (Washington, D.C.: The Animal Welfare Institute, 1983).

2. G. Pontecorvo, "Reminiscences on Genetics: From Mendelism to Recombinant DNA," *Current Science* 52 (1983): 382–390.

3. Some sense of the public perception of the exploitability of this new technology can be seen in popular accounts: "DNA Can Build Companies Too," *Fortune* (June 16, 1980); "On the Brink of Altering Life," *The New York Times Magazine* (February 17, 1980), pp. 16–80; "Shaping Life in the Lab," *New York Times* (March 9, 1981), pp. 50–59; "DNA's New Miracles," *Newsweek* (March 17, 1980); "Weaving New Life in Lab," *Life* (May 1980); "Cloning Gold Rush Turns Basic Biology into Big Business," *Science* 208 (May 16, 1980): 688–692; and "Biotechnology: Research that Could Remake Industries," *Chemical Week* (October 8, 1980): 23–38.

4. This issue has been discussed by M. Alexander, "Ecological Constraints on Genetic Engineering," paper given at the Seattle Conference on Genetic Control of Environmental Pollutants, August 31–September 3, 1983.

5. C. L. Marhert, "Cloning Mammals—The Current Reality and Future Prospects," *Theriogenology* 21 (1984): 60–67.

6. *The International Directory of Biotechnology* for 1984 lists 2,484 different companies in the Western world that participate in or support biotechnology.

7. See S. Krimsky, preface to the prospectus for an *International Network on the Social Impact of Biotechnology* (Medford, Mass.: Tufts University, 1983).

8. See in particular the article by M. L. Goggin, "The Life Sciences and the Public: Is Science Too Important to Be Left to the Scientists?" *Politics and the Life Sciences* 3 (August, 1984): 28–40.

9. See S. Krimsky, *Genetic Alchemy: The Social History of the Recombinant DNA Controversy* (Cambridge, Mass.: MIT Press, 1983) for an authoritative review.

10. L. Wofsy, "The Life and Sciences of the Public: Is the New Biology Too Important to Be Left to the Entrepreneurs?" *Politics and the Life Sciences* 3 (August, 1984): 65–68.

11. This was apparently the case for some early lines of recombinants developed at the University of California, San Francisco, in the mid-1970s that found their way to Genentech. A sealed, out-of-court settlement in which no blame was assigned was subsequently made between these two entities.

CHAPTER 1

Discovery
and Regulation

Discovery

The search for DNA was comparable in its ambitiousness to the medieval quest for the philosopher's stone. The seekers of DNA were looking for no less than the material that controls all the biological properties of life. Not until the mid-1920s did it become acceptable to think that a *chemical* might be responsible for controlling the basic biological properties of an organism. Credit for this concept belongs to the pathologist Frederick Griffith, a medical officer in the British Ministry of Health.

The work that was to prove revolutionary began inauspiciously enough. In 1927, Griffith observed a curious phenomenon in one of his pneumonia patients. Instead of finding a single bacterium, as was the dogma of his day, Griffith discovered that his patient carried multiple types of pneumonia-causing organisms *(Streptococcus pneumoniae)*.

More curiously to Griffith, his patient's type of pneumonia appeared to change over the course of the disease. Griffith's intellectual leap was to design a test of the idea that one type of pneumococcus bacterium could change into another.

He devised an experiment in 1928 that entailed injecting mixtures of disease-producing (virulent) and nondisease-producing (avirulent) cells into mice. Griffith injected test animals with what was presumably an innocuous mixture of dead virulent cells and live avirulent ones. To his amazement, animals receiving the mix of presumptively benign microorganisms (plus *dead* lethal ones) died almost as promptly as those receiving the live, disease-causing cells. Though dead, the virulent cells had conferred their lethal biological property on normally nonpathogenic pneumococcal bacteria.[1]

This observation stimulated a frenzy of activity. Was it possible that a *chemical* had survived in the dead virulent cells and converted a benign organism into a lethal one? Within a year, numerous laboratories had duplicated Griffith's feat. It was no fluke. Something other than living matter could carry genetic information. Three years later, the transformation of benign into lethal pneumococci had been duplicated in culture dishes using both whole cells and their nonliving extracts. By 1930, everyone knew that they were on to a transforming principle—but no one thought of DNA as the vehicle. Instead, all attention—mistakenly, as it developed—turned to the proteins that inevitably contaminated extracts of living cells.[2]

It remained for a group of three researchers at the Rockefeller Institute—Oswald T. Avery, Colin MacLeod, and Maclyn McCarty—to show that the transforming principle was almost certainly DNA. (DNA, or deoxyribonucleic acid, had been discovered in 1869 by the Swiss physiologist Friedrich Miescher, who later succeeded in isolating it from the sperm of Rhine River trout.) In early 1944, the Rockefeller Institute team published a paper in the *Journal of*

Experimental Medicine that contained a single, fateful sentence: "The evidence presented supports the belief that a nucleic acid of the deoxyribose type is the fundamental unit of the transforming principle of Pneumococcus Type III."[3] With this line, the Rockefeller researchers announced to the world that DNA was the vehicle for genetic information.

The philosophical impact of this discovery impressed itself on Oswald Avery, the principal investigator: While all the members of the team undoubtedly knew they had discovered a way in which the properties of organisms change from one generation to the next, Avery was transfixed by the notion that they had in fact discovered a way to *control* that change.

Writing to his brother Roy in 1944, the year of the initial discovery, Avery pointed out that their finding was "something which has long been the dream of geneticists. Up until now, the mutations [have been] . . . unpredictable and random and chance changes."[4] Now, Avery believed, scientists had the ability to direct that change. (The discovery of "site-directed" mutagenesis would bear Avery out some thirty-five years later.)

From 1869 through the turn of the century, DNA, though known, remained on the back shelves of science. Interest perked up with Griffith's work in 1929, and began to peak with Avery's work in 1944. Over the next forty years, the genetic revolution was heralded by a cascade of findings. By 1950, Erwin Chargaff had correctly perceived that the regularities in the amounts of purines and pyrimidines (the two classes of bases that make up DNA, which are found in equal portions in almost all life) could be related to DNA's structure. But Chargaff was, in his own words, "perhaps the wrong man to make these discoveries"[5] because he lacked the training in X-ray crystallography that would allow visualization of the binding of the bases in a complete molecule that could be obtained from an X-ray diffraction picture.

Breaking the Code

In 1943, J. D. Watson and F. H. Crick deduced the double-helical structure of the DNA molecule, putting to rest the theory that protein carried genetic information. Ironically, the publication of Chargaff's organizing principle of base pairing—admitted privately by Watson to be the key to his double-helical model—was ignored in the seminal 1953 article. As Watson and Crick delicately stated in their article in *Nature,* this double-helical structure would allow the DNA molecule to be self-replicating *and* to carry information.[6] In such a way, DNA could be transmitted faithfully from cell to cell and be used to direct protein synthesis.

The next step was to decipher the way in which genetic information was coded in the DNA molecule. Such researchers as Sydney Brenner adduced that the code might use the complementary pairings of the four bases that made up the DNA molecule: adenine (A) and thymine (T), and cytosine (C) and guanine (G). Brenner correctly predicted that the code could be determined by groups of three of these bases facing each other across the two strands of the DNA helix (see Figure 1.1). Brenner's group of three would allow for sixty-four different instructions from four bases— i.e., 4^3—more than enough to instruct the assembly of the twenty amino acids into protein.

Within a dozen years of the discovery of DNA's structure, researchers correctly predicted that a gene was a sequential instruction written in the alphabet of the base pairs (1956), that the way genetic information was transferred entailed its transmission from DNA to a "messenger" RNA molecule (1960), and that a three-base sequence was indeed used to direct the order in which amino acids would be assembled into proteins (1961). By 1966, just thirteen years after the discovery of the double helix, researchers had established a

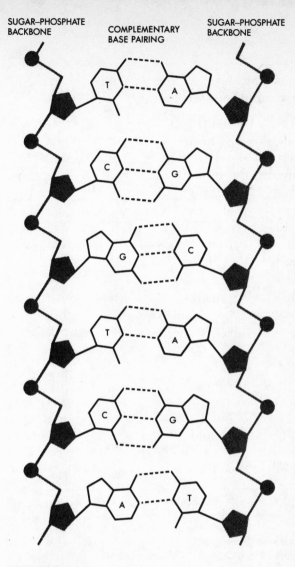

SUGAR–PHOSPHATE BACKBONE   COMPLEMENTARY BASE PAIRING   SUGAR–PHOSPHATE BACKBONE

FIGURE 1.1
The four bases that make up the DNA helix. Each base is connected to its complement by hydrogen bonds to form a "base pair." (*Source:* J. D. Watson, J. Tooze, and D. T. Kurtz, *Recombinant DNA: A Short Course,* New York: W.H. Freeman & Co., 1983. Used with permission.)

complete genetic code, which specified each of the twenty major amino acids, including "start" and "stop" instructions. This code is shown in Table 1.1.

Table 1.1
The Complete Genetic Code: Codon Dictionary*

| First Base | Middle Base | | | | Third Base† |
	U	C	A	G	
U	Phe‡	Ser	Tyr	Cys	U
	Phe	Ser	Tyr	Cys	C
	Leu	Ser	STOP	STOP§	A
	Leu	Ser	STOP	Trp	G
C	Leu	Pro	His	Arg	U
	Leu	Pro	His	Arg	C
	Leu	Pro	Gln	Arg	A
	Leu	Pro	Gln	Arg	G
A	lle	Thr	Asn	Ser	U
	lle	Thr	Asn	Ser	C
	lle	Thr	Lys	Arg	A
	Met	Thr	Lys	Arg	G
G	Val	Ala	Asp	Gly	U
	Val	Ala	Asp	Gly	C
	Val	Ala	Glu	Gly	A
	Val‖	Ala	Glu	Gly	G

*Groups of three bases code for specific amino acids. The repeat appearance of amino acids at different places in the code book illustrate that the code is "redundant"—that is, more than one three-base group codes for most amino acids. **Examples:** *Phenylalanine:* UUU or UUC; *Isoleucine:* AUU, AUC or AUG; or *Serine:* UCU, UCC, UCA, UCG, or AGU, AGC.

†Assumes code is read from the 5'-OH terminal base to the 3'-OH terminal base.

‡Abbreviations: *Ala*, alanine; *Arg*, arginine; *Asn*, asparagine; *Asp*, aspartic acid; *Cys*, cysteine; *Gln*, glutamine; *Glu*, glutamic acid; *Gly*, glycine; *His*, histidine; *lle*, isoleucine; *Leu*, leucine; *Lys*, lysine; *Met*, methionine; *Phe*, phenylalanine; *Pro*, proline; *Ser*, serine; *Thr*, threonine; *Val*, valine.

§Termination signal for ending amino acid chain.

‖Codes for Met if in the initiator position.

Splicing Life

The next ten years saw the discovery of the tools of the revolution in genetic engineering. By 1967, researchers had isolated the enzyme that joins DNA chains together (DNA ligase). Three years later, the first enzyme that could cut DNA molecules at specific sites (so-called restriction enzymes) was isolated. In 1972, recombinant molecules were created for the first time in the laboratory of Paul Berg at Stanford University, where a team of graduate students became the first to assemble recombinant-DNA molecules from DNA fragments.[7] (Other laboratories, notably those of Daniel Nathans at Johns Hopkins University School of Medicine and Stanley Cohen at Stanford, later succeeded in using restriction enzymes and ligases to construct recombinant DNA in other systems.)

In 1973, researchers successfully annealed foreign DNA fragments into the DNA of *plasmids,* the tiny loops of free DNA that can be found in most bacteria. Figure 1.2 is a schematic diagram typical of these first experiments. Researchers showed that this "chimeric" DNA could function after the plasmids were returned to another bacterium. Most importantly, this recombinant DNA, or "rDNA"—that is, the DNA inserted into the new bacterium—could direct the production of proteins not normally made in bacteria. Researchers had long believed that the DNA code was "universal"—that all living things use the same "call letters" for their protein synthesizing. Now these experiments showed that it was possible to put foreign genes into rapidly dividing single-celled organisms and have those genes function as if they were in their native species.

By 1974, molecular biologists had gotten novel bacterial genes to work in different bacteria, but they were still not sure whether genes from more distantly related organisms—say, mammals—could function in single-celled

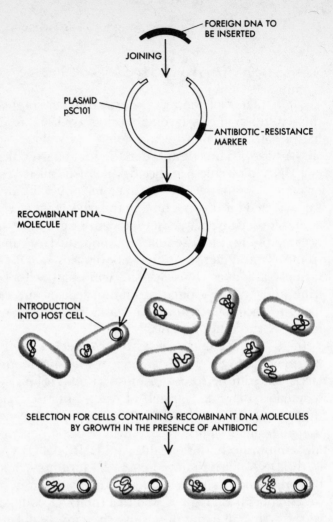

FIGURE 1.2
The cloning of DNA in a plasmid. (*Source:* J. D. Watson, J. Tooze, and D. T. Kurtz, *Recombinant DNA: A Short Course,* New York: W.H. Freeman & Co., 1983. Used with permission.)

hosts. After all, the species in question had diverged from a common evolutionary path hundreds of millions of years earlier! To get these higher genes to function in bacteria or yeast cells, researchers had to find the proper control signals that would cue bacteria or yeasts to read mammalian DNA. Without this key, new genetic instructions lying inside single cells like yeast *(Saccharomyces cerevisiae)* or the commonly used intestinal bacterium *Echereschia coli* would remain silent.

The next steps involved understanding how to tell bacteria to make multiple copies of desirable genes, when to start producing a desired protein, and how to stop doing so. This feat was achieved in the mid 1970s, setting the stage for the full-blown use of recombinant DNA to make novel proteins.

Biohazard

Before the production of novel genes could happen, both scientists and a concerned public were to address the possibility that these techniques might generate unforeseen hazards. In 1973, the first concerns about possible biohazards from recombinant-DNA systems were broached at the annual Gordon Research Conference on Nucleic Acids, in New Hampshire. Much of the concern focused on the use of tumor-causing viruses, which were then thought to be the only vehicles for carrying rDNA into higher cells. At the end of the conference, the delegates voted to send a letter to the National Academy of Sciences (NAS) requesting that this larger forum consider the problem of hazards and recommend specific actions or guidelines. Under the leadership of National Institutes of Health researcher Maxine Singer, and Dieter Söll of Yale University, a small group of NAS scientists authorized publication of a letter that was to appear simultaneously in the leading science journals in the Western world—*Science, Nature,* and the *Proceedings of the National Academy of Sciences.*

Published first in *Science,* this letter took the extraordinary step of inviting fellow scientists to declare a moratorium on potentially hazardous research by deferring certain experiments, "until the potentials of such recombinant DNA molecules have been better evaluated or until adequate methods are developed for preventing their spread. . . ."[8] One year later, a second group headed by Paul Berg of Stanford University published a letter that proposed that the National Institutes of Health (NIH) begin to devise guidelines for researchers who wished to conduct research with potentially hazardous recombinant-DNA molecules and proposed a convocation of scientists around the world at the Asilomar Conference Center in Pacific Grove, California.[9]

Following the suggestion of the Berg committee, a group of 150 scientists from fifteen countries plus two American lawyers and a select group of invited press attended the conference. At this retreat on the Monterey Peninsula, delegates conducted an historic debate over issues spanning freedom of inquiry, scientific responsibility, and the need for formal recognition of potential biohazards in their work. In a particularly stirring speech, then University of Pennsylvania law professor Alexander Capron invited the delegates to regulate themselves or face the inevitable—and in his view justified—exercise of public control. Shortly afterwards, the delegates called for the adoption of guidelines that would regulate recombinant-DNA experimentation.

The first meeting of the NIH Recombinant DNA Advisory Committee (RAC) convened the day after the Asilomar Conference ended, and began work on what was to become the NIH Guidelines.

In May 1975, I chaired a conference held under the joint auspices of the New York Academy of Sciences and the

Institute of Society, Ethics and Life Sciences to explore the ethical and scientific issues posed by genetic engineering.[10] At the conference, Dr. Richard Roblin, one of the individuals who first encouraged the submission of the Singer-Söll letter to *Science* and the other journals, pointed out that in the past scientists could claim that basic science was detrimental only when misapplied, but that the attendees at the 1974 Gordon conference had to realize that their research itself could be dangerous.[11]

Asking basic researchers to accept greater responsibility for what might be done with their research was new and possibly revolutionary for the biological sciences. Although some atomic physicists showed similar sensibilities (with little effect), never before had the scientific community seen such a collective movement to consider the consequences of scientific work before it was undertaken. While most of the attention was directed towards hazards that have since been shown to be largely hypothetical, the exercise forced many scientists to ask a more basic question: To what degree, if any, are scientists responsible for what others do with their research? (This thorny issue is discussed in Chapter 11.)

In July of 1975, a subcommittee of the NIH chaired by David Hogness issued the first draft of what were to become the National Institutes of Health Guidelines on Recombinant DNA Research.[12] (A final draft of these guidelines was to be issued one year later.) This draft (1) called for the development of "fail-safe" bacterial strains that would die outside a laboratory environment, (2) proscribed five types of experiments, and (3) described gradated containment facilities for housing potentially risky experiments.[13] These initial guidelines also prohibited the construction of batch sizes of organisms greater than 10 liters. Obviously, with such prohibitions in place, the commercial development of recombinant DNA was all but impossible.

The NIH Guidelines

The first guidelines, released on June 23, 1976, consisted of a detailed set of containment requirements deemed necessary to conduct rDNA experimentation safely.[14] The introduction to the guidelines, written by Donald Fredrickson of the NIH, indicated the central theme the deliberations were to follow: "The scientific community must have the public's confidence that the goals of this profoundly important research accord respect to important ethical, legal, and social values of our society." Donald Fredrickson went on to declare that the guidelines were intended to "allow the promise of the methodology to be realized" while protecting against "what we and others view as *potential* hazards [italics added]."[15] But within the year, scientists—and later, according to one of his aides, Donald Fredrickson himself—began to doubt the wisdom of inviting public scrutiny of their work.

By mid-1977, many scientists were beginning to argue that the whole debate about risks was ill-founded. Some, like Cold Spring Harbor Laboratory's James D. Watson, declared intemperately that the risks were essentially nonexistent and that consequently no outside control of any rDNA research was necessary.[16] In its October 1977 environmental impact statement, the NIH itself offered human insulin, growth hormone, clotting factors, and antigens and antibodies as examples of benefits to be expected from rDNA.

In December 1978, the NIH issued a revision of the 1976 guidelines. This 136-page document contained the reasons for adopting or rejecting earlier versions of some sections and presented an environmental impact assessment that would prove to be a major stumbling block to the proposed release of rDNA organisms some seven years later (see Chapter 7).

The revised guidelines acknowledged that they "relax

some of the restrictions under which recombinant DNA research has been conducted since 1976," while stressing that they were intended "at the same time [to] increase the role of the public in monitoring recombinant DNA experiments."[17] This increased public involvement was to take place largely via local institutional biosafety committees (IBCs), which were to oversee recombinant-DNA research at individual institutions, plus the federal Recombinant DNA Advisory Committee (RAC).

Specific congressional and state proposals to extend the guidelines to private industry were also proposed during the late 1970s. However, with the exception of a few local ordinances and two state laws, since repealed, no substantial widening of the purview of these guidelines outside the university sector has been achieved.[18] In spite of intense legislative interest—sixteen different bills were introduced into Congress over the three-year period 1976–1979—no single piece of federal legislation was actually passed by both houses of Congress.

The reluctance of legislators to regulate genetic engineering more vigorously can be ascribed to three concerns: (1) that initial fears of portentous events stemming from rDNA research were unfounded; (2) that legislation would preempt a more elastic, evolutionary process of regulation that would permit the research strategies and product development to be molded to evolving knowledge about safety; and (3) that external political constraints on research would threaten freedom of inquiry. Less explicit was the concern that economic developments might be stifled.

These three factors—safety, developmental plasticity, and freedom of inquiry—were to become cornerstones of the rDNA debate. Between 1977 and 1982, the public's concern about biohazards was dampened by a series of events. During this period, the preponderance of testimony submitted to the NIH shifted toward recommendations for downgrading concerns about safety.[19] Scientists argued that the guidelines should be made voluntary or abolished altogether. At stake here was the delicate counterpoise between risks and benefits. No one wanted to be responsible for thwarting the most promising new technique since the discovery of the microscope. And yet no one wanted to create a monster. Somehow a balance had to be struck. But the impetus to move ahead had clearly eclipsed earlier concern and caution.

The guidelines were progressively weakened by the absence of demonstrable hazards, even though few experiments had been conducted that were expressly designed to test assumptions of safe conditions. In fact by 1981, most of the limitations on recombinant-DNA experiments using specially designed *E.coli* and yeast strains had been exempted from special laboratory controls by the NIH.

In 1982, the NIH guidelines were further relaxed, although they stopped short of a recommendation by an advisory committee (the RAC) that all compliance be made voluntary.[20] The current set of guidelines differs from its predecessors in at least four salient aspects: (1) it exempts entire classes of experiments from review; (2) it assigns lower levels of protection for the covered experiments; (3) it lessens the requirements for prior approval of certain experiments; and (4) it simplifies the requirements for organization and approval.[21]

The evolution of the guidelines from restrictive to permissive was predicated on the assumption that the systems needed to apply rDNA techniques were safe. A comprehensive review of this history is contained in Sheldon Krimsky's *Genetic Alchemy*.[22] As Krimsky points out, the basis for assuming absolute safety remains flawed. A pivotal experiment, published since Krimsky wrote his book, exemplifies the residual uncertainty. This example of a safety study was reported in the October 1983 issue of the *Journal of Infectious Disease*.[23] Under the direction of Stanley Falkow, a group of University of Maryland and University of Washington scientists tested the ability of potential recombinant-DNA organisms to colonize the human intestinal tract. None of the twelve volunteers who ingested the so-called "safe" vector became colonized with bacteria.

This finding further diminished scientific and public concerns about the inadvertent contamination of laboratory employees with large inocula of recombinant *E. coli* bacteria, and strongly suggested that the second route of contamination—through environmental "spills" via the sewage system—were highly improbable. Indeed, the Falkow research team calculated that the likelihood of human contamination with this rDNA-carrying organism could be as low as 1 chance in 36 billion! Theoretically, a whole century of worldwide experimentation using this bacterium to carry recombined DNAs into cells could ensue without a harmful event.

But this otherwise reassuring news was tempered by two observations: (1) Falkow's work also showed that the ingestion of oral antibiotics to which the recombinant was resistant (in this case, tetracycline) greatly increased the likelihood of colonization—to the point that Falkow and his colleagues recommended that no one taking antibiotics should work in a recombinant-DNA laboratory; and (2) the published report appeared more than two years *after* its results had been anticipated. (The rapid relaxation of the standards required by the NIH guidelines began fully three years before publication of this study!)

During this same period other scientists were expressing newfound concern over the laissez-faire attitude towards safety. A. Sibatani of New South Wales worried that the pendulum of safety considerations had swung too far in the direction of complacency. Noting that many of the so-called worst-case tests of rDNA systems were not conducted with worst-case organisms, Sibatani called for a reexamination of our assumptions of safety. Sibatani's view circa 1983 was that the ground[s] for assuming that the recombinant

DNA is not so dangerous has been lost" in light of current data that show greater plasticity and freedom of exchange of genetic material than was previously assumed.[24]

Comment

Thus, the relative safety of rDNA research remains a point of contention: whether or not relaxed precautions will in fact prove wise remains to be seen. In the meantime, simple expedients—for example, taking care not to put the entire gene sequence for a potent toxin into any one host—appear prudent. Ironically, we will remain ignorant of the ultimate safety of much rDNA work until it has actually been done.

A second point of contention has been the assertion that public involvement is now greatly enhanced as a result of the modified guidelines. The key requirement regarding the institutional biosafety committees specified in the 1976–1978 guidelines was that these committees be composed of a significant portion of disinterested parties. Specifically, 20 percent of the members of the IBCs were to be unaffiliated with the institution in which the work was to be carried out. This provision was substantially changed in May 1982.[25] In these revisions, only two of the members of the IBCs were required to "represent the interests of the surrounding community." This formal requirement, of course, does not prevent more than two from being conscripted, nor does it ensure that the full public has access to IBC proceedings. In fact, the lack of such access is underscored by the absence of open meetings when proprietary information is being discussed.

A third area of concern has been the adequacy of the environmental impact statements (EISs) issued to accompany the guidelines. For instance, it is now clear that when the NIH published the first draft of its environmental impact statement on August 19, 1976, they failed to meet a judicial standard for considering the full breadth of potential impacts of this new technology.

The actual justification for this rapidly assembled EIS appeared on the very first page: "It is widely anticipated that a variety of research—impacting on health and other areas of human concern—will benefit from recombinant DNA technology."[26] This early document presaged much of what was to follow. The progenitors of the guidelines and EISs, notably NIH scientists and aides in Donald Fredrickson's office, were aware that the Director wanted to ensure that research would not be unduly hampered by the guidelines.[27]

As reflected by the final version of the environmental impact statement,[28] the initial guidelines were already considered to have encompassed every possible objection to the expansion of this technology. The EIS advocated directly proceeding with research for three reasons: (1) that any possible hazard of rDNA research is purely speculative; (2) that extrapolation from our existing knowledge base indicates that newly constructed organisms are likely to be extremely attenuated and diminished in vitality; and (3) that the potential gains are so enormous that they outweigh these statistically remote risks.

But were these projections reasonable?

By early 1984, the predictions from the 1978 impact statement appeared to be fully realized. Risks were still hypothetical. Attenuated organisms were shown under most circumstances to have less likelihood of survival than robust natural strains. And the gains from the research, though still not fully realized, appeared to be just on the horizon.

Just when recombinant DNA was going to make its great

leap forward, however, a judicial review of the adequacy of the initial EIS cast profound doubt over the likelihood that biotechnology would proceed smoothly to its promised ends. On May 16, 1984, Judge John Sirica ruled on a suit that challenged the adequacy of the original EIS (see chapter 7 for a full discussion of environmental impacts) and declared—to an astonished and upset rDNA community—that the impact assessment had been imperfectly performed.[29] Sirica ordered the NIH not to authorize any additional experiments that would lead to the release of genetically modified organisms into the environment, specifically those whose genetic makeup had been rearranged through use of recombinant DNA. Any future release, if cleared, would require a fuller assessment of environmental impact than had yet been done.

Thus, while the NIH guidelines have proven a useful and flexible series of documents for assuring *interior* safety of rDNA experimentation—that is, laboratory work per se—they have failed to anticipate adequately the much more complex and significant issues attending the *exterior* safety of such experimentation.

Notes

1. E. Griffith, "The Significance of Pneumococcal Types," *Journal of Hygiene* (Cambridge) 27 (1928): 113–118.
2. The history that preceded the discovery of DNA is eloquently described by one of the participants: Erwin Chargaff, *Heraclitean Fire* (New York: The Rockefeller University Press, 1978) pp. 82–88.
3. O. T. Avery, C. MacLeod, and M. McCarty, "Studies on the Chemical Nature of the Substance Inducing Transformation of Pneumococcal Types," *Journal of Experimental Medicine* 79 (1944): 137–158.
4. "Letter from Oswald Avery to Roy Avery, May 17, 1943," *Readings in Heredity,* John A. Moore, ed. (New York: Oxford University Press, 1972).

5. Chargaff, *Heraclitean Fire*, p. 96.

6. J. D. Watson and F. H. C. Crick, "Molecular Structure of Nucleic Acids," *Nature* 171 (1953): 737–738.

7. D. A. Jackson, R. H. Symons, and P. Berg, "Biochemical Method for Inserting New Genetic Information into DNA of Simian Virus 40: Circular SV40 DNA Molecules Containing Lambda Phage Genes and the Galactose Operon of *Escherichia coli*," *Proceedings of the National Academy of Sciences* 69 (1972): 2904–2909.

8. M. Singer and D. Söll, "Guidelines for DNA Hybrid Molecules," *Science* 181 (1973): 1114.

9. P. Berg et al., "Potential Hazards of Recombinant DNA Molecules," *Science* 185 (1974): 303. For a report of the resulting conference, see P. Berg et al., "Asilomar Conference on Recombinant DNA Molecules," *Science* 188 (1975): 991–994.

10. See M. Lappé and R. Morrison, "Ethical and Scientific Issues Posed by Human Uses of Molecular Genetics," *Annals of the New York Academy of Sciences* 265 (1976).

11. R. Roblin, "Reflections on Issues Posed by Recombinant DNA Molecules," *Annals of the New York Academy of Sciences* 265 (1976): 59–65.

12. The history of the guidelines is reviewed by Bernard Talbot in "Development of the National Institutes of Health Guidelines for Recombinant DNA Research," *Public Health Reports* 98 (1983): 361–368.

13. The five types of proscribed experiments were (1) those in which recombinant DNA would be derived from particularly pathogenic organisms or cancer-causing viruses; (2) those that embodied the deliberate use of DNA-containing toxins; (3) the use of DNA from plant pathogens that might increase the host range or virulence of resulting recombinant organisms; (4) the deliberate transfer of resistance to antibiotics or other therapeutic agents to organisms already having the genes for such resistance; and (5) the intentional release of any recombinant organism into the environment. All have since been made voluntary, subject to review by institutional "biosafety committees" and the federal Recombinant DNA Advisory Committee (RAC).

14. "Recombinant DNA Research—Guidelines," *Federal Register* 41 (July 7, 1976): 27902–27943.

15. Ibid., p. 27911.

16. J. D. Watson, "An Imaginary Monster," *Bulletin of the Atomic Scientists* 33 (May 1977): 12–13.

17. "Guidelines for Research Involving Recombinant DNA Molecules," *Federal Register* 43 (December 22, 1978): 60080–60131; I have reviewed the deficiencies in implementing this public representation elsewhere: See M. Lappé, "Recombinant DNA: The Case for Controls," In: Prospect for Man: Genetic Engineering, J. G. Little, ed. (York University, Toronto, 1979), pp. 91–102.

18. Much of this history is ably reviewed in a monograph by Sheldon Krimsky, Anne Baeck, and John Bolduc, *Municipal and State Recombinant DNA Laws, History and Assessment* (Medford, Mass.: Tufts University, 1982).

19. See National Institutes of Health, *Recombinant DNA Research* (Washington, D.C.: Government Printing Office, August 1976–December 1982), Vols. 1–7.

20. "Guidelines for Research Involving Recombinant DNA Molecules," *Federal Register* 46 (July 1, 1981): 34454–34487.

21. See Talbot, "Development" (no. 12).

22. Sheldon Krimsky, *Genetic Alchemy: The Social History of the Recombinant DNA Controversy* (Cambridge, Mass.: MIT Press, 1983).

23. M. M. Levine, J. B. Kaper, H. Lockman, R. E. Black, M. L. Clements, and S. Falkow, "Recombinant DNA Risk Assessment Studies in Humans: Efficacy of Poorly Mobilizable Plasmids in Biologic Containment," *Journal of Infectious Disease* 148 (1983): 699–709.

24. A. Sibatani, "Recombinant DNA Safety," *Search* 14 (1983): 245–246.

25. "Recombinant DNA Research—Actions and Guidelines," *Federal Register* 47 (May 26, 1982): 23110.

26. The statement appeared as a Draft Environmental Impact Report in the *Federal Register* (September 9, 1976). Its principal author is NIH scientist Maxine Singer.

27. Burke Zimmerman, National Institutes of Health Congressional Liaison, personal communication, February 10, 1984.

28. National Institutes of Health, *Environmental Impact Statement on NIH Guidelines for Research Involving Recombinant DNA Research for June 23, 1976,* parts 1 and 2 (October 1977), USDHEW publication numbers (NIH) 1489 and 1490, respectively.

29. P. B. Boffey, "Judge Bars Outdoor Test of Genetic Engineering," *New York Times* (May 17, 1984), p. A20.

CHAPTER 2

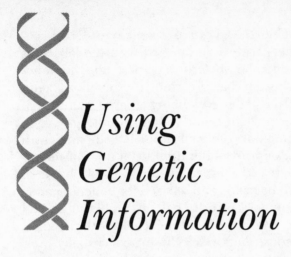

Using Genetic Information

The ability to control DNA is comparable to the ability to control the resources of a great library. Genetic engineering permits scientists to study and isolate the vast domains of genetic information contained in any species. It also allows researchers to use this information to produce specific proteins, to alter cells, and ultimately to modify whole organisms by giving them novel genetic characteristics. For a detailed technical description of the scientific basis for recombinant DNA, see Appendix A. The following summary is intended to highlight some of the key applications of this new technology.

Isolating Genes

Among the most powerful tools of recombinant DNA is the newfound ability to study the inner structure of the genome—the composite of genes in a species—of

higher animals. Until the advent of recombinant-DNA techniques, researchers had to be satisfied with the laborious
process of isolating the *products* of genes, not the genes
themselves. This meant that discerning the genetic makeup
of higher organisms required looking at large numbers of
enzymes or other proteins found in body fluids.

The long generation times of animals compared with
bacteria, viruses, or yeasts—the traditional tools of molecular biologists—created another limitation. Unlike bacterial
cells, which could be mated and selected for genetic characteristics in hours or days, with animals researchers often had
to wait months or even years to see the results of the simplest
crosses. These constraints were eliminated virtually overnight by the advent of recombinant DNA. A host of new
techniques now permits us to visualize the genome of the
most complex organism and to isolate its components in
greatly compressed time frames. The power of this technique requires a brief technical explanation.

To isolate genes from the DNA of a higher organism,
recombinant-DNA researchers characteristically break
down long lengths of DNA into smaller bits, using various
restriction enzymes. When the researchers remain "blind"
to the actual location of desired genes, this process is appropriately known as "shot-gunning." Once reduced to
manageable lengths on the order of fifty thousand to a
hundred thousand bases, the scattered fragments are
placed into bacterial hosts. These fragments are carried into
bacteria by means of suitable *vectors*, such as bacterial plasmids. To assure that enough of the desired gene is present,
the foreign DNA can be greatly amplified by forcing the
bacterial cell to make multiple copies of newly acquired
genes. The last step in the process is known as *cloning;* it
entails propagating all the descendants of the original bacterium that carry the desired piece of DNA. Once grown
into suitably large batches, the bacterial products made

from the cloned gene can be harvested from the culture medium and purified.

Researchers can also parse out DNA fragments into "book length" sections for closer study. Characteristically, each clone of bacteria carries a piece of genetic data that may include one to several genes, each about ten thousand to one hundred thousand base sequences long. Even with so many bases, the constellation of distinct bacterial clones needed to carry the genetic data borne on a single chromosome may number in the tens of thousands, because many sequences overlap. In the case of a human chromosome, the final "library" of genetic information may require more than fifty thousand different bacterial clones, each with a random "sentence" of genetic information. Researchers must then assemble each sentence into the proper order to re-create the chromosome's original message.

This seemingly Herculean task is greatly facilitated by the use of computerized libraries of sequences. By rapidly scanning the overlapping base sequences, the computer can string together long maps of genetic information. In 1982, the National Institutes of Health gave high priority to assembling a magnetic tape file of such sequences. Two organizations under contract with the National Institute of General Medical Sciences, one at the Los Alamos National Laboratory and the other in Cambridge, Massachusetts (Bolt, Beranek, and Newman, Inc.), together form the Genetic Sequence Data Bank (GenBank™). GenBank is sponsored by the United States government and makes available to international researchers nucleic acid sequences that contain more than fifty nucleotides. Entries to this data base originate in Los Alamos and are then transmitted to Bolt, Beranek, and Newman, a software and time-sharing firm.

This data bank now contains a large number of scattered blocks of unrelated genetic data, much like bricks in a brickyard. Between April 1, 1982, and the first part of 1984, the number of bases that had been sequenced jumped from five hundred thousand to nearly 3 million. By January 4, 1984, GenBank had recorded the precise composition of 3,609 gene sequences representing 2,602,596 bases of genetic information. In mid-1984,[1] GenBank joined with its European counterpart, the European Molecular Biology Laboratory, to forge a powerful data base.

As shown in Table 2.1, as of January, 1984, this collection included more than 1,000 mammalian base sequences, half of which are from human genetic material. Considering that the genetic material of most mammalian species contains an estimated 1–10 billion base pairs of genetic information,[2] this first foray into gene isolation is but a tentative probe of a vast repository of information. Yet advances in recombinant technology are proceeding so rapidly that the complete genetic makeup of a representative of a multicellular species is likely to be assembled within the decade.

The final assembly of the genetic codes of living and endangered species would be one of the sublime achievements of the human intellect. Is it really likely we will do it? The answer is a conditional yes. Researchers currently estimate that the human genome contains at a minimum between thirty thousand and one hundred thousand fully expressed genes. In 1980, perhaps a dozen genes were known. By the end of 1983, 361 sequences representing parts of perhaps 600 human genes were "mapped." By 1984, researchers had cloned the complete base-pair sequences for 132 genes.[3] While this accomplishment embraces a scant 0.1–0.3 percent of the total, the rate of acquisition of these data is accelerating rapidly. If—and this is a big if—the private sector cooperates in transmitting its growing repertoire of genetic knowledge to this system, it is entirely plausible that we will have the full picture by 1995.

Whether or not genetic data will continue to be as-

Table 2.1
Genetic Data Assembled by the Genetic Sequence Data Bank

Major Group	Number of Bases Known	Number of Sequences Studied	Number of Studies
1. Mammals	704,008	1,098	889
Cow	(36,390)	(57)	(45)
Dog	(1,303)	(1)	(1)
Goat	(8,179)	(9)	(8)
Guinea pig	(766)	(1)	(1)
Hamster	(4,596)	(13)	(12)
HUMAN	(261,196)	(361)	(283)
Monkey	(15,184)	(25)	(25)
Mouse	(245,798)	(431)	(338)
Pig	(2,795)	(3)	(2)
Rabbit	(21,735)	(47)	(40)
Rat	(104,841)	(149)	(133)
Sheep	(1,225)	(1)	(1)
2. Vertebrates (other than mammals)	149,972	246	215
3. Invertebrates	179,215	288	263
4. Plants	151,635	178	154
5. Organelles (mitochondria, etc.)	221,561	175	152
6. Bacteria	385,089	454	343
7. Structural RNA	29,252	313	286
8. Viruses	599,575	706	587
9. Bacteriophages	169,180	108	80
10. Synthetic DNAs	13,109	43	43
TOTAL:	2,602,596	3,609	3,012

Source: GenBank™ Release No. 16, January 4, 1984, Cambridge, Massachusetts.

sembled at the present accelerating rate depends to a substantial degree on the willingness of private researchers to file their base sequences with the national repository—and not exclusively within the private data banks of their respective companies. According to a representative of Bolt,

Beranek, and Newman who wished to remain anonymous, substantial quantities of genetic data are kept in the files of major genetic-engineering companies. Unlike the NIH-sponsored tapes, much of the data stored by private firms are considered proprietary information. Since even the nature of the information stored could cue competitors about the types of programs being pursued, a significant portion of the genetic data base being assembled is unlikely to become part of the universal file envisioned by the NIH unless major policy changes are implemented. Making more data available on a confidential "need to know" basis may be one answer. Whatever happens, it is clear that commercial interests have already proven to be a damaging factor in the acquisition and sharing of new genetic knowledge by the scientific community as a whole.

Practical Applications

Because of the almost limitless variety possible, the choice of which rDNA-directed molecules to make has been influenced by numerous forces. A key factor for the scientific community has been *feasibility*. How much is known about the molecule? How readily can it be cloned? Which lab team is prepared to make it? These variables lead to choices of molecules that are well characterized and easy to synthesize. Thus, feasibility explains the choice of somatostatin as the first rDNA-synthesized molecule. However, it hardly accounts for the choices of biotechnology firms, such as the selection of the much more complex Factor VIII, which corrects blood-clotting deficiency in males with classic hemophilia.

As we will discuss in Chapter 10, choices in the recombinant-DNA industry are rarely neutral. The ineluctable appeal of producing and selling something previously either so scarce or so valuable that no one could own it has been a force behind some choices. That is not to say that much of what will be produced with recombinant DNA will not be intrinsically useful, valuable, or even essential to human well-being. This may well be the case for human growth hormone (HGH), an essential polypeptide for persons with familial isolated growth-hormone deficiency, or for Factor VIII in treating hemophilia.[4] But these disorders are almost by definition rare because of their origins in single gene mutations. No more than fifteen to twenty thousand males have hemophilia in the United States, and approximately six thousand have pituitary dwarfism. No, it was not the frequency of human disorders that prompted these initial searches, nor was it the critical need for such hormones as insulin or HGH, or such blood proteins as Factor VIII, since, while scarce, all these substances are available from other sources. (As subsequent events have shown, it was almost certainly the potential applications of HGH genes for promoting the growth of livestock that kept commercial investment high.) In fact, one has to ask why researchers chose to synthesize *any* commercially duplicative proteins in light of the importance of rDNA to basic research.

Basic Investigation

Many of the earliest researchers believed that the principal value of recombinant-DNA techniques was linked to basic research into the structure of the DNA of higher organisms. Such pioneers as James Watson, writing with John Tooze and David Kurtz in the first real textbook on recombinant DNA identify the "most important" possibilities of recombinant-DNA techniques as those that lend themselves to the analysis of DNA from plants and animals.[5] While the gene-banking work points to substantial progress toward these and related ends of basic research, the preponderance of recombinant-DNA research now appears to be directed to applied rather than basic goals.

The differences between these two forms of inquiry are often largely academic, but some observers, such as Leon Wofsy, of the University of California at Berkeley, are beginning to question the balance between the public and private sectors.[6] A rough index of the preponderance of one form of inquiry over the other is the extent to which collaborative industrially sponsored recombinant-DNA research has evolved in the university. Appendix B is an abbreviated listing of 31 major university/corporate agreements made between 1974 and 1984. A full discussion of these relationships is outside the scope of this book. However, the nature and extent of these relationships reveal a clear pattern: the corporate sector has become the dominant force in applied recombinant-DNA research.[7]

Most observers of this development consider applied rDNA research to be effectively neutral. Watson, Tooze, and Kurtz, for instance, simply describe the aims of the industry as being "to harness for commercial ends our ability to manipulate, change, and transfer genes,"[8] without declaring their beliefs regarding the relative desirability of any particular application. Elsewhere, I have questioned whether the ends of the public and private sectors are comparable at all.[9] One concern is that given the fundamental differences in goals and means to attain them between the corporate and academic worlds, it is unlikely that corporate-based studies will yield comparable advances in basic knowledge or that their findings will be as widely shared as university-based research. The testing of this hypothesis will require at least another dozen years of research. Meanwhile, we can critically examine corporate goals and products.

Notes

1. D. T. Anderson, "U.S.-European Collaboration Makes NIH's Gen-Bank More Powerful than Ever," *Genetic Engineering News* 4 (May/June 1984): 1, 34.

2. D. C. Tiemeier, "The Recombinant DNA Technology," *Journal of Veterinary Pharmacology and Therapeutics* 6 (1983): 3–12.

3. M. H. Skolnide, H. F. Willard, and L. A. Menlove, "Report of the Committee on Human Gene Mapping by Recombinant DNA Techniques," *Cytogenetics and Cell Genetics* 36 (1984): 210–273.

4. See A. B. Rabson and A. S. Rabson, "Recombinant DNA Technology and Laboratory Medicine," *Archives of Pathology and Laboratory Medicine* 107 (1983): 505–508, for an excellent discussion of these and related opportunities.

5. J. D. Watson, J. Tooze, and D. T. Kurtz, *Recombinant DNA, A Short Course* (New York: W. H. Freeman, 1983), pp. 67–68.

6. Leon Wofsy, "The Life Sciences and the Public: Is the New Biology Too Important to Be Left to the Entrepreneurs?" *Politics and the Life Sciences* 3 (August, 1984): 65–68.

7. This fact is documented in the 1984 report of U.S. Congress Office of Technology Assessment, *Commercial Biotechnology, An International Analysis* (Washington, D.C.: OTA, 1984).

8. Watson, Tooze, and Kurtz, *Recombinant DNA*, p. 231.

9. M. Lappé, testimony before the Senate Subcommittee on Technology, November 1977.

CHAPTER 3

The Commercialization of DNA

Commercial interests have largely shaped the goals of the biotechnology industry and, in turn, the choices of many of the key products developed through the use of recombinant-DNA technology. Some of these choices carry with them "opportunity costs"—that is, often unforeseen consequences of electing one option in lieu of another. What is not done with recombinant DNA can be as important as what is done. To effectively critique the consequences of choices we must explore the definitions, scope, and justifications for commercial objectives in biotechnology.

At least three interrelated interpretations of biotechnology and its relationship to genetic engineering have emerged in recent years. The first can be considered the *commercial view*. Endorsed by the editors of major trade publications, advocates of this definition consider biotechnology to be the exclusive province of the commercial sector. A typical definition holds biotechnology to be the "application of scientific and engineering principles to the processing of materials by biological agents to provide goods and services."[1] Proponents of this view often conceptualize biotechnology as an extension of the group of industrial processes that rely on microorganisms to produce commercially valuable products from suitable raw materials. Examples include fermentation systems to make beer, wine, or doughs, or metallurgical processes that use microorganisms to extract certain metals from ores.[2]

A second conceptual frame places biotechnology squarely in the field of genetic engineering. In this view, biotechnological processes are intended to modify biological systems, irrespective of their eventual utility. The basic premise here is that biotechnology can be applied as much for assisting basic scientific inquiry as for developing products. This definition can be termed the *biosynthetic view*. In this framework, any biological system that assists in defining, isolating, or producing biological molecules is part of biotechnology. This definition thus puts biotechnology at the crossroads between academic and commercial applications by emphasizing the continued role of biological systems and biotechnical apparatus in basic research. This view, unlike the first and third, is found only rarely and when it appears it is in publications like *Bio/Technology*, which attempt to combine articles of commercial interest with those of a more basic scientific orientation.

The third view is the broadest. According to Dr. J. Coombs, joint secretary of the British Anaerobic and Biomass Association and editor of the *International Biotechnology Directory*,[3] biotechnology embraces the full gamut of applications of recombinant-DNA-based and other biological systems in all their potential aspects. We can call this conceptualization the *universal view*. As such, biotechnology is seen as aiding animal and human medicine, waste and pollution management, enhanced oil recovery, mineral leaching, advanced plant breeding, diagnostics, and the development of analytic equipment. It was this universal framework that the U.S. Office of Technology Assessment adopted in its publication *Commercial Biotechnology, An International Analysis*. The OTA considers biotechnology to include "any technique that uses living organisms (or parts of organisms) to make or modify products, to improve plants or animals, or to develop micro-organisms for specific uses."[4]

The Nonneutrality of Genetic Manipulation

This last, universal view is in fact an open-ended definition that connotes a scientifically neutral view of biotechnology. Such a view suggests that biotechnology can be incorporated into a broad spectrum of commercial applications depending solely on the ingenuity of their developers. Such a neutral viewpoint treats genetic technologies as analogous to the basic discoveries in physics and electronics. But genes are *not* transistors. They have their origins in the evolutionary systems of the natural world. From the viewpoint of naturalist ethics, recombinant-DNA systems should be applied to ends that are congruent with these origins rather than to ideas of a purely commercial bent. The countervailing view is that there is no value structure to DNA, and the forces of evolution do not necessarily indicate the most appropriate applications of rDNA. Thus it is that the human choices regarding the applications of biotechnology have emerged as issues of great moment to some groups (e.g., the concern of animal rights groups over transspecies movement of human growth hormone genes into animals) and not to others.

A contrasting viewpoint is that researchers isolated and developed recombinant-DNA technologies to study nature, not to control it.[5] Because its roots were in the domain of public health and not the commercial sector, this argument holds that rDNA should be used to foster human well-being, not acquisitiveness. And because its most powerful applications are those that allow control over existing biological systems, not *de novo* creation of untested new ones, biotechnology should be geared to minor (i.e., single-gene) manipulations, not to the major ones contemplated by some plant and animal engineers. But the realities of the rapid expansion of applied recombinant DNA make such purist thought moot, and dictate that we examine critically how and where it is being used, not whether it should be.

The Scale of Commercialization

To date, most assessments of biotechnology have centered on its market prospects, not its potential social impact. The articles that have glutted the pages of trade journals promise their readers the most up-to-date estimates of the products, markets, and ultimate size of the biotechnology sector. Other reports, like one in *Chemical Marketing Report,* project only modest increases in the market for rDNA-generated pharmaceuticals and other biotechnology products. In the November 23, 1981, issue, the editors of this journal estimated that the market for advanced biotechnology processes would grow to half a billion dollars by 1990. This same article carried an unflattering comparison of the ability of Western European industry to keep pace with American know-how, pointing out that as of

1981 some 170 Western European firms were involved to some extent in biotechnology, but only 20 were prepared to handle the high technology needed to establish a production base.

Some European observers, too, have taken the view that biotechnology is being grossly oversold. R. Batchelor, of Beecham Pharmaceuticals in Great Britain, points out that biotechnology processes will only be adopted if they can be perfected to a point that exceeds the efficiency of the processes currently in place—a limitation he asserts will take some time to overcome.[6]

The consensus of where biotechnology is going now appears to center on those companies that can put diagnostic products on the market quickly, utilize their present expertise in fermentation technologies to make "fine" chemicals (i.e., those that sell for more than a dollar per pound, such as enzymes, antibiotics, or hormones) or develop more efficient methods for using simple carbohydrates as energy sources. Such companies include massive Japanese firms, such as Suntory or Ajinomoto, which have traditionally used fermentation systems to produce alcohol or other large-scale commodities (e.g., Suntory's whiskey or Ajinomoto's fermented soy products). Microorganisms have already been developed that can produce amino acids such as serine, threonine, tryptophan, and phenylalanine, as have—in collaboration with American firms—simple biologicals such as monoclonal antibodies. (These products and their applications are discussed in Chapter 4.)

The OTA report *Commercial Biotechnology* spells out in more detail just where industrial applications will most likely be and identifies the factors that impede the most efficient development, but it fails to assign priorities to industry objectives. The OTA staff gives equal weight to using biotechnology as a vehicle for producing commodity chemicals and for fabricating basic foodstuffs. In fact, the OTA intentionally limits its recommendations to those factors needed for maintaining the current competitive advantage of the United States in world markets. To this end, OTA recommends to Congress that it

- improve the education base,
- change antitrust laws to promote more research collaboration among domestic firms,
- regulate imports to protect domestic industries,
- regulate and limit the transfer of technology from the United States to countries abroad, and
- offer federal assistance to specific industries or technologies.

These actions to serve American biotechnology assume that international biotechnological development will proceed along the lines identified for OTA by its panel of consultants. Most of the developments projected by OTA forecasters emphasize the value of biotechnology to the pharmaceutical, agricultural, and industrial sectors. But some private technology-forecasting companies under contract with industry have recommended divergent strategies for development that ensure profitability at the possible expense of social utility. European assessments of this new field have struck a similarly opportunistic note.

International Perspectives

Not unexpectedly, industry projections have concentrated on opportunities and untapped markets for biotechnology applications. In 1980, the British technology-forecasting company Information Research Limited (IRL) examined the prospects for biotechnology in the production of human and animal foods, medicines, and industrial and agricultural products. This study emphasized the value of veterinary and livestock products over their human counterparts because of more favorable regulatory conditions for developing agricultural commodities than for medical ones. IRL projected a $500 million industry for 1990 (to be worth $50 billion by 2000) as long as the major economies of the world powers continued to reinforce the patterns of consumption envisioned in 1980.

This and similar reports charted the future for biotechnology solely in terms of its market opportunities.[7] In 1980, the Federal Republic of Germany independently targeted biotechnology in its *Leistungsplan* (see Table 3.1 for an accounting of this and other international developments). Four separate funding groups, each with a pharmaceutical or chemical t at its center, have since been set up to accelerate biotechnological development.[8] In 1981, France published its program for making biotechnology a national priority (the Pelissolo report), and it has accelerated development accordingly. Japan has taken a similarly aggressiveposture in the biotechnology field, with more than 150 separate Japanese companies engaged in research and product development.[9] As suggested by these national priority programs, the various private-sector companies in the European Common Market and Japan are engaged in an internecine struggle to secure their share of the market for the most profitable rDNA commodities. In early 1982, the European Parliamentary Council sponsored a special report designed to identify those strategies and guidelines that would ensure the most efficient expansion of this technology in the European community.[10] The council recommended that the various European governments coordinate and standardize their applications of genetic engineering, but failed to spell out the potential consequences—or advantages—of heavy governmental involvement in biotechnology as a means of enhancing certain social goals.

According to Dr. Fritz Gautier, an attendee of the council and a member of the European Parliament in Brussels, the conferees neglected several key social issues. Chief among them were the individual needs of less fully developed countries in the European community and a critical valuation of the social ends to which recombinant DNA might be put.[11]

In contrast to the Americans, Europeans have only rarely expressed concern over the broad social implications of biotechnology. One voice has been that of Wolf-Michael Catenhausen, a member of the West German Bundestag. As a leader of the minority Social Democrats (SPD) and the Bundestag Committee on Research and Technology, Catenhausen submitted a motion in early 1984 to set up a special Bundestag committee to deal with the issues of industrial safety and human genetic engineering. Catenhausen subsequently drafted a white paper for the SPD that highlighted the social implications of genetic engineering, including issues generated by cloning, human modification, and rDNA experimentation.[12] Currently (circa 1984) this committee promises to look at the full gamut of biotechnology's social implications.

Like the SPD report, the European Parliamentary Council stressed the urgency of protecting human rights that might be jeopardized by the rapid expansion of biotechnology into genetic engineering. While the council's concern was focused primarily on biological hazards and public health effects, Gautier believed that these two efforts signaled the beginning of an awareness in some European communities that biotechnology had far-reaching social implications.

The Parliamentary Council urged that European states

collaborate to become publicly involved and offer mutual assistance in the effort to achieve identified priorities. But two years after the council made this plea for cooperation, the European community appears fragmented, with most

Table 3.1
Major Events in the Commercialization of Biotechnology

Year	Event
1973	• First gene cloned.
1974	• First expression of a gene cloned from a different species in bacteria. • Recombinant DNA (rDNA) experiments first discussed in a public forum (Gordon Conference).
1975	• U.S. guidelines for rDNA research outlined (Asilomar Conference). • First hybridoma created.
1976	• First firm to exploit rDNA technology founded in the United States (Genentech). • Genetic Manipulation Advisory Group (U.K.) started in the United Kingdom.
1978	• First product made with rDNA (somatostatin). • Nobel Prize given to Hamilton Smith and Daniel Nathans (restriction enzyme discovery).
1980	• *Diamond* v. *Chakrabarty*—U.S. Supreme Court rules that microorganisms can be patented under existing law. • Cohen/Boyer patent submitted for the construction of rDNA. • United Kingdom targets biotechnology (Spinks report). • Federal Republic of Germany targets biotechnology *(Leistungsplan)*. • Initial public offering by Genentech sets Wall Street record for fastest price per share increase.

Table 3.1 *(continued)*

Year	Event
1981	• First monoclonal antibody diagnostic kits approved for use in the United States. • First automated gene synthesizer marketed. • Japan targets biotechnology (Ministry of International Trade and Technology declares 1981 "The Year of Biotechnology"). • France targets biotechnology (Pelissolo report). • Hoechst/Massachusetts General Hospital agree to ten-year, $70-million collaboration. • Initial public offering by Cetus sets Wall Street record for the largest amount of money raised in an initial public offering ($125 million). • Industrial Biotechnology Association founded. • DuPont commits $120 million for life sciences research and development. • More than 80 NBFs* had been formed by the end of the year.
1982	• First rDNA animal vaccine (for colibacillosis) approved for use in Europe. • First rDNA pharmaceutical product (human insulin) approved for use in the United States and the United Kingdom. • First R & D limited partnership formed for the funding of clinical trials.
1983	• First plant gene expressed in a plant of a different species. • $500 million raised in U.S. public markets by NBFs.
1984	• Judge John Sirica thwarts the scheduled environmental release of rDNA organisms. • Stanford awarded Cohen/Boyer patent on basic rDNA process.

Source: Adapted from the Office of Technology Assessment, *Commercial Recombinant DNA: An International Analysis* (Washington, D.C.: U.S. Government Printing Office, January, 1984), p. 4.
*NBF = New biotechnology firm.

of the key individual nations (France, England, West Germany and Switzerland) preoccupied with securing hegemony in biotechnology.

Genetically Engineered Products

By the end of 1984, at least 202 companies in the United States, out of the 2,484 in the Western world, were developing recombinant-DNA products and supporting the basic industry. Several major companies, notably Genentech, Genex, Cetus, Bethesda Research Laboratories, DuPont, Eli Lilly, International Plant Research Institute, Monsanto, Phillips Petroleum, and Biogen, compose an inner circle of highly competitive companies. Worldwide, other major firms are currently exploiting genetic-engineering techniques to produce feedstuffs, energy products, pharmaceuticals, fragrances, reagents that facilitate diagnosis of disease, and any product with sufficient value to justify small-scale production. Table 3.2 displays the areas of interest of the major U.S. companies as charted by the OTA in its report on *Commercial Biotechnology* (Appendix C is a complete roster of companies active as of the end of 1983). In the year since these data were acquired, the aggregate investment in human health-related products has grown to more than half a billion dollars, representing 83 percent of all capital investment.[13]

The targeted products for major development in health in particular provide a baseline for assessing the relationship of these choices to human needs. This roster of major investments, in turn, gives us a rough way of evaluating the degree to which different industry members re-

Table 3.2
Major Areas of Research and Development among U.S.
Biotechnology Firms

Product(s) or Major Research and Development Effort	No. Companies Engaged in Work	No. Companies Specializing in this Area†
A. Pharmaceuticals	133	70
B. Animal agriculture	59	5
C. Plant agriculture	53	16
D. Specialty chemicals and food	40	8
E. Commodity chemicals and energy	28	3
F. Microbial application to the environment*	21	6
G. Electronics	7	2

Source: U.S. Congress Office of Technology Assessment, *Commercial Biotechnolgy* (Washington, D.C.: U.S. Government Printing Office, 1984), pp. 67–70; adapted from Table 4.
*Microbial enhanced oil recovery; microbial mining, pollution control, and toxic waste treatment.
†Companies that list only a single specialty in their prospectus or annual report.

spond to societal (extrinsic) and corporate (intrinsic) pressures. Among the potential factors that can influence these choices are health needs, economic attractiveness, and scientific value. (The general mode by which some of the major companies set priorities is reviewed in Chapter 10.) Appendix D is a representative roster of existing products and their respective companies. It lists twenty-three major substances now being produced.

One major contributor to the shift toward human health-related products is the increased attractiveness of potent small-molecular-weight hormones or their releaser molecules. This shift is evident in Appendix D, where substances such as interleukin 2, growth-hormone releasing factors, and human sex hormones are prominent. Other health products, such as insulin, blood-clot-dissolving enzymes, anticancer drugs, reflect the dominant role of diseases in developed countries as shapers of the product choices of the biotechnology industry generally. Thus, high "value-added" commodities have become the mainstay of the industry.

This observation suggests that the disease patterns of the more affluent nations of the world have a greater weight in product choices than those of the poorer nations. This hypothesis is underscored by independent observers such as Professor J. Coombs, editor of the *International Biotechnology Directory*. Coombs believes that it is the shift of major mortality towards viral infections, cancer, heart disease, and problems of aging that has "prompted the rapid growth of companies producing diagnostics, controlled drug delivery systems and automated delivery systems" designed to diagnose and treat these diseases.[14]

More difficult questions arise in the nonhealth sector, where protein-rich corn or grain is subjected to rDNA-generated enzymes and fermentation systems to produce high-fructose sweeteners or feedstock for biotechnology-derived energy-production systems. Here, obvious ethical questions surround the use of otherwise vital foodstuffs for secondary conversion into energy-rich substances, such as methanol, fructose, or ethanol. From an ethical standpoint, one might expect that research into converting nonutilizable lignocellulose from corn or wheat stalks, pulp mills, and the like into a feedstock for fermentation systems producing valuable single-cell protein would be more attractive to investors. But while single-cell protein has been produced, most notably by Britain's Imperial Chemical Industries (ICI), it has been markedly unsuccessful in comparison to low-volume, high-value products.

Existing regulatory obstacles and ready markets in the veterinary health field have led to an emphasis on animal vaccines, antibiotics, and growth stimulants as biotechnology products. Table 3.3, which lists some of the major biotech products selected for development, shows that the majority of products actually developed to date are in the veterinary sector. Ronald Cape, president of Cetus Corporation of Emeryville, California, interprets the rationale for this pattern as a complex mix of regulatory and market pressures shaping the choice of biotechnology products.[15]

Regulatory Obstacles

Beginning in the mid-1970s and continuing to the present day, representatives of the biotechnology industry such as Genex's J. Leslie Glick have asserted that companies were discouraged from focusing on what would be valuable pharmaceutical products by the severe obstacles posed by federal regulatory agencies such as the FDA.[16] In fact, where biotechnology firms have attempted to put products on the market, they have been remarkably successful.

This is not to say that the process of product development is simple. Quite the contrary. Before an agent can receive federal approval for use as a drug, it must pass rigorous tests of safety and efficacy, beginning with animal tests and culminating with a three-step sequence of human clinical trials. An elaborate sequence of protocol development, human-subject recruitment, and human-subject review plus clinical trials must occur before products that have shown promise in animal testing may be marketed for human use.

The dogma in the pharmaceutical industry is that products might progress with relative ease through the gauntlet of regulations that govern research and initial development stages only to encounter unanticipated hurdles when subjected to clinical testing. In actuality, rDNA patenting and product review have been granted favored status, resulting in the remarkably swift processing of applications for Patent Office and FDA review. As shown in Table 3.3, which lists many of the nondrug products under development, even more rapid success has been achieved for agricultural products.

When such accelerated processing occurs, imperfectly purified products may be prematurely tested. Such a phe-

Table 3.3
Introduction of Genetic Engineering Products

Product	Predicted Year* (circa 1981)	Year First Reported
1. Rennin	1985	1984
2. Casein	1985–89	———
3. Animal growth hormone	1985	1983
4. Foot & mouth vaccine	1985	1981
5. Hog diarrhea vaccine	1985	1982
6. Blue tongue vaccine	1985	———
7. Methanol bacteria	1985	———
8. Bacterial/misc. feeds	1985	1981
9. Amino acids	1981	1981
10. Antibiotics	1985	1983
11. Anabolic steroids	1985	1984
12. Pesticides	1985	1984
13. Pesticide-resistant plants	1985–89	1983
14. Cloned livestock	1985–90	1984
15. Gasohol-fermentation bacteria	1985	———
16. Improved yeasts	1985–89	1983
17. Cellulose-digesting bacteria	1985	1983
18. Salinization osmoregulation	1985–89	———
19. Nitrogen-fixation cereal enzyme	1985–90	1984
20. Cereal nitrogen-fixation synthesis	1990	———

*The source of the predicted years is the Chicago Group for Policy Research, Chicago, Illinois, 1981.

nomenon appears to have occurred in the rush to put human growth hormone into clinical practice. The successful production in bacteria of this hormone, which is 191 amino acids long, was reported in 1979.[17] By the fall of 1984, Genentech's David Goeddel was able to report to an appreciative audience at a conference in Boston called Thirty Years of DNA that his team had attained FDA approval for the finished human product. Goeddel noted, however, that the first human patients given experimental treatment experienced unanticipated reactions.

Human Growth Hormone

As reported by Goeddel at the Boston conference, the human growth hormone produced was initially so impure that a significant proportion of the growth-deficient children in the first clinical trials showed evidence of reaction to bacterial contaminants. Most experienced fever, malaise, and soreness at the injection site. Only after the hormone preparation was retested twice more—and purified after each test—was it possible to demonstrate that it both accelerated growth and was without significant side effects. But even with such setbacks, human growth hormone set a new marketing record for the ease with which it passed through FDA's regulatory process.

It remains to be seen if this new product will find acceptable clinical use. While demonstrating its ability to reverse pituitary dwarfism in children, the authors of a recent clinical study warned their readers that neither the criteria for defining the conditions that are suitable for treatment with HGH nor the extent of its side effects are known.[18] (The ethical implications of the marketing strategies and uses of this product are discussed in Chapter 5.)

Insulin

Other companies that put their recombinant-DNA-generated molecules into clinical trials were also remarkably successful in accelerating the commonly tedious process of approval. Thus, just over a year elapsed from the announcement of a bacterial system for producing human insulin (July 11, 1979) to the commencement of human clinical trials (July 22, 1980). Less than two years later, on April 12, 1982, Eli Lilly opened the first plant for producing insulin from genetically modified *E. coli* in the United Kingdom. On October 30, 1982, the FDA granted Eli Lilly's synthetic human insulin, Humulin, final approval. On that date, Humulin became the first genetically engineered product intended for human use to be offered for sale in the United States.

Even faster processing was accomplished by Novo Industri of Denmark. This company had developed an enzymatic technique of converting pork insulin into human insulin that was much simpler than Lilly's. When the terminal amino acid is cleaned from pork insulin, the latter becomes molecularly indistinguishable from human insulin. Within a year of submitting its papers, Novo announced that it had begun to sell its product in both Britain and Ireland. The firm received its U.S. license to sell human insulin on September 16, 1982.

Part of the explanation for the remarkable success of this product was the ability of both Lilly and Novo to demonstrate their products' molecular equivalence to human insulin—i.e., the purity of their products. But even more important was their ability to stimulate a dramatic number of clinical studies over an extremely short period. One symposium published in 1983 under the auspices of the journal *Diabetes Care* exemplifies the extraordinary amount of good will (and financial investment) needed to ensure cooperation among research centers.[19] This symposium brought together thirteen research teams from all over the world to share their data and results. In spite of Lilly's high expectations for the recombinant or enzymatically derived products, researchers showed that the new products were generally no better—and no worse—than the traditional porcine insulin. An additional property of the rDNA products—their faster absorption rates after injection—might even be considered a disadvantage. While the synthesized human insulin was expected to offer a significant advantage over pork insulin in being less likely to provoke an immune reaction, subsequent reports have suggested immune reactivity even to the rDNA product.[20] On balance, the feat these companies achieved was simply to show that rDNA could be used to make something commercially valuable at a time when the industry needed a much-vaunted boost. This interpretation is underscored by the realization that for most diabetics, rDNA insulin offers no real advantage except as a hedge against future shortages. In fact, Eli Lilly now advertises its accomplishment as a way of protecting us against a future when pigs won't be available for making the traditional form of insulin.

Interferons

Many scientists once believed that one or more of the three interferons—leukocyte, or alpha; fibroblast, or beta; and immune, or gamma interferon—held great promise as a pharmaceutical agent for treating cancer or viral diseases. Originally cloned with rDNA techniques, alpha and beta interferons have already been the objects of intense medical interest. Alpha interferon, which the Finns produced in unpurified form and in bulk from their blood-banking industry, was the first to be successfully synthesized and subjected to clinical testing. Beginning in the early 1980s,[21] biotechnology entrepreneurs used the public enthusiasm for the "wonder drugs" to encourage rapid, and sometimes premature, clinical testing of these new rDNA products.

On January 24, 1980, Biogen announced production of a precursor to interferon from recombinant DNA. Clinical trials began that same year. By June 4, 1980, Genentech and Hoffman-La Roche had announced synthesis of both leukocyte (alpha) and fibroblast (beta) varieties of human interferon in recombinant-DNA systems. By March 1981, Genentech had begun clinical trials of its alpha interferon. (They tested two subtypes out of at least fourteen possible varieties.) ICI Corporation announced in September 1981 that it had used bacteria containing recombinant DNA to synthesize alpha interferon in its entirety. Later in 1981, Suntory of Japan announced that it had achieved purification of an alpha interferon that was ten to a hundred times more effective than previous products. And in August 1983, Collaborative Research announced that it had successfully produced batch quantities of fibroblast interferon.

Clinical trials of the Finnish product were reported in a 1983 issue of the *New England Journal of Medicine*. These studies showed that even though it was more impure than its cloned counterpart, alpha interferon derived from blood leukocytes was unexpectedly effective against one form of human leukemia (hairy cell leukemia). Ironically, the same issue contained potentially discouraging news about the pure alpha product. It produced side effects and kidney toxicity in patients being treated for another form of cancer.[22]

Except for its success in treating some forms of lymphatic cancer,[23] boosting the immune response in weakened cancer patients,[24] and perhaps treating some forms of herpes virus infections,[25] alpha interferon has failed to live up to its expectations. More seriously, some patients using it have died. And when it was used to counteract the depressed immune function of kidney-graft recipients, it was found actually to exacerbate their condition by accelerating an irreversible rejection episode.[26]

With very few exceptions, interferon has only rarely caused the complete regression of a malignant tumor, a feat now routinely accomplished by many forms of chemotherapy. (For this reason, some researchers now combine interferons and chemical antitumor agents.[27]) In fact, according to a 1982 report of the World Health Organization, "no response [to interferons] has been observed in the majority of patients" with malignant disease. And while objective improvement has been reported for some malignancies, WHO concluded with a stern warning to its international colleagues that "interferons are not a panacea for the cure of human virus infections or cancer, and there is no case for their use at present except in properly conducted clinical trials."[28]

The interferon story illustrates another generic problem of developing rDNA-based pharmaceuticals. Some U.S. firms have established overseas bases of operation for doing their clinical trials, in large part to avoid stringent FDA regulations that protect human subjects of research. In early 1982, Southern Biotech announced that it had begun the manufacture and export of interferon in Jamaica, leaving uncertain whether or not it had conducted suitable clinical trials according to FDA protocols. By September 1982, Southern was able to announce that the FDA had approved its Caribbean clinical trials of one of its interferon preparations for treating lymphoma patients. Biogen, S.A., the parent company of the American firm of the same name, conducted interferon trials against cold viruses abroad as well.

As with early batches of human growth hormone, inter-ferons are sometimes contaminated with bacterial by-products such a pyrogens. Even when made in yeast, which are pyrogen-free, they can still cause adverse reactions. Gen-entech's leukocyte interferon, for instance, can produce objective responses in lymphoma patients, but at the cost of producing sometimes severe side effects, including fever, chills, loss of sensation and appetite, weight loss, and depres-sion of white blood cells and granulocytes.[29]

The limitations of this drug as a therapeutic agent were stressed by other researchers who have conducted studies. One group concluded: "There is a role for IFLrA [alpha interferon] in the treatment of cancer patients, but its pre-cise indications, optimal doses, and schedules remain to be determined."[30]

Monoclonal Antibodies

Monoclonal antibodies (MCAs) are so-named because they are molecules of antibodies with (usually) just one specificity or targeted antigen and are derived from the descendants ("clones") of a single, fused cell. In an unusual departure from recent practices, British researchers Cesar Milstein and G. Kohler, who discovered the technique of making monoclonal antibodies in 1975,[31] chose not to pa-tent the process, thereby making it available to the bio-technology field as a whole free of royalty payments. In recognition of the vast implications of their technique—and perhaps their altruism—the Nobel Committee awarded Milstein and Kohler the Nobel Prize for Medicine in October, 1984.

To produce these antibodies in sizable quantity, re-searchers take spleen cells of an animal that has been immunized against a given antigen and fuse them with a type of tumor cell. The descendants from such a pairing, called a *hybridoma,* carry with them the characteristics of both parental cell lines: those of the cancerous cell partner confer on the hybridoma the capability of replicating indefinitely, and those of the spleen cell make a single type of antibody. The resulting hybridoma is distinctly different from normal antibody-producing cells in that it can be maintained in tissue culture for protracted periods and hence can mass-produce specific antibodies almost indefinitely.

Certain companies have taken advantage of the power and availability of this technique to move monoclonal antibodies aggressively into the commercial sector. One of the promising applications of MCAs is their clinical use in detecting evidence of disease or dysfunction.[32] In May 1980, Hybritech, one of the earliest developers of monoclonal-antibody products (such as diagnostic antibodies that react with human pregnancy hormones), announced that it had three commodities on the clinical diagnostics market. A competing firm, Monoclonal Antibodies, subsequently developed a new pregnancy diagnostic kit, which also promised early and accurate determination of pregnancy. (In keeping with the times, Monoclonal Antibodies received its FDA clearance a bare six weeks after filing for approval.) Another biotech firm, Damon Corporation, announced in December 1981 that it had developed a way to mass produce monoclonal antibodies. (Ironically, in light of Milstein and Kohler's altruism, competition among these firms is sometimes fierce.[33])

Latecomers have also fared extremely well in the monoclonal-antibody market. On March 16, 1982, Bio-Response, Inc., announced that it was seeking $10 million to finance research into a commercial plant for producing MCAs using whole animals as living factories to make homogeneous antibodies in quantity. This firm has subsequently patented several of the elements of this process. Cetus Corporation has been granted a patent in the same area, having demonstrated that its monoclonal antibodies can pick out human leukocyte antigens (HLAs) with greater precision than existing methodologies. One of these antibodies is directed at an antigen (HLA-B27) that signals the presence of an arthritis-like condition (ankylosing spondylitis) in symptomatic men[34] and can be used at least in theory to indicate others at high risk for disease (see the discussion of this controversial point in Chapter 11).

As an index of the breadth of interest in diagnostic monoclonal-antibody preparations, established pharmaceutical companies rapidly developed their own techniques or acquired them outright from MCA companies. Damon Corporation has ceded its patent rights on an exclusive basis with the pharmaceutical giant Hoffman-La Roche. Abbott Laboratories launched a major effort to get into the field in the early 1980s. By April 14, 1982, it had been cleared by the FDA to use its MCAs to monitor the success of cancer therapy.

Other companies are capitalizing on the success of researchers in using MCAs to detect cancer antigens.[35] In May 1982, the Genetic Systems Corporation made an agreement with Syntex Corporation's Syva Company of Palo Alto to develop cancer-antigen-specific MCAs. Five months later, Hybritech announced a coventure with Tei-jan to develop monoclonal antibodies that could be used to treat a variety of cancers.

A ready market for MCA reagents that can type blood as well as other serum constituents[36] has also been tapped. For instance, on October 5, 1982, Genetic Systems announced that it had contracted with New England Nuclear and Laiichi Pure Chemicals of Japan to develop a worldwide marketing strategy for monoclonal antibodies that could rapidly and precisely type human blood cells.

Other diagnostic uses of MCAs include the detection of herpes viruses (both simplex and zoster), especially herpes genitalis, which is sexually transmitted. Such companies as Biotech Research Laboratories of Rockville, Maryland, have developed reagents for both type 1 and 2 herpes simplex viruses. These viruses are characterized by a latent state that makes detection of an infected individual or infected cells very difficult. Herpes' infectivity makes the uncovering of such carriers extremely valuable. According to Biotech Research Lab reports, MCAs directed against one or both antigenic types are on the horizon. This same company produces MCAs against other viral causes of human disease or congenital malformation, such as the cytomegalovirus, and an MCA against a potent toxic contaminant of foodstuffs, alflatoxin B1. However, none of these products is yet at the stage of direct clinical application.

While exhibiting strong interest in developing MCAs that are saleable in developed countries, biotechnology companies have expended little effort to develop commercially available monoclonal antibodies directed against the bacterial or parasitic diseases of great health significance in Third World countries. Evidence is at hand that such MCAs could be produced: MCAs against the liver fluke *(Fasciola hepatica)*, the causative agent of schistosomiasis *(Schistosoma mansoni)*, and malaria *(Plasmodium falciparum)* have all been produced in the research laboratory.[37] On the other hand, potentially more profitable MCA tests, such as one for meningitis, have been aggressively pursued. On August 8, 1983, Becton Dickinson, of Paramus, New Jersey, announced such a test.[38]

Other potentially lucrative applications for MCAs would be passively administered antibodies that could augment or replace the body's own immune system products as a form of immunotherapy.[39] A buy-out venture in May 1982 by

Schering-Plough of DNAX led to the formation of a new company to produce antibodies that would mimic those generated by the body when it fights infections. DNAX has emphasized antibody products that could be used in the therapy of allergies (such as the IgE molecules needed to desensitize allergic patients) as being among the items chosen for development by 1986–1987.

Ironically, more health-directed products have been marketed by biotechnology firms with relatively modest financial backing. In September 1983, Biotest Serum Institute announced the development of a series of three products, at least one of which would be useful in Third World countries. That product is a specific immunoglobin to protect exposed persons against hepatitis B viral infection, a problem common to many West African countries. A second product would be used to protect severely infected adults who lack the childhood immunity against the effects of chicken pox. The third would be used as a pretreatment to reduce the likelihood of immune-mediated rejection of organ transplants.

At least one residual concern about the possible safety of monoclonal antibodies for human use has been broached. Writing in the May 7, 1983, issue of *Lancet,* three British researchers emphasized that most human monoclonal antibodies are potentially contaminated with a human herpes virus (Epstein Barr Virus, or EBV) carried in latent form in blood lymphocytes. Since these lymphocytes are commonly used to make MCAs, these authors recommend that a rigorous purification procedure be used in all clinical tests of EBV-transformed cell lines.[40]

Theoretically, MCAs can be directed against the bacteria responsible for diarrheal diseases of livestock as a means of passively protecting animals that would otherwise receive protective antibodies through their mother's milk. Such a product was announced in June 1982 by Molecular Genetics. In July, this firm announced that it had conducted successful field trials of an oral preparation of a product that could prevent toxic diarrhea in dairy calves. As I have documented in my book *Germs That Won't Die*,[41] such infections are largely the result of poor husbandry practices, not inevitable infection. Protecting dairy calves intended for early slaughter is only cost-effective in economies willing to pay the high cost of veal. And veal is not on the tables of most households in middle-income America, much less those in the developing world.

Vaccines

Companies with an interest in producing vaccines lagged behind their biochemically oriented counterparts. In April 1981, Damon Corporation formed a subsidiary company called Damon Biotech to capitalize on a newly patented microcapsulation technique to make vaccines as well as cancer diagnostics and interferons. During this same period, Cetus embarked on its Palo Alto venture to set up a subsidiary for concentrating on small polypeptide vaccine products, and in 1981 Johnson & Johnson announced development of a major research program in San Diego. According to its director, Ralph Arlinghaus, J & J's Biotechnology Research Center plans to concentrate on long-term projects based on polypeptides.[42] Products would include vaccines against eight major human diseases, such as human leukemias, where viral antigens have been implicated as causative agents.

Other more common but nonetheless highly profitable diseases have attracted considerable attention as candidates for recombinant-DNA-engineered vaccines in the United States. A case in point is genital herpes. In fall 1982, Molecular Genetics, of Minnesota, announced a vaccine against the herpes simplex virus.[43] This new immunologically active peptide was developed with American Cyanimid. Judged by the success of acyclovir, a topical drug product developed by Burroughs-Wellcome (Avirax), an effective vaccine could be a major money winner for this company were it to prove successful in clinical trials.

In contrast to these human vaccine projects, which have to pass close FDA scrutiny, progress on the veterinary-vaccine front has been considerably easier. Several rDNA companies have been competing to develop the first effective hoof-and-mouth virus vaccine. On June 20, 1981, Genentech and the U.S. Department of Agriculture announced the successful testing on the USDA's Plum Island, Massachusetts, quarantine facility of an effective hoof-and-mouth disease vaccine. Biogen announced on October 19 the same year that it had successfully cloned the key protein for hoof-and-mouth disease virus. (See Table 3.3 above to gain a sense of the rapidity of these developments.)

Related work on other viruses has also progressed rapidly. On March 17, 1982, Connaught Laboratories and the Canadian government signed a contract for the commercial development of a rabies vaccine. And in August 1982, a French biotechnology company produced an immunologically active fraction of the rabies virus based on material supplied to it by the Wistar Institute of Philadelphia.

Following the lead of Cetus Corporation, which conducted the ground-breaking work on isolating the key bacterial antigens involved in producing a devastating diarrheal disease known as hog scours, in March 1982, Norden Laboratories announced that it was marketing a vaccine based on the Cetus antigens. As an indicator of the intensity of the race to develop this single livestock product, still another company announced that it had developed the first hog-scours vaccine barely one month later. On April 29, 1982, Intervet International claimed that it had successfully marketed the first hog-scours vaccine. In June 1982, the AKZO group in the Netherlands announced that it, too, was marketing a recombinant-DNA-produced vaccine against hog and cattle scours.

Cetus, capitalizing on its early success with its own hog-scours vaccine, signed an agreement in July 1982 with Tech American Corporation for the research and development of a set of animal health care products that would include a vaccine for bovine calf diarrhea.

Thus, with the notable exception of a vaccine for hepatitis B (developed by two Emeryville, California, firms, Genentech and Chiron) virtually all the vaccine-related research in the American biotechnology industry has been directed to commercially saleable products that would either serve the veterinary industry or control mild but highly contagious diseases, such as herpes simplex, likely to draw considerable consumer attention. While some major companies have agreed to offer some support to international development of major vaccines against parasitic diseases such as malaria,[44] this effort is likely to fall short of the full-scale commitment needed to achieve rapid success in this complex area of research.

Blood Products

In the early 1980s, the development of blood products accelerated as concerns grew regarding contamination of donor blood by the agent responsible for acquired immune deficiency syndrome (AIDS). Many blood agencies came to believe that they would have greatly enhanced needs for recombinant-DNA-produced blood products as a result of the discovery that AIDS could be transmitted to hemophiliacs by transfusion from the multiple donors needed to produce Factor VIII.[45]

By mid-1984, fifty hemophiliacs, representing about 1 percent of all cases, had contracted AIDS, presumably from such contaminated blood. In spite of the fact that most blood can be safely used if donors are suitably screened, a high premium on uncontaminated blood products led several companies to embark on crash programs to make Factor VIII, the essential clotting factor for classical hemophilia. Connaught Labs in Canada contracted with the Canadian government to make a relatively inexpensive version of such a product in the spring of 1982, and Travenol Laboratories and Genetics Institute agreed to use a proprietary technique under an exclusive license to make Factor VIII. In April 1984, Genentech became the first company to announce successful development and approval of this product. In the United States, this means that some fifteen to twenty thousand male hemophiliacs may now receive a product free of contamination with AIDS. (The residual question of whether Factor VIII should have been a health priority is discussed in Chapter 5.)

Other blood products have comparable value as adequate supplies of uncontaminated natural blood decline. Thus, in May 1982, Genentech announced that it had signed a major agreement with the massive Mitsubishi Chemical Industry group in Japan to produce commercially synthetic human serum albumin.

Cardiac Therapeutics

Economically attractive medical uses of enzymes are now being developed in the area of cardiac research. Clot-digesting enzymes such as urokinase and streptokinase have shown dramatic success in reducing the damage to heart muscle in patients who have had recent heart attacks. (Genentech, which pioneered the cloning of these and related enzymes, signed a contract with the German firm Gruenthal for mass-producing urokinase in June 1982).

A molecule similarly effective in reducing the consequences of blood clots is tissue plasminogen activator, a thrombolytic agent that degrades red blood cells. Genentech signed a contract with two Japanese firms that have substantial fermentation expertise—Mitsubishi Chemical Industries and Kyowa Hakko Company—to produce sufficient amounts of this substance for clinical tests involving humans. In July 1982, Genentech announced that it had succeeded in producing tissue plasminogen activator and that animal trials would begin within two months, with human testing scheduled six to nine months later.[46]

In a move common to much of the biotechnology industry, the U.S. developer of this recombinant product looked to Japan for its full-scale production. Biogen and Fujisawa Pharmaceutical announced on October 2, 1982, that they would collaborate in developing the plasminogen activator.

Chronic Diseases— Replacement Therapy

One would expect to see the substantial investment of biotechnology venture capital in the area of chronic disease control, since chronic diseases are now the primary cause of disability in the developed world. Such investments are in fact the rule, although not all are necessarily biomedically sound. A case in point is chronic obstructive pulmonary disease (COPD) and its linkage to a critical enzyme.

COPD and related conditions are the fifth most common cause of death in the United States, accounting for some three percent of all deaths.[47]

One rDNA product designed to combat COPD is a molecule that is a potent enzyme inhibitor known as alpha-1-antitrypsin (AAT). Adequate amounts of functional AAT are essential to protect sensitive lung tissue against enzyme-mediated damage following the physical injury of cells within this tissue. Individuals who have a genetically based disorder in the protease inhibitor series of genes have a deficiency of this inhibitor. Rare homozygous affected individuals who have the ZZ marker are prone to develop cirrhosis and later chronic obstructive pulmonary disease. The more common carrier of this Z gene may also develop a predilection to COPD.[48] It is the first group, numbering some 54,000 in the United States, that the Zymos Corporation hopes to reach with a synthetic antitrypsin product announced in November 1982. But little evidence exists to suggest that product replacement will in fact cure—or prevent—this constitutional deficiency.

Hormones

The commercial marketing of hormones for pharmaceutical use in humans has followed a tortuous evolution. While animal growth hormones, both rat and bovine, had been isolated one to two years earlier, human growth hormone or its evocative hypothalamic hormones were not tested until 1982.

Polypeptide hormones such as insulin and HGH have already been described. But others, such as thymosin alpha-1, relaxin, glucagon, and growth-hormone releasing factor, will soon undergo or are now undergoing clinical testing. Recombinant-DNA-derived hormones such as these promise greater control over basic disease processes, but as a result of patent laws they also make available to the pharmaceutical sector exclusive control over extraordinarily scarce and expensive commodities. This last observation points to a lingering concern over the commercial control of rDNA: that products needed for protecting or enhancing human health and well-being may be kept prohibitively expensive while others that may be critically needed in Third World countries are given a back seat.

Notes

1. *Chemical and Engineering News* (October 18, 1982): 17.
2. A. L. Demain and N. A. Solomon, "Industrial Microbiology," *Scientific American* 245 (1981): 67–75.
3. J. Coombs, ed., *International Biotechnology Directory* (London: Nature Press, 1984).
4. U.S. Congress, Office of Technology Assessment, *Commercial Biotechnology: An International Analysis* (Washington, D.C.: OTA, 1984), p. 6.
5. See C. W. Harris, "The Gene Age," *Biotechnology* (February 1984): 173–174.
6. Cited in *European Chemical News* (May 3, 1982): 16–17.
7. See *Biotechnology Europe,* an Imsworld Report, London, September 1981.
8. See S. Yanchinski, "Biotechnology Takes Root in West Germany," *Bio/Technology* 2 (April 1984): 291–292.
9. For an extensive survey see C. G. Edwards, J. Elkington, and A. M. Murray, "Japan Taps into New Biotech," *Bio/Technology* 2 (1984): 307–321.
10. Council of Europe, Parliamentary Assembly, 33rd Session, 21st and 22nd sitting, January 18, 1982 (Geneva, 1982).
11. F. Gautier, Member of the European Parliament, personal communication, of September 20, 1983.
12. "Report by the SPD Working Group on Research and Technology: Limits in the Handling of Genetic Engineering," undated white paper made available on April 20, 1984 through the West German Consulate, Walter Stechel, Consul.

13. J. R. Murray, "1983 Financing for Health Applications Increases over Agriculture," *Bio/Technology* 2 (1984): 332–333.

14. *International Biotechnology Directory*, p. 76.

15. Interview with Ronald Cape, March 1, 1984.

16. Telephone interview with J. Leslie Glick, February 10, 1984.

17. D. Goeddel, H. Heyneker, T. Hozumi, et al., "Direct Expression in *Escherichia coli* of a DNA Sequence Coding for Human Growth Hormone," *Nature* 281 (1979): 544–548; and D. V. Goeddel, D. G. Kleid, F. Bolivard, et al., "Expression in *Escherichia coli* of Chemically Synthesized Genes for Human Insulin," *Proceedings of the National Academy of Sciences* 76 (1979): 106–110.

18. G. Van Vliet, D. M. Styne, S. L. Kaplan, and M. M. Orumbach, "Growth Hormone Treatment for Short Stature," *New England Journal of Medicine* 309 (1983): 1016–1022.

19. *Diabetes Care 6: Supplement 1* (March–April 1983).

20. For example, L. C. Grammer, B. E. Metzger, and R. Patterson, "Cutaneous Allergy to Human (Recombinant DNA) Insulin," *Journal of the American Medical Association* 251 (1984): 1459–1460.

21. S. Nagata, H. Taira, A. Hall, et al., "Synthesis in *E. coli* of a Polypeptide with Human Leukocyte Interferon Activity," *Nature* 284 (1980): 316–320; R. Derynck, E. Remaut, E. Saman, et al., "Expression of Human Fibroblast Interferon Gene in *Escherichia coli*," *Nature* 287 (1980): 193–197; and D. Goeddel, E. Yelverton, A. Ullrich, et al., "Human Leukocyte Interferon Produced by *E. coli* Is Biologically Active," *Nature* 287 (1980): 411–416.

22. J. R. Quesada, J. Reuben, J. T. Manning, et al., "Alpha Interferon for Induction of Remission in Hairy Cell Leukemia," *New England Journal of Medicine* 310 (1984): 15–18.

23. H. Ozer, M. Garigan, J. O'Malley, et al., "Immunomodulation by Recombinant Interferon-DC$_2$ in a Phase I Trial in Patients with Lymphoproliferative Malignancies," *Journal of Biological Response Modifiers* 2 (1983): 499–515.

24. J. C. D. Hengist, R. A. Kempf, J. Kam-Mitchell, et al., "Immunological Effect of Recombinant Interferon-DC$_2$ in Cancer Patients," *Journal of Biological Response Modifiers* 2 (1983): 516–527.

25. D. J. Freeman and S. L. Spruance, "Topical Recombinant Interferon in the Treatment of an Experimental Herpes-Simplex Virus-Infection," *Clinical Research* 32 (1984): A42.

26. P. Kramer, F. W. J. Fen Kate, A. B. Bijnen, et al., "Recombinant

Leukocyte Interferon A Induces Steroid-Resistant Acute Vascular Rejection Episodes in Renal Transplant Recipients," *Lancet* I (1984): 989–990.

27. T. I. Mughal, N. Robinson, W. A. Thomas, et al., "Evaluation of Recombinant Interferon-Alpha-2 (IFN) and Cimetidine in Metastafic Malignant Melanoma Resistant to IFN Alone," *Clinical Research* 32 (1984): A59.

28. "Interferon Therapy," Report of a WHO Scientific Group, *WHO Technical Report* Series No. 676 (Geneva, 1982), p. 25.

29. Such problems sometimes reflect inadequate quality control of the biologicals produced by rDNA. This subject has been a concern of the World Health Organization since 1983. See the WHO consultation team article, "Quality Control of Biologicals Produced by Recombinant DNA Techniques," *WHO Bulletin* 61 (1983): 897–911.

30. J. R. Quesada and J. U. Gutterman, "Clinical Study of Recombinant DNA Produced Leukocyte Interferon (Clone A) in an Intermittent Schedule in Cancer Patients," *Journal of the National Cancer Institute* 70 (1983): 1041–1046.

31. C. Milstein and G. Kohler, "Continuous Cultures of Fused Cells Secreting Antibody of Predefined Specificity," *Nature* 256 (1975): 495.

32. E. G. Engelman, "The Clinical Use of Monoclonal Antibodies," *Western Journal of Medicine* 138 (1983): 707.

33. In March 1984, Hybritech sued Monoclonal Antibodies for patent infringement. See *Science* 224 (1983): 594–596.

34. E. G. Engelman, A. Colin, and F. C. Grumet, "Analysis of HLA-B27 Antigen with Monoclonal Antibodies," *Journal of Rheumatology* 10 (1983): 56–61.

35. See, for instance, T. Masuko, H. Yagita, and Y. Hashimoto, "Monoclonal Antibodies Against Cell-Surface Antigens Present on Human Urinary Bladder Cancer Cells," *Journal of the National Cancer Institute* 72 (1984): 523–530; and E. D. Bal, R. F. Graziano, O. S. Pettengi, et al., "Monoclonal Antibodies Reactive with Small Cell Carcinoma of the Lung," *Journal of the National Cancer Institute* 72 (1984): 593–598.

36. See, for instance, the broad-ranging discussion by J. F. Bach, A. E. Vondembo, D. B. Cines, et al., "What Will Be the Impact of Monoclonal Antibodies on the Reagent Spectrum for the Characterization of Genetic Makers of Cellular and Humoral Constituents of Human Blood," *Vox Sanguinus* 45 (1983): 166–179.

37. R. E. B. Hanna and A. G. Trudgett, "Fasciola Hepatica: Use of Monoclonal Antibodies to Characterize and Localize Somatic Antigens," *Parasitology* 87 (1983): R1; M. A. Smith and J. A. Clegg, "Monoclonal Antibodies Against *Schistosoma monsoni*," *Parasitology* 87 (1983): R19; and A. Saul, P. Myler, L. Schofiel, and C. Kidson, "A High Molecular Weight Antigen in *Plasmodium falciparum* Recognized by Inhibitory Monoclonal Antibodies," *Parasite Immunology* 6 (1984): 39–50.

38. See, for instance, "Monoclonal Antibodies Test for Meningitis," *Chemical Engineering News* 61 (1983): 4–5.

39. A. Estabrook and J. A. Patterson, "Immunotherapy Using Monoclonal Antibodies," *Journal of Cutaneous Pathology* 10 (1983): 559–566.

40. D. H. Crawford, E. R. Huehs, and M. A. Epstein, "Therapeutic Use of Human Monoclonal Antibodies," *Lancet* I (1983): 1040.

41. M. Lappé, *Germs That Won't Die* (Garden City, NY: Anchor/Doubleday, 1982).

42. Interview with Ralph Arlinghaus, September 20, 1983, Boston, Massachusetts.

43. C. Wenz, "Vaccines Show the Way," *Nature* 303 (1983): 648–649.

44. Telephone interview with David Martin, Jr., vice president for research at Genentech, February 8, 1984.

45. See A. L. Bloom, "Benefits of Cloning Genes for Clotting Factors," *Nature* 303 (1983): 474–475, for a discussion of the value of providing virus-free agents.

46. See the *Wall Street Journal* (July 23, 1982), p. 28 for the way in which such annoucements are inflated for the press.

47. *Monthly Vital Statistics Reports* 31 (October, 1983): 5.

48. The controversy over whether or not the carrier of the Z allele (the MZ heterozygote) is at increased risk for lung disease has apparently been resolved in the affirmative. See D. Kozarevic, M. Laban, and M. Budmir, et al., "Intermediate Alpha-1-Antitrypsin Deficiency and Chronic Obstructive Pulmonary Disease in Yugoslavia," *American Review of Respiratory Disease* 117 (1978): 1039–1043; cf., J. Lieberman, "Heterozygous and Homozygous Alpha-1-Antitrypsin Deficiency in Patients with Pulmonary Emphysema," *New England Journal of Medicine* 281 (1969): 279–282; the penultimate study showing the predictive power of the Z allele when in the SZ state is T. Sveger, "Prospective Study of Children with Alpha-1-Antitrypsin Deficiency: Eight-year-old Follow Up," *Journal of Pediatrics* 104 (1984): 91–93.

CHAPTER 4

Health Objectives

Second only to profitability, the core corporate question facing the biotechnology industry is whether its products accurately anticipate the ongoing needs of the public. The moral corollary to fulfilling the corporate goal of profitability is fulfilling bona fide public needs by producing the most critical and essential commodities at reasonable cost. This commitment to the public weal is underscored by Monsanto's senior vice president for research, Howard Schneiderman. Speaking about his firm's commitment to biotechnology, Schneiderman warned that "we cannot lose sight of the fact that our products must benefit humanity if they are to be of enduring commercial worth."[1]

Such a dictum presumably already undergirds the pharmaceutical industry. (Whether or not the industry discharges that ethos is, of course, debatable.) For biotechnology, the balance point of corporate responsibility is more tenuously set between the poles of simple self-interest and pure altruism. This set point is determined to some substantial degree by the origins of the technology and its capabilities.

In a sense, biotechnology is cursed by the virtual omnipotence of its technological capabilities. Through recombinant-DNA-based techniques (as we have seen), an enormous spectrum of products offers itself up for development. For the industry to be publicly responsible, it has to compare choices dictated by pure commercial interest and feasibility with those dictated by human need.

Needs

In recent years, several independent assessments have been made of the specific ends that biotechnology could serve. International agencies or health organizations such as the United Nations Industrial Development Organization (UNIDO), Pan American Health Organization (PAHO), and the World Health Organization (WHO) have considered the international implications of biotechnology and identified broad public health objectives that might be served by biotechnology.[2] American panels and assessment teams have tended to be more parochial, either weighing the ethical implications of clinical uses of genetic engineering or, like the Office of Technology Assessment's *Commercial Biotechnology*, assessing the competitive standing of the U.S. biotechnology industry.

As an example of the latter study, consider the President's Commission for the Study of Ethical Problems in Medicine and Biomedical and Behavioral Research. It was convened by Congress in 1975 to review the ethical implications of human genetic engineering. In doing so, it has generally declined to make normative judgments about the desirability of commercial applications of biotechnology.

The presidential commission's report, *Splicing Life*,[3] favorably described virtually all developments in recombinant DNA that held any promise for medical application. In keeping with the desires of religious groups, the members concentrated their critical analysis on the implications of rDNA-based technologies for modifying the human genome rather than on exploring the relative value of other applications. As evidence of its limited perspective, the commission emphasized the question of using rDNA to enhance human qualities, a prospect that the commission itself recognized as being beyond the technical capabilities of the field. It gave particular attention to human genetic engineering, owing to concern expressed by some religious groups over the likelihood of genetic engineers entering the human realm.

The commission tended to be cautious in criticizing the field as a whole, in part because of its perception of biotechnology's potential for doing good—and in part because of the lack of substantive evidence of imminent perils. In an apology for its failure to consider the broader implications of human genetic engineering, the commission noted that "assessing this new technology through cost/benefit or risk/benefit analysis is complex because decision making about gene splicing is characterized by several types and levels of uncertainty . . . consensus is lacking about whether a particular outcome is in fact a benefit or a detriment."[4]

The commission justified ignoring questions of international priorities and human health needs related to applications of recombinant DNA because of its limited time to examine the moral and philosophical questions raised by genetic engineering. In examining the clinical applications of rDNA, the commissioners simply noted that drugs produced through gene splicing did not pose problems that differed radically from those encountered in the development and marketing of any new pharmaceutical product. In fact, the commission took pains to distinguish its concerns about the intrinsic propriety of gene-splicing research from those about possible negative aspects of some of its applications and consequences. On the first question, the commissioners unanimously held the view that genetic engineering was not intrinsically wrong or irreligious per se. Instead, they argued, "the issue which deserves careful thought is: by what standards, and toward what objectives, should the great new powers of genetic engineering be guided?"[5] Perhaps because of the limited time given for preparation of their analysis, the commissioners did not materially advance our understanding of these questions.

The Office of Technology Assessment produced its first report on genetic engineering in 1981.[6] Like the commission's report, this paper was limited in its critical analysis of the field. Instead, the OTA study noted a broad range of areas in which developments were likely, and left to Congress the question of which developments should receive priority.

These reports have tended to reinforce a laissez-faire governmental attitude toward the biotechnology industry. This view is exemplified by OTA's more recent study on commercial biotechnology, discussed in Chapter 2. An alternative approach might have been to examine the overall human needs for commodities, particularly those in the health sector. We can get some idea of the direction that might be taken by looking at the major public health objectives set by the World Health Organization (WHO).

World Needs

According to WHO, a single category of disease is responsible for 80 percent of illness worldwide. Broadly classed as the enteric diseases, this group includes the bacteria-produced dysenteries, cholera, typhoid fever, and amoebic dysentery. Together, WHO estimates that these diseases are responsible for 20 million deaths annually, including 5 million deaths in children under the age of five in developing countries.[7] Second in importance are the parasitic diseases—namely, leishmaniasis, malaria, trypanosomiasis, filiariasis, and river blindness. The third category includes leprosy, which is experiencing a resurgence worldwide.

Among the first statements urging a broader role for biotechnology in reducing the public health impact of this constellation of diseases was a 1982 report based on a multinational workshop held under the auspices of the National Research Council (NRC).[8] Several specific recommendations for how biotechnology might meet public health priorities emerged from a consensus of the workshop participants.

Four key points stand out: (1) all the diseases earmarked for intensive, high-priority biotechnological investigation are very common in the Third World and less so in developed countries; (2) most have been undervalued as problems worthy of research investment by major pharmaceutical houses in the developed countries; (3) many promising avenues exist for prophylaxis or treatment that relies on genetic-engineering techniques; and (4) a high degree of cooperative effort is essential for realizing the success of any of the identified goals. This last point was underscored at a round-table discussion sponsored by the International Center for Law in Development (ICLD) on Biotechnology and the Third World as being at the crux of the present disparity between biotechnology in the developed and developing countries.

Unlike the OTA or presidential commission reports from the United States, neither the NRC report nor the ICLD discussion touched on treatment of genetic disease or rare disorders. Instead, they downplayed the desirability of concentrating on the development of commercially saleable drugs for disorders such as diabetes or growth insufficiency in favor of encouraging developments deemed to fit public health needs of the large masses of the world's population. The diseases identified by the NRC group for rapid development of vaccines included rabies, dengue fever, Japanese encephalitis, certain bacterial respiratory and enteric diseases, chlamydial infections (such as those causing river blindness), and two parasitic diseases, malaria and leishmaniasis, or *kalaazar*. Indeed, many commentators and scientists have long urged the biotechnology industry to get into the vaccine business, citing this area as holding the greatest promise for health benefits worldwide.[9]

Some biotechnology firm spokespeople, such as Genentech's David Martin, Jr., counter that vaccines are simply too complex and difficult to produce (Martin's position is analyzed at length in Chapter 10). The facts suggest otherwise. Many vaccines are well within the industry's current technological capabilities. The core of these capabilities rests in the ability to rapidly isolate the genes responsible for directing the synthesis of antigenic (i.e., immunity-producing) sections of the surface of targeted organisms. (A second approach, which entails "disarming" the toxin-producing capacity of disease-causing organisms such as the cholera vibrio, the causative bacterium of cholera, is discussed in Chapter 9.) These antigenic fragments, or toxoids, are actually small-length molecules, composed of a few to several dozen amino acids. A number of scientific teams have recently succeeded in isolating the polypeptides that compose small sections of the protein coat of viruses and, more recently, of malaria organisms.

The success of this new generation of vaccines depends on the likelihood that short sections of many protein molecules retain the ability to provoke an immune response against the whole viral organism without producing toxicity.[10] According to Syntex researcher Tony Allison, some such peptides, though less than twenty amino acids long, provide potent immune responses.[11] The remaining problem, according to Allison, is to augment the initial, limited immune response sufficiently to produce a lasting immunity. The trick to this achievement is to use chemically defined "adjuvants" to stimulate an immunity as long-lasting as that provoked by a live organism. Once perfected, this new composite (rDNA-synthesized peptides plus adjuvants) opens the door to an entire new field of immunologic products, which could fulfill some of the basic public health needs of large populations.

Currently, researchers rely on their ability to generate sufficient quantities of specially "attenuated," or weakened, strains of a specific virus or bacterium in tissue culture to inoculate an at-risk population. In pursuing a program for developing peptide vaccines, researchers can avoid working with potentially infectious substances (the blood of hepatitis patients, for instance) that are now the sole source of immunogenic material. Although successful, however, technical developments themselves do not assure commercial development. Of all the potential rDNA vaccines, by 1984 only hepatitis B vaccine had been marketed for human use, while several animal vaccines had been brought to market. Development of immunological controls for complex diseases such as malaria still pose substantial technical and development problems. But in view of the tremendous health need for such products, the absence of major investment capital in their resolution is still difficult to justify.

Short-Term Gains

One explanation is that medical researchers in developed countries such as the United States, Germany, and Great Britain (but not Japan) have tended to identify more easily achieved, short-range objectives for their biotechnological enterprises rather than long-term goals. This tendency is reinforced by the choice of products such as insulin, interferon, and human growth hormone, all of which have had preexisting markets.[12] A current case in point is the crash program undertaken by three biotech firms to market genetically engineered clotting factors for treating hemophilia.

In contrast to parasitic diseases and their extraordinarily high prevalence in some parts of the world (ranging up to 90 percent of some rural populations), hemophilia affects about six men in every one hundred thousand. Deficiencies in the blood-clotting factors that characterize these illnesses can in principle be restored by administering exogenous replacements. By far the most common deficiency is for Factor VIII (type A hemophilia). Were it possible to clone part or all of the Factor VIII molecule, an expensive and presently somewhat dangerous form of replacement therapy (because of potential contamination with hepatitis virus and/or the AIDS agent) would be replaced.

In part because of its extraordinarily inflated value— Factor VIII replacement therapy costs $5,000–7,000 a year and a major bleeding episode costs $10,000–20,000—this commodity became a highly attractive product in spite of the difficulties entailed in its isolation and production.[13] When Factor VIII was first successfully produced, in the spring of 1984, it was the largest rDNA-manufactured protein to date: more than 2,000 amino acids long.

At a forum reported in 1983,[14] a group of international researchers assessed the value and prospective impact of using recombinant DNA for producing other human plasma derivatives. As with Factor VIII, the principal value of these commodities is in acute-care medicine. The participants were unanimous in their strong endorsement of the value of research directed towards the mass production of marketable plasma substances. Since the use of plasma derivatives such as albumin or Factors VIII and IX is largely limited to high-technology-dependent care centers, such a perspective tends to minimize broader public health benefits that could come from development of field blood replacement kits or improved home-base self-administration kits for substances such as Factor VIII precipitate.[15]

In general, the pharmaceutical industry has looked to rDNA techologies to augment traditional acute-care medicine rather than deal with the major killers identified by WHO and the NRC.[16] Putting aside the moral implications of such short-sightedness, we still need to determine the extent to which diseases targeted as world priorities lend themselves to biotechnological solutions.

Enteric Infections

As discussed above, diarrheal diseases of childhood are the single greatest threat to the overall health of the developing world.[17] Individuals currently at risk for cholera, the most devastating of these diseases, need either heat-killed suspensions of the causative agent to prevent infection, or if sick, simple oral hydration therapy, which replaces lost vital fluids. Part of the problem stems from the limited ability of heat-killed *Vibrio cholerae* to provoke a lasting immune response. Similar limitations plague the development of heat-killed bacilli responsible for typhoid fever organisms, which produce reasonably strong immune responses (as gauged by antibody production) but little proven long-term protection in populations living under primitive conditions.

The key for gaining control over these organisms now appears to be the deliberate engineering of their genetic makeup to weaken but not kill them. This feat has been accomplished for cholera by a research team from the University of Maryland, which successfully produced a nontoxic but immunogenic strain of *V. cholerae*.[18]

A similarly attenuated vaccine was made from the agent that causes typhoid fever by Professor Réné Germainer of the Swiss Serum and Vaccine Institute, in Berne. Germainer's work led to the production of the strain called Ty21, which undergoes only four or five cell divisions after it has been swallowed and provokes an immune reaction just before it dies by penetrating the intestinal wall. According to *Nature* correspondent Peter Neumark, this novel organism may soon be made available for wide-scale use under the aegis of the WHO Expert Committee on Biological Standardization.[19]

With a little help from the recombinant-DNA industries, such self-destructing organisms could be armed with plasmids that would carry the instructions to make proteins capable of inducing an immune response to more pathogenic microorganisms, such as the *Pseudomonas* bacterium. Such an extraordinary feat has already been accomplished for adding the antigenic material of hepatitis and herpes virus to normal vaccinia virus.[20]

This form of genetic engineering, in the words of the editor of the *British Journal of Hospital Medicine,* is the way in which "genetic tinkering" could make its first major impact on world health. Unfortunately, as he observes, "the area concerned may not be the most glamorous but the repercussions [of development] could be of momentous importance."[21] But it is precisely the lack of this "glamorous" element—along with the absence of substantial economic returns on investment—that threatens to dissuade serious investment from the private sector. As indicated by WHO's assessment of health needs, one of the least glamorous—and most important—potential applications of rDNA technology lies in the identification, prevention, and treatment of parasitic diseases. But within the commercial bio-technology community, this work is currently being under-written to any substantial degree by only one company, New England Biolabs of Beverly, Massachusetts[22] (more about this in Chapter 11 on Priorities).

Parasites

Recombinant-DNA technology has proven to be an extremely powerful tool in identifying those charac-teristics of parasites that may make them amenable to con-trol. At least three different avenues of parasitology research have benefited from this technology: (1) studies on funda-mental cell-differentiation control mechanisms leading to better understanding of the antigenic changes that occur with sequential infections[23] and of the surface charac-teristics of parasite cells;[24] (2) work on cloning of specific proteins of the parasite's cell surface needed for vaccine production and diagnostic testing;[25] and (3) basic research into the evolutionary relationships of various types of para-sites. Here researchers have identified various fractions of the special DNA found in a subcellular organelle called the *kinetoplast,* which can identify substrains of trypanosomiasis and leishmania parasites.[26] The prime candidate for much of this work has been the malarial parasite.

Malaria

Since there are more than 300 million cases of malaria annually in the Third World, even marginal success in its control would be a boon for public health in developing countries. A key problem in developing a successful vaccine for malaria is that each stage in the complex life cycle of the malaria parasite has its own antigenic spectrum. A second problem is that the causative agent lives and divides within red blood cells, making it relatively inaccessible to chemotherapeutic agents and antibodies. (The parasite eventually kills the infected red blood cell, leading to anemia and other complications that often result in death.) Indeed, the emergence and spread of chloroquine and now mefloquine resistance, coupled with the resurgence of the *Anopheles* mosquitoes (the principal carriers of this agent), suggest that malaria will grow rather than diminish in public health importance over the next few years.[27]

Three possible means of malaria control are linked to breakthroughs in recombinant-DNA technology. The first means involves attacking the sporozoite stage of the organism—the form it assumes during the infective period when it leaves the mosquito's gut. On biting a potential host, the infected mosquito injects a few thousand of these sporozoites into the bloodstream, from which they rapidly enter the liver. The attractiveness of this approach is that the sporozoites of many plasmodium strains contain a similar antigen, making cross-immunization between strains feasible.[28] The second means involves attacking the merozoites, the second stage of the parasite's life cycle, when it is dividing and is periodically released from the host's red blood cells. The third means involves an attack upon the parasite's gametes, or gametocytes, during its sexual stages.

Precise biochemical analysis has revealed that the surface of the sporozoite of the malarial species infecting humans (*P. vivax* and *P. falciparum*) is composed in part of an antigen made up of repeating units of just twelve amino acids each.[29] Related work on isolating the gene responsible for this repeating sequence has been done in the laboratory of

Ruth and Victor Nussenzweig, a husband and wife team at New York University.[30]

This sequence of twelve amino acids is sufficient to mimic the antigenic configuration of the entire surface coat of the sporozoite. Whether or not this peptide will work as a vaccine against malarial parasites per se is currently being tested in squirrel monkeys. Further progress in spotting vulnerabilities in the other stages of the parasite's life may turn on the successful cloning of larger *P. falciparum* antigens in *E. coli.*[31]

The blood stage has proven to be the most difficult to work with because the merozoites express numerous antigens on their cell surface. Several of these antigens have nonetheless been isolated and cloned—the resulting antigens produced in appropriate bacterial hosts show a gratifying reactivity with the blood of recovered malarial victims. This result strongly suggests that the antigenic preparation might be able to provoke similar antibodies and thus protect hosts at this stage of infection.

A gametocyte vaccine, while affording no protection to an infected person, would nonetheless prevent malaria from spreading by breaking the cycle of reinfection of new mosquitoes.

Most commentators now agree that a malaria vaccine is still only a hypothetical reality, because a literal cocktail of antigens, mixing not just the first two stages but the later stages as well, will probably be needed to effectively immunize human hosts against this disease. Apparently, nothing less than an international effort is needed to achieve such a complex victory. But such cooperation, at least among the large biotechnology firms that have the capacity—with their pharmaceutical house sponsors—does not appear to be in the offing.

While most scientists agree that such cooperative genetic-engineering research is the best bet for a solution to the malaria vaccine problem, few firms (with the notable exception of New England Biolabs in Beverly, Massachusetts)[32] have invested outside their own doors to solve it. To be effective, the vaccine must be mass-produced and inexpensive, allegedly prohibitive considerations for even the largest biotech firms. As I document in Chapter 10, at least one company has shied away from investing heavily in this area for just this reason.

One means for rescuing this essential development from obscurity was proposed in 1983 by a group of international planners that convened under the auspices of the UN in Tbilisi, USSR.[33] A summary of this meeting that appeared in June 1983 contained the suggestion that malaria vaccine be designated a "technology for humanity," thereby qualifying under the UN charter as a development of "clear and urgent character to the human community." If so designated, malaria vaccine would be prepared as an international venture, with the technical skills of major genetic-engineering companies provided freely in all countries.

Based on my conversations with the research directors of major U.S. biotechnology companies, such an humanitarian appeal is unlikely to sway key biotechnology firms. It is unlikely that any company would undertake such a risk-laden and unprofitable venture without substantial government subsidy or the support of a major pharmaceutical firm.

Hepatitis

Hepatitis poses an unusual opportunity for cooperative efforts across nations because of its unusual pattern of distribution. This virus-induced illness poses a particularly vexing problem in developing countries, especially those in Africa, because of its endemicity (up to 20–30 percent of the population has been infected in some countries) and its association with liver cancer. It is simultaneously a major health problem in the U.S. because of its spread through contaminated blood products and the existence of specific high-risk groups such as the gay community.

Presently, the vaccine being used must be laboriously prepared from blood products—posing a danger to the preparers as well as a problem of sufficient supply. The production of a truly suitable vaccine is thus constrained by a limited supply of viral particles, and the fact that the virus once isolated will not grow in other than primate cells. But the value of such a noninfectious product made with rDNA is inestimable. In the words of G. R. Barker, from the Department of Biochemistry at Manchester University, "this would be much more than just an improvement in an existing therapy; it would be the production of a vaccine which would have been impossible without the new [rDNA] technology."[34]

A genetically engineered vaccine for this debilitating disease will soon be widely available, achieved as a result of the collaborative efforts of Chiron Laboratory of Emeryville, California, and the Institute of Therapeutic Research at West Point, New York, a subsidiary of Merck Sharpe and Dohme Research Laboratories.[35] This work built on the successful incorporation of the viral genes that code for the antigen protein, or B antigen, into a vector that could survive and direct the synthesis of the antigen alone—without the infective virus—first in *E. coli*[36] and later yeast.[37] The resulting proteinaceous material, when injected into rabbits, produces antibodies indistinguishable from those needed for producing effective immunity in humans.

In spite of the dramatic success of the hepatitis vaccine, it remains to be seen just how much investment will be directed towards parasite-directed vaccines in the foreseeable future. According to parasitologist and immunologist Tony Allison of Syntex Laboratories in Palo Alto, California, most of the current investment is going toward the more readily achieved successes in virus-antigen isolation—and in the development of suitable adjuvants to enhance the immune reaction to pure polypeptide preparations. As to the relative weight given to parasitic diseases such as malaria and leishmaniasis, Allison's view is that both the more difficult technical problems posed by vaccine development for these diseases and their location in Third World countries has caused genetic engineering firms to scale down their investments. ·

In Allison's words "The major focus is not on these diseases at all, but rather on virally produced diseases."[38] If universally true, such an emphasis suggests that the priorities of the biotechnology industry are focused on diseases of the wealthier, more developed countries at the expense of diseases causing major morbidity and mortality in the developing world.

Heart Disease

One index of the soundness of this hypothesis is to compare the attention given to a major disease that is heavily concentrated in developed countries. One disease that differentiates the health problems of the developed from the developing countries is heart disease. Since this disease is highly prevalent among populations in the developed nations, but relatively infrequent among people living in the less developed ones, evidence for a skewing of significant investments in the biotechnology industry towards it would support the hypothesis of preferential priorities.

Heart and vascular-related diseases, according to the most recent figures of the National Center for Health Statistics, hold indisputable first place among the major killers in the U.S. In the United States atherosclerotic and thrombotic (clot-related) causes of death, such as stroke, heart attack or other forms of ischemic heart disease, are responsible for almost half of all deaths annually.[39]

While many public health officials consider a high proportion of these deaths preventable (through proper diet, exercise, etc.), most of the attention of pharmaceutical companies has been aimed at treating blood clots or vessel disease *after* they have appeared. As we saw in Chapter 3, clot-dissolving enzymes and inhibitors of thrombin formation (part of the clotting process) were among the earliest to be produced with genetic engineering. Genentech alone produces three of these agents: antithrombin III, urokinase, and tissue plasminogen activator.

The choice of these products suggests that biotechnology companies are following in the footsteps of major pharmaceutical companies, which concentrate on secondary- or tertiary-care products. Exploration of preventive approaches to cardiovascular disease is largely left to major university centers, which are using rDNA techniques to elucidate the genetic basis for heart disease as well as identifying the structure of cell-surface lipid receptors and related molecules[40] (e.g., the genetic control of the receptors for low-density lipoproteins).

Cancer

Genetic-engineering firms are also investing heavily in agents that will prove valuable in the fight against cancer. Second only to heart disease, cancer ranks as a major killer in the Western world. While environmentally oriented epidemiologists try to piece together its complex origins, university-based molecular biologists have been pressing hard on the frontiers of the genetic causation of malignant transformation. Substantial research and progress have been made towards elucidating the structural genes that may contribute—singly, or more likely in tandem—to the carcinogenic process. Through the use of restriction enzymes and sophisticated detection techniques, researchers have been able to identify almost thirty different "oncogenes" associated with tumors as diverse as lymphomas, leukemias, and bladder cancer.[41]

In the latter instance, a single base substitution was found to distinguish the genetic makeup of a human bladder-cancer cell from its normal counterpart. This feat entailed finding a single base substitution in a human gene—equivalent to finding one change out of perhaps 6 million possible base sequences. The discovery of the gene, made possible by rDNA techniques, showed that a single nucleotide had changed, resulting in a substitution of one amino acid for another—a valine for a glycine in the twelfth amino acid residue.[42]

University scientists have also put monoclonal antibodies to use in detecting surface characteristics of malignant cells,[43] a possible step towards prevention. In contrast, industry researchers have concentrated on the more lucrative treatment market with drugs and agents such as toxin-conjugated MCAs. An example is the "magic bullet" linking diphtheria toxin with MCAs directed against breast cancer cells being developed at Cetus Corporation.

Diabetes

Further evidence for biotechnology firms' concentration on diseases of developed countries comes from the intensity of their efforts to develop an insulin substitute. As discussed in the previous chapter, the successful production of human insulin has been touted as evidence for the prowess of rDNA researchers. It is less clear why commercial development has occurred on the large scale now taking place. One reason offered by Eli Lilly vice president Irving S. Johnson is that the 2 million insulin-requiring diabetics in the United States present a ready market for synthetic insulin. Writing in the special biotechnology issue of *Science* magazine, Johnson pointed out that this population represented a rapidly growing market (and clearly one with a readily predictable high rate of demand) for insulin.[44]

Among the factors Johnson identified as accelerating the growth of demand among the insulin-using diabetic population were (1) the availability of insulin itself, which enables present-day diabetics to live longer—and use more insulin; (2) the survival and reproduction of future generations of diabetics; and (3) greater public awareness of the disease. Left unspoken is the fact that present supplies of porcine pancreases are more than sufficient to supply existing needs, and that Eli Lilly has a monopoly in the United States of all forms of insulin.

According to Johnson, this stockpile and the availability of the porcine insulin supply could be adversely affected by the vagaries of market conditions, hence justifying the development of a permanent and unlimited supply of this essential pharmaceutical.

This pattern of health investments and objectives suggests but does not prove that the biotechnology industry takes many of its cues for its product lines from the needs of the industrialized world. To resolve residual uncertainty about the actual mechanisms of product selections we need to examine more closely the industry's priority-setting mechanisms. This we do in Chapter 10.

Notes

1. Howard Schneiderman, "Some Thoughts on Biotechnology," *Chemical and Engineering News* (February 1, 1982): 4.
2. See in particular World Health Organization Advisory Committee on Medical Research, "Genetic Engineering: Benefits and Dangers," *WHO Chronicle* 32 (1978): 465, 508.
3. President's Commission for the Study of Ethical Problems in Medicine and Biomedical and Behavioral Research, *Splicing Life: The Social and Ethical Issues of Genetic Engineering with Human Beings* (Washington, D.C.: U.S. Government Printing Office, 1982).
4. *Splicing Life,* p. 51.
5. *Splicing Life,* p. 77.
6. U.S. Congress, Office of Technology Assessment, *Impacts of Applied Genetics—Micro-organisms, Plants, and Animals* (Washington, D.C.: U.S. Government Printing Office, 1981).
7. J. Snyder and M. H. Merson, "The Magnitude of the Global Problem of Acute Diarrhoeal Disease: A Review of Active Surveillance Data," *Bulletin of the World Health Organization* 60 (1982): 605–613.
8. National Research Council, *Priorities in Biotechnology Research for International Development* (Washington, D.C., 1982).
9. See especially the appraisal made by D. G. Kleid, "Using Genetically Engineered Bacteria for Vaccine Production," *Annals of the New York Academy of Sciences* 413 (1983): 23–30; and statements appearing in Council on International and Public Affairs, *Biotechnology and the Third World* (New York: International Center for Law in Development, October 31, 1983); and in the report on the Fifth Meeting of the Scientific Working Group on the Immunology of Malaria, held in

Geneva on March 8–10, 1982, which appeared in the *Bulletin of the World Health Organization* 61 (1983): 81–92.

10. P. Newmark, "Will Peptides Make Vaccines?" *Nature* 306 (1983): 9.

11. Telephone interview with Tony Allison, January 20, 1984.

12. N. Stebbing et al., "Biological Comparisons of Natural and Recombinant DNA Derived Polypeptides," in *Insulins, Growth Hormone and Recombinant DNA Technology*, J. L. Overiguian, ed. (New York: Raven Press, 1981), pp. 117–131.

13. A. L. Bloom, "Benefits of Cloning Genes for Clotting Factors," *Nature* 303 (1983): 974–975.

14. L. M. Aledort et al., "What Is the Prospective Impact of the rDNA Technique on the Production of Human Plasma Derivatives?" *Vox Sanguinus* 44 (1983): 390–395.

15. L. M. Aledort, "The Availability of Plasma Products and the Care of Hemophilia Patients," *Journal of the American Medical Association* 248 (1981): 157.

16. M. Konrad, "Applications of Genetic Engineering to the Pharmaceutical Industry," *Annals of the New York Academy of Sciences* 413 (1983): 12–22.

17. See, for instance, the discussion in D. C. Turk and I. A. Porter, *Short Textbook of Medical Microbiology* (London: English Universities Press, 1979).

18. J. B. Kaper, H. Lockman, M. M. Baldwin, and M. M. Levine, "A Recombinant Live Oral Cholera Vaccine," *Bio/Technology* 2 (1984): 345–349.

19. Newmark, "Peptides."

20. E. Poolett, B. R. Lipinska, G. Samsonof, et al., "Construction of Live Vaccines Using Genetically Engineered Poxviruses: Biological Activity of Vaccinia Virus Recombinants Expressing the Hepatitis B Virus Surface Antigen and the Herpes Simplex Virus Glycoprotein D," *Proceedings of the National Academy of Sciences (Biology)* 81 (1984): 193–197.

21. Anonymous, "Gene Manipulation," *British Journal of Hospital Medicine* 29 (1983): 389.

22. Telephone interview with Donald Coomb, president of New England Biolabs, September 4, 1984.

23. M. Parsons, R. G. Nelson, G. Newport, et al., "Genomic Organization of *Trypanosma brucei* Variant Antigen Gene Families in Sequential

Parasitemias," *Molecular and Biochemical Parasitology* 9 (1983): 255–269.

24. E. N. Miller, L. M. Allan, M. J. Turner, et al., "Analysis of the Antigenic Determinants of a *Trypanasoma brucei* Variant Surface Glycoprotein Using Monoclonal Antibodies," *Parasitology* 84 (1983): R50.

25. J. S. Cordingle, D. W. Taylor, D. W. Dunne, et al., "Clone Banks of rDNA from the Parasite *Schistosoma mansoni*—Isolation of Clones Containing a Potentially Immunodiagnostic Antigen Gene," *Gene* 26 (1983): 25–39.

26. M. Mukich, L. Simpson, and A. M. Simpson, "Comparison of Maxicircle DNAs of *Leishmania tarentolae* and *Trypanosoma brucei*," *Proceedings of the National Academy of Sciences* 80 (1983): 4060–4064; and M. Milhausen, R. G. Nelson, M. Parsons, et al., "Molecular Characterization of Initial Variants from the ISTAT 1 Serodene of *T. brucei*," *Molecular and Biochemical Parasitology* 9 (1983): 241–254.

27. F. E. G. Cox, "Malaria and Babesiosis," *Nature* 306 (1983): 114–115; "Development of Mefloquine as an Antimalarial Drug," *Bulletin of the World Health Organization* 61 (1983): 169–178; and, WHO Expert Committee on Malaria, Seventeenth Report, *WHO Technical Report Series*, No. 640 (WHO, Geneva, 1979), pp. 7–71.

28. J. L. Marx, "Human Malarial Gene Cloned," *Science* 225 (1984): 607–608.

29. F. E. G. Cox, "Cloning Genes for Antigen of *Plasmodium falciparum*," *Nature* 304 (1983): 13–14; see also J. B. Dame, J. L. Williams, T. F. McCutchan, et al., "Structure of the Gene Encoding the Immunodominant Surface Antigen on the Sporozoite of the Human Malaria Parasite *P. falciparum*," *Science* 225 (1984): 593–599.

30. L. S. Ozaki, P. Svec, R. S. Nussenzweig, W. V. Nussenzweig, and G. N. Godson, "Structure of the *Plasmodium knowlesi* Gene Coding for the Circumsporozoite Protein," *Cell* 34 (1983): 814–822; and V. Enea, J. Ellis, F. Zawata, et al., "DNA Cloning of *P. falciparum* Circumsporozoite Gene: Amino Acid Sequence of Repetitive Epitope," *Science* 225 (1984): 628–629.

31. R. G. Odink, S. C. Nicholls, M. J. Lockyer, and Y. Hillman, "Cloning of Malarial Genes Coding for High Molecular Weight Antigens: Isolation of *Plasmodium falciparum* Genes Coding for Proteins of 145,000 Molecular Weight," *Molecular and Biochemical Parasitology* 10 (1984): 55–66.

32. This company has assigned almost a third of its staff to study parasitic diseases, has assisted the Nussenzweigs at NYU and routinely sends its top management and senior scientists to conferences on major world health problems, the most recent being in Paris, France, in fall 1983.

33. High-Level Expert Group Meetings Preparatory to the Fourth General Conference of UNIDO, April 12–16, 1983, ID/WG 389.

34. G. R. Barker, "Biochemistry of Genetic Manipulation," *Journal of Biological Education* 17 (1983): 101–104.

35. W. J. McAleer, E. B. Buynak, R. Z. Maigette, et al., "Human Hepatitis B Vaccine from Recombinant Yeast," *Nature* 307 (1984): 178–180.

36. C. J. Burrell et al., "Expression in *Escherichia coli* of Hepatitis B Virus DNA Sequences Cloned in Plasmid pBR 322," *Nature* 279 (1979): 43–47; and M. Pasek et al., "Hepatitis B Genes and Their Expression in *E. coli*," *Nature* 282 (1979): 575–579.

37. P. Valenzula, A. Medina, and W. J. Rutteretal, "Synthesis and Assembly of Hepatitis B Virus Surface Antigen Particles in Yeast," *Nature* 298 (1982): 347–350.

38. Allison, personal communication.

39. Heart disease and cerebrovascular accidents accounted for 38.7 and 8.0 percent of all deaths in 1982, respectively; *Monthly Vital Statistics Report* 31 (Oct. 5, 1983): 5. The notion that cancer is the primary cause of death is belied by the facts: a recent survey of Metropolitan Life Insurance policy holders showed that twice as many (21,513 versus 11,543) died of major cardiovascular diseases as from cancer [*American Journal of Public Health* 74 (1984): 71–72].

40. Professor David Cox, University of California, San Francisco, personal communication, May 21, 1984.

41. M. J. Murray, B-Z. Shilo, C. Shih, et al., "Three Different Human Tumor Cell Lines Contain Different Oncogenes," *Cell* 25 (1981): 355–361.

42. M. Goldfarb, K. Shimitzu, M. Perucho, and M. Wigler, "Isolation and Preliminary Characterization of a Human Transforming Gene from T24 Bladder Carcinoma Cell," *Nature* 296 (1982): 404–409; and E. P. Reddy, R. K. Reynolds, E. Santos, et al., "A Point Mutation Is Responsible for the Acqusition of Transforming Properties by the T24 Human Bladder Cancer Oncogene," *Nature* 300 (1982): 149–152.

43. T. Masuko, H. Yagita, and Y. Hashimoto, "Monoclonal Antibodies

Against Cell-surface Antigens Present on Human Bladder Cancer Cells," *Journal of the National Cancer Institute* 72 (1984): 523–530; and E. D. Ball, R. F. Graziarro, and R. F. Petteng, et al., "Monoclonal Antibodies Reactive with Small Cell Carcinoma of the Lung," *Journal of the National Cancer Institute* 72 (1984): 593–598.

44. I. S. Johnson, "Human Insulin from Recombinant DNA Technology," *Science* 219 (1983): 632–637.

CHAPTER 5

The Quest
for Defective DNA

Human Genetic Disease

In spite of the potential and undeniably profound importance of biotechnology for the human condition generally, the area of impact that has sparked the greatest interest and most trenchant debates has been human genetics. It is here that the deepest religious, moral, and ethical concerns have been spawned. Some of this concern has focused on our newfound ability to plumb the human genome—diagnosing genetic disease, identifying high-risk groups for occupational illnesses or diseases, and designing treatments for previously intractable conditions. For this reason, this chapter is concerned with the extent of the developments most likely to affect human genetics and the likelihood that effective interventions will be developed to stem the often inexorable course of genetic disease.

Diagnosis

The prenatal use of recombinant-DNA techniques to diagnose human genetic disease has expanded markedly in the ten years since this application became feasible. Because of the great power of this technique to reveal incipient disease or susceptibility, there is value in examining how it fits into worldwide patterns of disease generally and the clinical practice of medicine specifically.

In the developed world, the proportional contribution of genetic disease to childhood illness and disease has increased dramatically in the last two decades. In 1960, the major causes of childhood death and disability in the United States were respiratory and disorders linked to prematurity diseases. By 1980, congenital malformations and disorders attributable to genetic makeup accounted for more early disability and hospitalizations than did the previously predominant infectious diseases. Some estimates ascribe as many as 40 percent of all pediatric hospital admissions to genetically determined or associated disorders.[1] With infant mortality in the United States at an all-time low in 1981—10.5 per 1,000 for whites and 20.0 per 1,000 for blacks—genetically based disorders may now account for the majority of early childhood deaths. They are certainly a major factor. Congenital malformations, many of which include a genetic component, account for 2.45 deaths per 1,000 births, making them currently the major cause of death in infancy.[2]

Marcus E. Pembrey, of the London Institute of Child Health, and Robert Williamson, of St. Mary's Hospital Medical School, also in London, have both argued for the desirability of using rDNA for detecting human gene defects. Writing in the *British Journal of Hospital Medicine*, Pembrey advocated the advantages of using recombinant DNA to allow the direct analysis of genetic defects and to discover carriers of genetic disease. But he limited his advocacy of the technique to families already shown to be affected by genetic disease.[3]

Pembrey's cautious advocacy contrasts with more expansive comments that Williamson made two years earlier in a talk at Case Western University.[4] Williamson had made reference to the technique of using single-stranded lengths of DNA as "probes." These segments mirror a base sequence in a defective or aberrant gene and can be labeled with an easily detected radioisotope. Williamson proposed that these small DNA probes plus the so-called blotting techniques (developed earlier by Southern) lent themselves beautifully to the diagnosis of a broad range of human genetic disease. He cited the ability of researchers to use DNA hybridization made possible by the availability of precisely sequenced DNA probes to identify abnormal hemoglobin in tissues taken from the fetal chorion early in pregnancy, and urged that human DNA sequences be catalogued and maintained in a library of human DNAs. One such center already exists at Oxford, where the gene sequences that code for red blood cell abnormalities are catalogued.[5] One can appreciate the magnitude of the total exercise Williamson proposed by considering the size of the total human genome.

The human genome carries upwards of 100,000 different genes, of which 600 will have been mapped by the mid-1980s.[6] Of the 3,669 single-gene-determined genetic diseases catalogued in 1983,[7] about 160 involve a deficiency where there is an identifiable gene product. Currently (circa 1984), clinicians can diagnose about a third of these 160 disorders, and it is projected that they will be able to identify all but 8 to 10 of the remainder in the next few years.[8] Given the genetic tests that rely on the new recombinant-DNA technologies plus the new techniques for obtaining early fetal tissue, virtually all couples known to be at risk for a genetic disorder will be able to get information about their fetuses in time to request abortion or, more rarely, a new therapy.

Clearly, the large array of genetic diseases caused by identifiable, single-gene disorders now strains our technical ability to the limit. The key question is whether or not a sustained effort to identify each one individually is justified. Elsewhere I have argued for the value of developing generalizable techniques for identifying and treating related groups of disorders.[9]

Even though this projected composite of detectable disorders would greatly expand the repertoire of diseases that could be diagnosed in pregnancy, even collectively the disorders in question are rare. This means that even with all potentially diagnosable conditions counted, fewer than 1 percent of births are likely to be at risk from them. In developing countries where infant mortality stands at 5–14 percent of births and up to 20 percent of the survivors die after the first year, progress in the diagnosis of genetic disorders is swamped by the overwhelming reality of malnourishment and infant diarrheal disease. It is also important to realize that the alternatives presented by such early diagnosis are presently limited to abortion—and only in rare instances to attempts at fetal therapy. Furthermore, without question, the ability to detect diseases that are only marginally impairing in the prenatal period will raise even more significant moral questions than does our present ability to detect uniformly fatal disorders such as Tay-Sachs disease, a progressive neurological disorder that affects Jewish children of Eastern European ancestry.

In 1982, when rDNA-based tests were still largely experimental, about thirty thousand patients in the United States used prenatal diagnostic services.[10] In 1982–1984, the number of these patients who relied on rDNA-mediated tests still represented a bare handful. Most were done at experimental centers such as Yale Medical School, Johns Hopkins University, or the University of California, San Francisco. By 1990, most prenatal testing will probably be done with rDNA-related techniques.

In theory, recombinant-DNA methods allow an obstetrician to examine the actual gene that a fetus is carrying and to advise parents regarding the prognosis for normal or abnormal development. Many of the recombinant-DNA techniques presently used to enhance the physician's ability to detect diseases in the fetus can also be used to accurately pick out the members of the adult population who carry genes that might place their offspring at risk.

As originally construed, many mass screening programs for disorders such as Tay-Sachs disease or sickle-cell anemia were intended to allow informed couples to make knowledgeable choices about their reproduction. Unfortunately, such screening programs were often conducted in ignorance of their full ramifications for stigmatizing participants. Sometimes compulsory testing was also seen as an invitation for discrimination.[11] In the early 1970s, mass programs for sickle-cell-trait testing in children and adults were often done without clearly formulated goals and little or no education of the recipient population. Many of the targeted groups (mainly blacks) were tested without their informed consent and with virtually no protection of the confidentiality of the collected data. As a result, some "affected" individuals were denied employment opportunities or life insurance coverage, even though the uncovered "defect" of a single sickle-cell gene posed no limitations on job performance or longevity. Now genetic screening has extended into the workplace, with the greatest attention going to tests of putative value for identifying high-risk groups or particularly susceptible workers.[12]

Newly perfected recombinant-DNA techniques will allow physicians to detect adults whose genetic makeup preordains them to develop certain late-appearing diseases such as Huntington's chorea or chronic obstructive lung disease. Of greater ethical complexity is the realization that these techniques will also allow employers, insurers, and health insurance carriers to presumptively identify persons with particular risk profiles for disease—and to permit them to take certain steps to limit their employability or coverage. Of course, the same findings could also be used benevolently to provide advance warnings of diseases to certain individuals, permitting them to take steps to reduce their impact or likelihood.[13]

These new prospects are possible because of specific developments in recombinant-DNA genetics that allow diagnosticians to identify a region of a chromosome or even examine a gene itself. The growing "library" of different restriction enzymes (now numbering over 350) can be used rapidly to identify very small regions of the human genome or—as in the case of Huntington's disease[14]—map adjacent regions with enough certainty to provide a high degree of assurance that the nearby gene in question is either normal or defective.

Among the genetic techniques that can be used to accomplish these feats are Southern blotting, restriction fragment-length analysis, and gene cloning. *Southern blotting* uses a radioactively labeled probe carrying gene sequences that are directly complementary to the gene being sought and that can selectively bind to the restriction fragment of the DNA containing the desired sequence. After separation under electrophoresis, a "blot" of the fragments is made. Autoradioactive bands identify the targeted fragments. *Restriction analysis* refers to the ability to measure the length and—with some greater refinement—the actual base sequence of gene fragments produced by restriction enzymes. And *gene cloning* (discussed in Chapter 2) takes spliced sequences of a larger genome and encourages their proliferation in bacterial hosts for isolation and further analysis.

To date, a large proportion of the research in applying these techniques has concentrated on identifying diseases of the synthesis or control of hemoglobin production. This orientation is in part due to the fact that the molecular basis—and gene sequence—for such diseases as classical sickle-cell anemia and the thalassemias were well worked out by the time rDNA technologies became available.

The series of investigations that revolutionized prenatal diagnosis for hemoglobinopathies was done by a group of University of California at San Francisco researchers, headed by Yuet Wai Kan. The first successful test for sickle-cell anemia was reported in 1978; it was followed by a more definitive assay four years later.[15] A collaborative research group from Johns Hopkins and Children's Hospital Medical Center of Boston reported an even more precise way to perform this diagnosis.[16] The significance of the two studies was that they permitted an analysis for the presence of a human gene that could be performed early in pregnancy without the need for the laborious culture of cells from the amniotic fluid or the hazards attendant to collection of fetal blood.

The Boston group extended this work further in the direction of identifying single genes through the use of restriction enzymes. Restriction enzymes can recognize the particular base change in the gene for sickle-cell hemoglobin that distinguishes it from the one for normal hemoglobin (from CCTGAGG to CCTGTGG). Enzymes that recognize the GAGG but not the GTGG sequence cut the DNA coding for normal hemoglobin at the specified point but do not alter the length of the one coding for sickle-cell hemoglobin. In practice, this means that researchers find either one segment of DNA 370 bases long, which signals the presence of sickle-cell hemoglobin genes, or two smaller molecules 170 and 200 bases long, signifying the successful cut of the GAGG, or a normal sequence.

Two other developments have made the rapid diagnosis of human genetic disease possible: (1) the tissues in which these genes are expressed have become more accessible to clinical geneticists through the ability to sample the fetal placenta directly through the cervix;[17] and (2) the presence of defective DNA can now be inferred through the use of synthesized probes. The prenatal tissue biopsy of chorionic villi early in the first trimester permits amniocytes themselves to be obtained, thereby permitting early confirmation of the presence of a genetically abnormal fetus. And where the gene sequence is unknown, it can be re-created from cells from the fetal placenta or other cell types that contain the requisite messenger RNAs for synthesis of the target molecules.[18] The mRNA in turn can be used as a template for making the complementary DNA that actually codes for the defective protein in question. This DNA can then "probe" the targeted cells for the presence of the defective gene by binding to the DNA in the host cell.

Linkage analysis, in contrast, lacks this molecular fine-tuning. It only locates a chromosomal *area* in the fetus that was contributed by one or the other parent known to carry the defective gene in question. Unless it is possible to detect the defective gene itself, or to find a "marker" gene on the parental chromosome very closely linked with the one being sought, it is always possible that crossing-over will occur between the marker and a *normal* gene at the same site. Were this to occur, researchers would make a false diagnosis of the presence of a mutant allele and families would be misled about the presence of the genes leading to incipient disease.

The earliest rDNA-based tests for sickle-cell anemia were also limited because of their dependence on accurate measurements of the different lengths of DNA split off by restriction enzymes.[19] Sometimes both factors limit the success of a test. Because of its dependence on linkage analysis, for instance, Dr. Kan's first test system could provide useful information to only 70 percent of blacks tested.

As pointed out in an editorial in the December 17, 1983, issue of the British medical journal *Lancet*,[20] partial or incomplete information can invite disaster. Patients and their doctors are likely to seize on any information that suggests that they carry a disease possibly fatal or crippling to their offspring. With the ability to identify only a portion of the at-risk fetuses, parents can be left in the dark or given confusing probability estimates. Obviously, highly intensive genetic counseling is needed to educate parents to the limitations of the information they receive where probabilities rather than certainties are cited.

Three Examples of Work in Progress

Recombinant-DNA technologies have opened new possibilities for the clinical diagnosis and treatment of serious and previously inaccessible diseases. A close look at one of these diseases, Duchenne muscular dystrophy, will provide insight into how this can be done. This form of muscular dystrophy causes severe wasting of muscle tissue and eventual paralysis of its almost always male victims. Because it is a *sex-linked* condition—caused by a gene on the X chromosome—males (XY) who receive a defective X chromosome will be affected, while females (XX) are "protected" by the presence of the normal gene on their other X chromosome.

Recognizing the importance of the X chromosome in

sex-linked diseases generally (there are some 343 X-linked disorders),[21] a research group at St. Mary's Hospital in London has used rDNA technologies to develop a library of human DNA sequences taken from the X chromosome that can be maintained in clones of bacteria[22] (see Chapter 2 for an explanation to this process).

Each group of bacterial descendants carries a small portion, commonly no more than several thousand base pairs, of "cloned" gene segments from along the length of the X chromosome. In the St. Mary's group's work, this bacterial library contains some fifty thousand separate clones—an astonishing feat in itself—enough to represent almost the entire length of the X chromosome. Using a radioactive labeling technique, the British researchers can tell which of her X chromosomes a mother has passed on to the fetal son in her uterus. With this information, the researchers have been able to assist some of the families at risk for having a child with a sex-linked disorder who want to have more children. Previously, most such families simply stopped having children or aborted all male fetuses rather than taking the risk of having another affected son.

Another test based on recombinant-DNA techniques led to development of a linkage analysis that permits the detection of the location of the gene responsible for Huntington's disease. This discovery marks the first time clinicians have been able to provide meaningful information to families facing this dread disorder.[23] This new research, while not yet affording definitive diagnosis of the defective gene itself, nonetheless is a major breakthrough, for it shows how much genetic data can be accessed through linkage studies based on restriction-fragment analysis as well as the amount of work still needed to establish a knowledge base of the human genome.

That the knowledge is at our doorstep is suggested by the discovery of the molecular basis for yet another crippling disease discussed in the preceding chapter: that caused by a defect in the gene for AAT, or alpha-1-antitrypsin.[24] This group of proteins is needed to ensure that elastase enzymes released from white blood cells do not degrade the elastic fibers needed for the resilience of lung tissue. In the presence of defective antitrypsin, these elastases damage the alveolar structure of the lung, leading to emphysema, particularly in heavy smokers. This predilection is common to both the homozygous (where both genes are defective) and, to a lesser extent, to the carrier person deficient in AAT.

Reporting in the July 21, 1983, issue of *Nature* magazine, a group from the City of Hope Research Institute in Duarte, California, and another group at Baylor University in Houston, Texas, described their success in identifying the molecular basis for AAT deficiency—and for identifying the defective gene through the use of specially synthesized DNA sequences that mimic the region of the antitrypsin gene responsible for the defect.[25]

As with many other medical breakthroughs, this one was achieved by a piece of basic research that was to have unforeseen reverberations. Just three months after the report was published, an article appeared in the *New England Journal of Medicine*[26] announcing another rDNA-mediated discovery: a single gene mutation in the alpha-1-antitrypsin molecule that was responsible for converting AAT into a different but biologically active protein. Through analysis of the amino acid composition of the now known sequences that make up antitrypsin, a group of New Zealand researchers identified a genetic change that led to the conversion of the 358th amino acid in the antitrypsin molecule from a methionine to an arginine. This simple change was responsible for a fatal bleeding disorder, as the reversal converted the antitrypsin molecule into one that inhibited thrombin, a key factor in the cascade of reactions needed to ensure efficient blood clotting.

Taken to its logical conclusion, rDNA-mediated diagnostics would permit a test for virtually every known human genetic disease. If and when this occurs, we will be faced with a cornucopia of diagnostic procedures for a set of extraordinarily rare and initially untreatable disorders. But when these tests appear and are integrated into the clinical diagnostic routine, there is a risk that some of them will be used in an attempt to preempt what clinicians cannot yet do: pick out people at risk for socially or occupationally dysfunctional disorders. While genetic testing for susceptible workers has not yet begun on a wide scale, interest in its implications has prompted the Office of Technology Assessment to evaluate workplace testing.[27]

rDNA in the Workplace

Modern genetic techniques, particularly those based on recombinant-DNA methodologies, have thrown open the door to employment-screening uses by promising rapid identification of a wide constellation of genetic markers for human disorders and disease. Among these conditions are some that interfere with the self-recognition component of the immune system, leading to autoimmune disease and neuropsychiatric conditions. Recombinant DNA opens a window on the gene-mediated elements of these and other profoundly significant diseases, such as diabetes, hypertension, and heart disease.[28] The temptation to use what are now barely experimental test systems as predictive mechanisms for identifying individuals whose future health is in doubt raises serious questions about the control and scientific limitations of this new technology.

In theory, new recombinant-DNA-based tests do indeed promise to allow a clinician to predict the likelihood of late-onset diabetes, heart disease, rheumatoid arthritis, and neuropsychiatric disorders.[29] But to "work"—in the clinical sense of confirming a diagnosis with enough certainty to begin preventive treatment—all such genetic tests must be evaluated in conjunction with a broader panel of clinical tests. Unfortunately, in most life and health insurance examinations in occupational settings, a traditional doctor/patient relationship does not exist. The absence of this relationship means that the confidentiality of the data gathered will remain unprotected.[30] Nor is there much assurance, given the setting of such exams, that the usual follow-up testing will be done, or that the results will be fully interpreted and described to a prospective employee or annuitant. At least part of the attraction of these tests rests on their unproven ability to reduce the costs of chronic absenteeism, disability or premature retirement. Thus, the new tests that seem to be broadly indicative of a higher-than-normal risk for employees are likely to prove so attractive to some employers that they will be used without confidentiality, however highly recommended.

The potential for misuse of information so obtained will be high. Even where such tests indicated the risk status of an employee only broadly, they would still give employers an ostensibly more scientific way for excluding workers than the poorly predictive methods now in use.

Predicting Susceptibility

Four specific examples demonstrate the attractiveness of certain recombinant-DNA-based tests. Recent advances in this technology—including restriction-frag-

ment-length polymorphisms (RFLPs), monoclonal antibodies, and direct gene probes or sequencing using libraries
of recombinant-DNA-derived genes—make possible the
identification of a large number of previously inaccessible
genes. Among those genes are variants, like those for
alpha-1-antitrypsin, where tests are capable of remarkable
precision. Others, like tests that pick out special "receptor"
molecules to predict the amount of different fats that will
appear in the blood, are still only inferential means of identifying high-risk persons.

Still, uncovering a special genetic marker or nearby gene
makes it theoretically possible for testers to say something
about the likelihood that certain persons will develop conditions such as emphysema or chronic obstructive lung
disease,[31] heart disease,[32] arthritic and autoimmune phenomena,[33] or psychiatric disorders.[34] For some of these disorders, the newfound predictive ability is good enough to
encourage physicians to recommend to their genetically
at-risk patients that they take certain medications (e.g., cho-
lestyramine for high cholesterol levels), avoid specific infections where possible that could precipitate a major flare-up
of their arthritis (*Brucella* or other bacteria for the human
leukocyte antigen [HLA] B27-positive individual), or eliminate nonspecific pollutants (cigarette smoking for the persons with the ZZ form of alpha-1-antitrypsin deficiency).

Surprisingly, for many of these disorders the increased
risk is only determined through discovery of a gene that is
near the actual risk-generating gene. This is true for conditions such as familial hyperliproproteinemia, where affected individuals are at increased risk of developing
hardening of the arteries[35] or the marker on human chromosome 4 that is associated with Huntington's disease. In
these cases, most clinicians usually consider the correlation
of markers with disease too imprecise to be used to identify
with certainty who is *really* at risk. But because it is possible

to predict a greater (or lesser) likelihood of occurrence of such potentially disabling or major handicapping conditions as macroangiopathy, atherosclerosis, and Huntington's disease, it is highly likely that life insurance underwriters, health plan membership directors, and workers' compensation underwriters will begin to request such data. This prospect warrants concern, since these linkage tests might also be used in preemployment settings, particularly where high-level executive positions are at stake.

In all these applications recombinant-DNA-based biotechnology firms have a special responsibility. If they continue to develop and aggressively promote the diagnostic kits for picking out these uncertain markers, they may invite the very abuses we have described here. But these same tests have great value in doing the family studies and linkage analyses essential for uncovering human genetic disease. Avoiding abuse calls for prudence, while successful research and development proceeds in synchrony with medical and social needs. In the most egregious instances, the answer may be industry-encouraged restraint or regulation, at least initially. Without such limitations, the uncontrolled use of such incomplete diagnostic tests as that for HLA B27 will generate confusion and misinformation and possibly even stigmatization and unwarranted discrimination.

A Historical Overview

To understand how far we have moved towards genetic discrimination, let's look briefly at how genetic screening tests have been used historically, particularly in employment situations. In the last ten to fifteen years, a few firms (the OTA counted only seventeen of the Fortune 500 companies that responded to their queries) used genetic tests as a way of predicting or at least testing the idea that certain workers might adversely react to a specific work-place hazard. Some of these tests focused on sickle-cell trait or G6PD deficiency, where red blood cells are more likely to break open at lower than usually toxic levels of carbon monoxide or some twenty-eight to thirty other toxic sub-stances. But the newest generation of tests only permits an employer to identify individuals who are *prone* to disability.

The person who has *both* defective genes for alpha-1-antitrypsin deficiency (the ZZ allele)—referred to as a *homozygote* for this trait—is at high risk to develop cirrhosis of the liver and probably emphysema *irrespective* of additional en-vironmental insults. Similarly, the homozygote who has a shortage of receptors for low-density lipoproteins (LDL) will normally have a series of heart attacks before the age of 21, irrespective of diet.

People with a double-dose of these risk-conferring genes are exceedingly rare in the population (on the order of 1 per 100,000–1,000,000). The carrier who has *one* defective gene (known as the *heterozygote*) is much more common. As many as 1 in 40 prospective workers could have one of the carrier states (e.g., SZ) for the Z allele. Similarly, about 1 in 500 individuals (depending on ethnicity) will carry the LDL receptor gene that predisposes to hypercholesterolemia. And about 1 in 12–14 persons will carry the HLA B27 allele.

From our experience with sickle-cell-trait screening, it is likely that the more common carrier, or heterozygote, of a defective gene will be the one hurt by testing. Such genet-ically positive individuals are also presumed to be collec-tively at higher than normal risk for their respective diseases compared to the average, noncarrier person (although not as high as the homozygote). Under most environmental circumstances, the proclivity of the heterozygote for developing clinically significant illness is still imperfectly understood for all but a few conditions.

The great majority of persons in occupational settings who carry a single dose of a gene will not manifest symptoms. This is true under all but the most stressful conditions for sickle-cell heterozygotes. Carriers of a defective gene for a protein that activates a fat-digesting enzyme only experience symptoms when they maintain high-cholesterol diets, and the MZ or SZ heterozygote for alpha-1-antitrypsin usually has symptoms only in extremely dusty or smoky places.[36] Still, employers and insurers who presumably wanted to avoid the likelihood of having job-related disability claims or high-risk life insurance annuitants used the test for sickle-cell trait to exclude high-risk blacks from consideration despite the rarity of symptoms.[37]

Legally, little stands in the way of employers' use of presumptive markers for emphysema or heart disease to exclude risky workers regardless of whether they are simply carriers or doubly affected individuals. Ironically, under present laws, an employer could use these tests preemptively to exclude affected workers after establishing only that the tests were scientifically sound and that they address a harm that occurs only in the groups in question. Conceivably a case could be made for any of the linked conditions in question, including individuals determined to be at risk for Huntington's disease. Employers could also claim that a given exclusionary policy, say, for heterozygotes, was dictated by "business necessity," a legalism for any intervention deemed essential for the safe and efficient operation of a business.

Theoretically, an employer can only use "business necessity" as a reason for excluding genetically detected workers if there are overriding issues of safety involved.[38] In principle, then, no one should be able to use the newly developed monoclonal antibody against HLA B27, because the linked condition (ankylosing spondylitis) is not usually disabling nor compromising to workplace safety. In practice, however, nothing prevents an employer from including this test in a battery of preemployment workups—as long as the employer's *ultimate* reason for excluding a worker hinges on the person's lack of a "bona fide occupational qualification."

The markers we have discussed fail to meet this last legal test of acceptability, because none of the respective genes is strongly correlated with an actual ability of the affected worker to perform his or her job. The employer might still claim that ascertaining the genetic status of workers is necessary to ensure that they do not put others at risk owing to a latent and potentially handicapping condition, such as epilepsy. Legally, as a provision of the Rehabilitation Act of 1973, the employer must establish that workers can perform their own tasks safely. Unlike specific genetic tests that suggest a likelihood of catastrophic insult or failure (such as hemolysis after a G6PD-deficient individual is exposed to naphtha or carbon monoxide), the genetic tests in question are broad nonspecific indicators of chronic disability or disease and do not predict safe or unsafe performance at work.

Thus, by most counts, the use of recombinant-DNA-developed assays of genetic status seems to be premature at best. Most if not all genetic markers would fail to qualify as legal grounds for excluding otherwise qualified workers from employment. But use of these tests is very near at hand, in large part because prospective employers are not now legally constrained to limit their tests to those that assess the ability to perform specific tasks. Accountability only exists when the employer is challenged by a prospective employee to demonstrate that a particular battery of tests was used in a nondiscriminatory fashion.

To prevent abuse of otherwise powerful and desirable genetic tests of risk status, occupational physicians need to be alert to the prospect of being asked to gather and interpret genetic data on prospective employees that are unrelated to the performance of a specific job. Where genetic markers indicate a higher-than-normal risk for future disability unrelated to job performance, any data collected should be the exclusive property of the employee. To prevent potential abuse of this provocative and potentially damaging information, further vigilance and perhaps regulation on the part of state and federal authorities appear essential.

In the past, the limited success of regulatory efforts to establish guidelines for applying medical diagnostic or treatment regimes (as with the computer axial tomography [CAT] scanner, for instance) has partly been due to a lack of critical analysis as to the greatest potential utility of the technique in question. Similarly, we do not now know where recombinant-DNA-mediated intervention offers the greatest benefit and where it offers the greatest risks. An evaluation of each of these issues has been distorted by the biased perspective of vested interest groups. One of the major distortions has been in the relative weight given to questions of medical priorities versus moral concerns.

Moral Concerns

Instead of focusing on the priorities to be given to practical applications of biotechnology, many ethicists have focused on the moral dilemmas implicit in human genetic engineering—a particular preoccupation of some groups has been with the direct manipulation of the genetic material of human germ cells. This focus on creating "new" humans has generalized confusion and distrust to more easily justified achievements, such as modifying body, or somatic, cells to correct genetic defects. Using genetic engineering to treat human genetic disease is one of the most significant and realizable achievements that biotechnology has made possible. The significance of this feat rests squarely on the fact that until now most genetic disease has been incurable.

Human
Genetic Engineering

In spite of the dramatic medical advances in using rDNA to diagnose previously inaccessible human disease, the public imagination continues to be caught up in the most exotic—and least likely—applications of biotechnology. According to public opinion polls, the public apparently perceives the use of recombinant DNA for genetically modifying a human being as an imminent and disturbing eventuality.[39] A Yankelovich poll found that the second most common application of genetic engineering expected by the public was the manipulation of embryos in vitro, although few geneticists are currently anticipating human experimentation of this kind, in part because of federal prohibitions on fetal research.

Part of the concern over fetal manipulation is kindled by a misunderstanding of the significance of the now established ability to incorporate genes into the germ cells (eggs or sperm) of animals and insects. This feat is a necessary precondition for genetic engineering where genes and their products must be perpetuated from one generation to the next. In fact, this eventuality has only been accomplished for fruit flies and mice, and then only for relatively easily detected genes such as those for eye color or growth hormone. How likely, then, is it that we will engineer humans? Given the testimony collected in the seven volumes of *Re-*

combinant DNA Research cited throughout this work, most scientists believe that such an event is decades away. As we saw with diagnostic techniques, many more pressing problems are closer at hand.

One way to distinguish among these possibilities has been proposed by Leroy Walters, director of the Kennedy Institute's bioethics program at Georgetown University. Walters has suggested separating genetic engineering into four categories, the first two embracing changes in the body or germ line cells to correct genetically based defects, and the second two dealing with attempts to enhance or augment basic human characteristics that may have a genetic foundation (see Figure 5.1).

The first key difference among the four types of engineering is that between involvements of germ cells and those of somatic cells—that is, whether the change produced is likely to be passed on to future generations or will only affect the person being treated. A second key distinction is whether the treatment being sought is intended to correct a defect or to enhance a desired quality.

	Correction	Enhancement
Germ line	1	3
Body cells	2	4

FIGURE 5.1
Somatic and germ-cell interventions and enhancements. This scheme classifies genetic interventions into four groups: corrections of defects or enhancements of specific characteristics, each involving somatic (body) cells or germ-line (sex) cells. Only in the germ-line changes do interventions become hereditary.

Gene Therapy

The use of rDNA techniques in category 2 in Figure 5.1—that is, to correct a defect in body cells—is the most promising and least controversial intervention. In part, the acceptability of this "gene therapy" hinges on its analogy to more traditional forms of therapy.

Gene therapy usually entails correcting the genetic dysfunction in some significant portion of genetically handicapped cells in an individual so as to restore normal function. This means that cells that are unable to carry out vital functions because of a genetically based deficiency themselves become the subjects of treatment. The production of hemoglobin for red blood cells in the reticulocytes of the bone marrow is a good example. In a person with sickle-cell disease, those reticulocytes produce a defective hemoglobin that is subject to collapse and crystallization when oxygen levels in the blood are low. By directly modifying enough of these bone marrow cells (but not the red blood cells, which lack DNA) and returning them to the affected individual, we can in theory correct the defect since reticulocytes are the precursors of hemoglobin-carrying red blood cells.

However, some observers doubt that we will be able to correct the defect in such cell lineages, despite how much we know about its cause. Stephen Budiansky believes that effective treatment of sickle-cell anemia (or its hemoglobin-regulatory-deficient counterpart, the thalassemias) is unlikely to be among the earliest successes of genetic engineering. His belief has been echoed by NIH director Dr. James Wyngaarden who has commented that today "exaggerated expectations as well as exaggerated fears are very common."[40] Similar views were voiced among researchers who spoke at a public forum on genetic engineering held in

Washington in late November 1983. According to Dr. French Anderson, director of the Laboratory of Molecular Hematology at NIH, a major obstacle to gene therapy for humans is presently our lack of a means of restoring cells containing "corrected" gene products to the sick person's body. However, the limited success of bone marrow grafts of transformed cells in hamsters and mice reported in 1980 suggests that this obstacle may be overcome in the near future.[41] An optimistic assessment was presented at the Cold Spring Harbor Symposium on gene therapy held in 1982, where both the ethical and technical limitations on successful intervention to correct genetic disease were downplayed.[42]

Even if successful, we presently lack any way to ensure the correct expression and precise regulation of transferred, gene-altered cells. This latter point is critical, because genes that are repositioned in the human genome through genetic engineering may be placed improperly, so that they fail to pick up the controlling sequences necessary to ensure their proper function. A mistake in position could lead to a kind of "runaway" gene that refuses to stop making its product—or a total "blackout," whereby no product is produced at all. A case in point may be the otherwise successful introduction of a growth hormone gene along with its regulating sequences into the germ cells of mice. In these experiments, rat or human growth hormone was expressed in the mice, leading to a dramatic increase in body size.[43]

Rather than belabor the problems generated by these still distant scenarios, it is worth considering the ethical problems raised by the much simpler *replacement therapy*, already being used to rescue genetically compromised persons.

It is important to distinguish between the use of replacement therapy, in which a missing gene product is injected or supplied through the diet, and *gene therapy*, in which a defective gene is replaced by a normal one. The use of human growth hormone to accelerate growth in children with short stature itself represents a paradigmatic case. Even the authors of one of the first successful uses of synthetic GH worried over the implications of their findings. In concluding their paper, they stated, "These preliminary results . . . raise important ethical, clinical and economic issues. Until we have more knowledge of its long-term effects and possible adverse actions in these children and more sharply defined criteria for the selection of patients . . . the extrapolation of these findings to support indiscriminate treatment of short normal children with this potent hormone is premature and unwarranted."[44] And one year later, an editorial in the *Journal of Pediatrics* could conclude that "the ultimate physical and psychologic benefits of GH therapy . . . are not known."[45]

In spite of these misgivings, at least one manufacturer has published ads that promote this recombinant-DNA-derived gene product. (To its credit, Genentech, the producer of biosynthetic HGH, has undertaken a controlled, multicenter study of the effects of its product.) However, only about 10 percent of children who are below the height norm and whom pediatricians consider warranting GH treatment (children who fall 2.5 standard deviations below the mean for their age and sex) actually have a *genetic* deficiency. This means that many short-normal children are likely to be treated. Some observers now feel that pediatricians are under extreme pressures to treat even moderately under-height children,[46] in spite of guidelines from the American Academy of Pediatrics to limit HGH to children with proven growth deficiency.[47] Thus, gene-product therapy raises difficult questions of priorities that have not yet been adequately addressed by the medical or bioethical community.

Limitations

In part to overcome the problems inherent in therapy, where complex and powerful balancing forces are at work, researchers plan initially to concentrate only on those genetic diseases where the site or regulation of gene products is not critical. In contrast to those with metabolic disorders, individuals who have diseases such as diabetes, thalassemia, hypopituitarism, and blood-clotting disorders cannot afford to have unregulated production of gene products. In each of these instances, control and precise regulation are essential to ensure that proper amounts of key substances are released at the right times. Hence, gene therapy for these disorders is likely to prove to be much trickier than simple enzyme replacement.

A good group of candidate diseases for nonspecific replacement therapy is that formed by the so-called classic inborn errors of metabolism. In diseases like phenylketonuria, Krabbes disease, and Lesch-Nyhan syndrome, a single missing enzyme is responsible for the toxic buildup of certain substances that would ordinarily be utilized or broken down in the body. These diseases would be particularly amenable to product *or* gene therapy, because the place or amount of the replacement product administered would be largely of no import. Theoretically, as long as a functional gene were working somewhere in the body, it would not matter for these metabolic-deficiency diseases how much of the missing enzyme were produced. Thus, unlike the hemoglobinopathies, in which restoring the genetically transformed cell back into an appropriate blood-producing tissue is probably critical, for a metabolic defect it is immaterial in which organ the genetically transformed cells or product-releasing material (e.g., lipid-lined carriers called liposomes) ultimately lodge.

A secondary limitation is that, once transformed with the corrected gene, the number of cells that can be successfully cloned from a corrected somatic (body) cell is severely restricted by the cell's limited life span. Success is also constrained by the questionable ability of a transformed cell to outstrip the still-survivng defective counterparts that the corrected cell finds on its return to the body. For this reason, Dr. Joseph Schulman of George Washington University Medical Center believes that the first success in gene therapy will be researchers' coercion of the body to confer a higher value on the survival of the corrected cells.[48] This kind of "selective survival" might first be achieved in correcting the defect for adenosine deaminase, an enzyme deficiency that reduces the effectiveness of the immune system.

Therapy in which only a portion of somatic cells are altered presents inherently fewer ethical problems than alterations that lead to direct placement of altered cells into the germ line (categories 1 and 3 in Figure 5.1). In the latter instance, whatever is achieved, whether success or failure, could be perpetuated over more than one generation. In the view of John Fletcher, bioethicist and adviser to the assistant director of NIH, a system of ethics to deal with such germ-line-altering manipulations is needed but simply unavailable.[49]

Enhancement

The most problematic intervention from an ethical viewpoint is covered in areas 3 and 4 in Figure 5.1. According to some protagonists, such as University of Virginia bioethicist Joseph Fletcher, the other broad objective of gene therapy is to use our growing knowledge of genetics to *enhance* human qualities such as intelligence and physical prowess or such qualities as altruism—or even aggressiveness.[50] Indeed, each of these properties or close analogs to them have been bred into our domesticated animals, suggesting that what may seem to be a futuristic and unattainable notion is actually closer than some would like to think. A short look at just one group in which we have invested intense breeding effort easily illustrates the point: among canines, we have successfully bred shelties and border collies for intelligence, huskies for stamina and prowess, seeing-eye dogs for "altruism," and pit bulls for aggressiveness.

These successes among dogs actually reinforce the improbability of doing the same for humans over the short run. Each breed required years of intensive selection and inbreeding to reach the level where the desired qualities would be passed on routinely. What nature or humankind has taken hundreds of generations to accomplish will not be done overnight by genetic engineering. At least four facts reinforce this argument: (1) virtually all the traits in question are "multifactorial" in inheritance, requiring a multiplicity of genes and environmental interactions to achieve their full expression; (2) our ability to identify "good" gene products is substantially less well developed than our ability to identify the "bad"; (3) to breed a super race, or even one that was subservient to us, would require generations of expansive and selective population growth, and in developed countries at least, the period when such growth could have occurred is now gone; and (4) success in such breeding would require the wholesale discarding or slaughter of so-called undesirable or intermediate types.[51]

The nearest analog to a genetically engineered prospect for humans was the ill-fated *Lebensborn* movement in Nazi

Germany. To qualify for this selective breeding experiment, the mates had to have physical features that matched a supposed Aryan ideal: blond hair, tall stature, blue eyes, and so on. Of the three hundred thousand or so "encouraged" marriages and the few hundred such matings that actually produced offspring, what little we know of the outcome suggests that the children resembled this Aryan model only most remotely, more predictably reflecting the mean or average of the physical types rather than the extremes that were being sought.

Most observers of the present scene doubt that intentional genetic engineering using the germ line will ever be done. In the view of the President's Commission, such alterations are not likely in the foreseeable future, mainly because the research now being done does not result in mature organisms—nor is it intended to do so. A more subtle risk of this research, in the view of the commission, "is that if genetically engineered changes ever become relatively easy to make, there may be a tendency to identify what are in fact social problems as genetic deficiencies of individuals or to assume that the appropriate solution to a given problem, whether social or individual, is genetic manipulation."[52] For the present, the use of rDNA technologies to assist in the replacement of missing or defective gene products appears to be the most important, least controversial, and most readily achieved objective. More exciting—and problematic—opportunities represented by gene therapy of somatic or germ-line cells need to be approached systematically. But to hold back from what may be the greatest medical achievements of rDNA-based medical research because of fears of misuse would be both short-sighted and a distortion of the values underlying medicine. Rather, these advances need to be put into perspective with other needed advances.

Notes

1. The 40 percent figure has appeared in several state, federal, and March of Dimes brochures. See, for instance, the federally funded House of Representatives, *Report on Human Genetics*, Report Number 498, 94th Congress, first 1975 Session (Washington, D.C.: U.S. Government Printing Office, 1975). More recent estimates of the number of hospitalizations attributable to genetic conditions have been much lower; see, for instance, C. R. Scriver, "Genetics and Medicine: An Evolving Relationship," in *Health Care*, P. Abelson, ed. (Washington, D. C.: American Association for the Advancement of Science, 1978), pp. 145–151. See also, J. A. F. Roberts, J. Chavez, and S. D. M. Court, "The Genetic Component in Childhood Mortality," *Archives of Diseases in Children* 45 (1970): 33–38.

2. National Center for Health Statistics, *Monthly Vital Statistics Report* 33 (June 22, 1984): Supplement 3, p. 4.

3. M. Pembrey, "Clinical Applications of Recombinant DNA Techniques in Families with Genetic Disease," *British Journal of Hospital Medicine* 29 (1983): 546–551.

4. R. Williams, presentation at Case Western University, June 22–26, 1981.

5. Anonymous, "DNA Probes for the Duchenne Carrier," *Lancet* 2 (1983): 497.

6. T. B. Shows, A. Y. Sakaguchi, and S. L. Naylor, "Mapping the Human Genome," *Advances in Human Genetics* 12 (1982): 341–452.

7. V. McKusick, *Mendelian Inheritance in Man*, 6th ed. (Baltimore: Johns Hopkins Press, 1983).

8. For example, G. A. Grabowski and R. J. Desnick, "Prenatal Diagnosis of Inherited Metabolic Diseases," *Methods in Cell Biology* 26 (1982): 95–179.

9. M. Lappé, "Ethical Aspects of Therapy for Genetic Disease," in *Genetic Disease: Diagnosis and Treatment*, A. A. Dietz, ed. (Washington, D.C.: American Association of Clinical Chemistry, 1981), pp. 282–296.

10. Cited in Anonymous, "Recombinant DNA Methods for Prenatal Diagnosis," *Annals of Internal Medicine* 99 (1983): 718–719.

11. See the discussion and documentation of stigmatization and discrimi-

nation from genetic screening in M. Lappé, *Genetic Politics* (New York: Simon and Schuster, 1979), Chapter 4.

12. See Office of Technology Assessment, *Genetic Screening and Monitoring in the Workplace* (Washington, D.C.: U.S. Government Printing Office, 1983); and commentaries for industrial employers such as "Genetic Testing Debate Grows as New Techniques Emerge from Labs," *BNA Employee Relation's Weekly* 2, 5 (March 1984): 259–262.

13. These issues were extensively reviewed in M. Lappé, "Ethical Issues in Testing for Differential Sensitivity to Occupational Hazards," *Journal of Occupational Medicine* 25 (1983): 797–808.

14. J. F. Gusella, N. S. Wexler, P. M. Conneally, et al., "A Polymorphic DNA Marker Genetically Linked to Huntington's Disease," *Nature* 306 (1983): 234–237.

15. Y. W. Kan and A. M. Dozy, "Antenatal Diagnosis of Sickle-Cell Anemia by DNA Analysis of Amniotic Fluid Cells," *Lancet* 2 (1978): 910–913; J. C. Chang and Yul Kan, "A Sensitive New Prenatal Test for Sickle-Cell Anemia," *New England Journal of Medicine* 307 (1982): 30–32.

16. S. H. Orkin, P. F. R. Little, H. H. Kazazian, Jr., and C. D. Boehm, "Improved Detection of the Sickle Mutation by DNA Analysis," *New England Journal of Medicine* 307 (1982): 32–34.

17. R. G. Elles, R. Williamson, M. Niazi, et al., "Absence of Maternal Contamination of Villi Used for Fetal Gene Analysis," *New England Journal of Medicine* 308 (1983): 1433–1435.

18. Anonymous, "Recombinant DNA and Genetic Disease—Answers and Questions," *Lancet* 2 (1983): 1404.

19. Kan and Dozy, "Antenatal Diagnosis."

20. Anonymous, "Recombinant DNA."

21. McKusick, *Mendelian Inheritance.*

22. Anonymous, "DNA Probes."

23. Gusella et al., "A Polymorphic DNA Marker."

24. S. Woo et al., "Alpha-1-antitrypsin Deficiency and Pulmonary Emphysema: Identification of Recessive Homozygote by Direct Analysis of the Mutation Site in the Chromosomal Genes," *Cold Spring Harbor Symposium on the Application of Recombinant DNA to Human Disease* (Cold Spring Harbor Laboratory, Long Island, N.Y., 1982).

25. V. J. Kidd, R. B. Wallace, K. Hakura, and S. L. C. Woo, "Alpha-1-antitrypsin Deficiency Detection by Direct Analysis of the Mutation in the Gene," *Nature* 304 (1983): 230–234.

26. M. C. Owen, S. O. Brennan, J. H. Lewis, et al., "Mutation of Antitrypsin to Antiprothombin," *New England Journal of Medicine* 309 (1983): 694–698.

27. Office of Technology Assessment, *Genetic Testing and Monitoring for Susceptibility to Occupational Hazards* (Washington, D.C.: U.S. Government Printing Office, 1983). See also, M. Lappé, "Ethical Issues"; B. Woolf, "On Estimating the Relation Between Blood Groups and Disease," *Annals of Human Genetics* 19 (1955): 251–253; David Landers, M. D., personal communication, October 21, 1981.

28. See, for instance, M. Pembrey, "Clinical Applications of Recombinant DNA Technology in Families with Genetic Disease," *British Journal of Hospital Medicine* 29 (1983): 546–551; and T. B. Shows, A. Y. Sakaguchi, and S. L. Naylor, "Mapping the Human Genome, Cloned Genes, DNA Polymorphisms, and Inherited Disease," *Advances in Human Genetics* 12 (1982): 341–452.

29. Such optimistic predictions have appeared in prominent medical journals and texts. Cf. Anonymous, "Molecular Genetics for the Clinician," *Lancet* 1 (1984): 257–259; and D. J. Weatherall, *The New Genetics and Clinical Practice* (London: Nuffield Provincial Hospitals Trust, 1982).

30. The special nature of patient/physician relations in occupational settings and the need to protect the gathered information is described in Judicial Council of the American Medical Association, "Current Opinions of the Judicial Council of the American Medical Association," Section 5.09, *Confidentiality: Physicians in Industry* (Chicago: AMA, 1984).

31. S. Woo et al., "Alpha-1-antitrypsin Deficiency and Pulmonary Emphysema: Identification of Recessive Homozygote by Direct Analysis of the Mutation Site in the Chromosomal Genes," *Cold Spring Harbor Symposium on the Application of Recombinant DNA to Human Disease* (Cold Spring Harbor Laboratory, Long Island, N.Y., 1982).

32. See, for instance, the studies that established the genetic linkage between high blood lipid levels and certain genetic markers indicative of enzyme deficiencies or receptors, W. C. Breckenridge et al., "Hypertriglyceridemia Associated with Deficiency of Apolipoprotein C-11," *New England Journal of Medicine* 298 (1978): 1265–1273; G. Utterman, K. H. Vogelberg, and A. Steinmetz, et al., "Polymorphism of Apolipoprotein E II. Genetics of Hyperlipoproteinemia Type III," *Clinical Genetics* 15 (1979): 37–62; and K. Berg and A. Heiberg, "A Linkage Between Family Hypercholesterolemia with Xantho-

matosis and the C3 Polymorphism Confirmed," *Cytogenetics and Cell Genetics* 22 (1978): 621–623.

33. The use of a monoclonal antibody to pick out a marker linked to arthritic conditions has been described recently by F. C. Grumet, "Monoclonal Antibodies to HLA-B27," *British Journal of Rheumatology* 22 (1983): 110–118.

34. See N. Suzan Nadi, J. I. Nurnberger, Jr., and E. S. Gershon, "Muscarinic Cholinergic Receptors on Skin Fibroblasts in Familial Affective Disorder," *New England Journal of Medicine* 311 (1984): 225–230.

35. T. Mandrup-Poulson, D. Owenbuch, S. A. Mortensen, and J. Nerup, "DNA Sequences Flanking the Insulin Gene on Chromosome 11 Confer Risk of Atherosclerosis," *Lancet* 1 (1984): 250–252.

36. See, respectively, National Academy of Sciences, *Genetic Screening: Principles, Programs and Research* (Washington, D.C.: NAS, 1975); A. M. Gotto, Jr., "Apolipoprotein C-II Deficiency Revisited," *New England Journal of Medicine* 310 (1984): 1664–1665; and D. Kozarevic et al., "Intermediate Alpha-1-antitrypsin Deficiency and Chronic Obstructive Pulmonary Disease in Yugoslavia," *American Review of Respiratory Disease* 117 (1978): 1039–1044; for a good general review of the relationship between genetics, cholesterol and heart disease, see M. S. Brown and J. L. Goldstein, "How LDL Receptors Influence Cholesterol and Atherosclerosis," *Scientific American* 251 (1984): 58–66.

37. Such discrimination is cited in M. Lappé, J. M. Gustafson, and R. Roblin, et al., "Ethical, Legal, and Social Aspects of Screening for Genetic Disease," *New England Journal of Medicine* 286 (1972): 1129–1136.

38. Under *Wright* v. *Olin Corporation* 697 F.2d 1172, 1189, 30 FEP Cases 889 (4th Cir. 1981), business necessity is defined as "an *overriding* business purpose . . . necessary for the safe and efficient operation of the business." (Emphasis added.)

39. Cited in T. Powledge, "Public Says Genetic Engineers Should Proceed Cautiously," *Bio/Technology* 1 (October 1983): 645–646.

40. J. Wyngaarden, quoted in S. Budiansky, "Gene Therapy: Quick Fixes Not in the Cards," *Nature* 306 (1983): 314.

41. See the experiments of M. Wigler et al., "Transformation of Mammalian Cells with an Amplified Dominant-Acting Gene," *Proceedings of the National Academy of Sciences* 77 (1980): 3567–3570; and K. E. Mercola et al., "Insertion of a New Gene of Viral Origin into Bone Marrow Cells of Mice," *Science* 208 (1980): 1033–1036. The implanta-

tion of genetically modified bone marrow corrected by so-called retroviral-vectors currently appears to be the method of choice for treating certain severe genetic diseases. See W. F. Anderson, "Prospects for Human Gene Therapy," *Science* 226 (1984): 401–409.

42. T. Friedmann, ed., *Gene Therapy: Fact and Fiction* (Banbury Public Information Report, Cold Spring Harbor, Long Island, N.Y. 1983).

43. See R. D. Palmiter et al., "Dramatic Growth of Mice that Develop from Eggs Microinjected with Metallothionein-Growth Hormone Fusion Genes," *Nature* 300 (1982): 611–615; and R. D. Palmiter, G. Norstedt, R. E. Gelinas, et al., "Metallothionein-Human GH Fusion Genes Stimulate Growth of Mice," *Science* 222 (1983): 809–814. In this latter report, the authors emphasized that the researchers had little control over the expression of the foreign genes.

44. G. Van Vliet, D. M. Styne, S. L. Kaplan, and M. M. Grumbach, "Growth Hormone for Short Stature," *New England Journal of Medicine* 309 (1983): 1016–1022.

45. L. E. Underwood, "Growth Hormone Treatment for Short Children," *Journal of Pediatrics* 104 (1984): 237–239.

46. See the discussion in M. Benjamin, J. Muyshans, and P. Spenger, "Growth Hormone and Pressures to Treat," *Hastings Center Report* 14 (1984): 5–9.

47. Ad Hoc Committee on Growth Hormone Usage, "Growth Hormone in the Treatment of Children with Short Stature," *Pediatrics* 72 (1983): 891–894.

48. J. Schulman, cited in Budiansky, "Gene Therapy."

49. John Fletcher, cited in Budiansky, "Gene Therapy."

50. Joseph Fletcher, *The Ethics of Genetic Control* (Garden City, N.Y.: Anchor Books, 1974).

51. These points are discussed in M. Lappé, "Ethical Issues in Eugenics," in *Encyclopedia of Bioethics*, W. T. Reich, ed. (New York: The Free Press, 1978).

52. President's Commission for the Study of Ethical Problems in Medicine and Biomedical and Behavioral Research, *Splicing Life: A Report on the Social and Ethical Issues of Genetic Engineering with Human Beings* (Washington, D.C.: U.S. Government Printing Office, 1982), p. 72.

CHAPTER 6

Agricultural
Developments

In the long run, agricultural innovations promise to be the most complex and potentially rewarding applications of biotechnology. Their complexity turns on two elements: (1) the intrinsic genetic variability and polygenic basis of the animal and plant characteristics most likely to be selected for improvement, and (2) the difficulties involved in assuring the safe environmental release of modified organisms. In general, direct genetic modification of plants now appears more likely than specific genetic engineering of animals (see Appendix E for a description of the basic technologies of genetic engineering in plants). Rapid selection of farm animals is now possible through artificial insemination and production of identical sets of animals through forced twinning. In the future, cloning of desirable stock will be possible.[1]

In the short run, though, the need to turn a quick profit may be dissuading many companies from investing in the long-term agricultural developments that offer the most promise for worldwide agricultural growth. Commodity analysts now routinely advise their genetic-engineering clients to concentrate on the rapid production of amino acid feed supplements for a healthy return on investment.[2] (The market for genetically engineered animal growth hormones alone is estimated to be $1.1 billion!)

In spite of these optimistic projections, investments in agriculture remained flat between 1982 and 1983, and actually declined from 27 to 6 percent when measured against the total investments in biotechnology during this period.[3] One possible explanation for the unattractiveness of agricultural investment strategies is that they often require a longer time to reach their objectives. Another is the failure by investors to recognize the strategic importance of genes themselves.

Germ Plasm

The crucial factor in assuring the long-term viability of agriculture is probably the viability of seed banking and research into the genetic makeup of crops, or germ plasm research. This is so because the continued survival of essential food crops often depends on the identification of naturally occurring genes for pest resistance and other essential traits. Paradoxically, given its primary emphasis on commercial profitability, Japan has initiated the major work in germ plasm banking activities. In Tusubuka Academic New Town, plans are under way to establish a comprehensive gene bank to study and map Japan's gene resources, particularly its animal, plant, and microorganism germ plasm resources.

A parallel effort in the United States to establish a national plant germ plasm system (NPGS) has been beset by problems generated by competing commercial interests. The intention behind this effort has been to preserve, evaluate, and distribute otherwise scarce or valuable plant germ plasm to assure genetic diversity for future crop improvement. While NPGS makes more than four hundred thousand accessions of germ plasm available free of charge to any U.S. scientist, little industry reciprocity in bequeathing such material to NPGS is evident. Given the commercial value of the germ plasm, the industry as a whole is perhaps understandably chary about giving out germ plasm to scientists who seek contributions from the private sector.[4]

As more and more seed companies have moved into the hands of multinational corporations, the germ plasm acquisition program has suffered serious setbacks. Cary Fowler, director of the Rural Advancement Fund, in a conversation with me in January 1984, noted oversights by some conglomerates that fail to reseed vital crops annually; he also noted outright losses of germ plasm and other problems associated with a displacement of investment priorities.[5] In Fowler's view, the very agencies charged with maintaining the germ lines of our key seed crops are letting more and more of the key plant types slip away and are eroding the genetic variability that adapts these crops to their native habitats. To illustrate this point, he gives the example of Hopi blue corn, a wild maize adapted to the arid Southwest. By spacing the essential germination and growing-out of seed at longer and longer intervals, and by testing these stocks in the more temperate climates of the Midwest, the new germ plasm conservators are subjecting blue corn to selective pressures that are likely to shift its genetic makeup away from adaptation to its native environment and towards adaptation to more temperate conditions.

In response to concerns about the serious losses of important gene resources among crop species, a nonprofit organization called the National Center on Gene Resources was founded in 1980. A spin-off organization in California, the California Gene Resources Program (CGRP), was started shortly afterwards to establish a gene-resource management and gene-conservation program in the Golden State. CGRP's purpose was to offset the potential loss of valuable germ plasms that is occurring as the genetic diversity of forestry, livestock, wild organisms, and crop species is reduced in California.

Under a seed grant from the Levinson Foundation, a nonprofit charitable trust in Boston, Massachusetts, the California group got support from the state legislature to study the genetic resources of Douglas fir, strawberries, barley, and anadromous salmonids such as salmon and sea run trout in a special sixteen-month program. The study, now complete, made key recommendations for maintaining the genetic diversity of these natural resources, including the avoidance of monocultures and special efforts to maintain species diversity. Unlike this nonprofit program, other more intensive agricultural investments less intent on preserving genetic diversity are focusing on capitalizing on the most rapidly exploitable resources.

On first inspection, there appears to be nothing seriously wrong with this approach. After all, we have a long history of selection and breeding of plant types to meet human needs. But too few researchers are looking beyond these preliminary goals to exploring the possible impact of recombinant-DNA-facilitated techniques on the long-term viability of forest and aquatic ecosystems as well as crop and animal diversity, or to selecting or enhancing the preservation of endangered plant or animal species. Given the commercial value of food crops, it is perhaps understandable that most researchers are focusing on just a few plant types.

Despite all the press given to our imminent control of the plant kingdom, our knowledge of the molecular basis for most of the genetic traits in plants is exceedingly primitive. In contrast to our minimal but growing familiarity with the genetic systems that contribute to human genetic disease, our knowledge about the genetic basis for plant diseases is extensive, but that about the sets of genes responsible for key traits, such as salt tolerance, drought resistance, and nutrient requirements, is minimal.

It is time to ask if some of the current attempts to apply genetic-engineering technologies to agriculture may be premature. Do we have a sufficient knowledge base to appreciate all the ramifications of our newly found ability to move key photosynthetic or nitrogen-fixation genes across species lines? We do know that our knowledge of the basic genetic factors that regulate—and balance—the relationships among the key species that make up the biosphere is extremely limited. We have little appreciation of the factors needed to balance symbionts and parasites with their hosts. We know still less of the forces that assure ecological—and possibly evolutionary—harmony. (It was in part for this reason that Judge John Sirica's decision on May 16, 1984, to bar outdoor testing of genetically engineered plants was sound and timely.[6])

We know too little about the dependencies, interrelationships, and codependencies among the species at stake to perform major transformations—such as replacing whole stands of soft-wood trees[7]—with any measure of sagacity. What is at stake is nothing less than the survival of the major ecosystems now being threatened with extinction on this planet, and the productivity of some of the most important food crops that serve humankind.

Yet here we are about to pull genetic material from exotic bacterial species and mix it with the genome of bacteria that colonize the roots of commercially desirable food crops. Where our ambitions are modest—say, in attempting a minor increase in nitrogenase production to provide more efficient nitrogen fixation—it is unlikely that we will do any great harm. Where they are more extreme—as in the attempt to move whole genetic systems for fixing nitrogen from one species to another—the risks are considerably greater. And genetically redesigning a whole forest, as some genetic engineers envision doing with clones of some profitable woody perennial species, is about as wise as putting an entire life's savings into a single over-the-counter stock. Fortunately, as Michigan State University's Larry Tombaugh, a forest economist, observed, "We're so far behind [the other fields of applied biotechnology] that by the time we come up with something that's ready for field-testing, the issues will be settled."[8]

The limits to our understanding of the factors that go into selectively encouraging or discouraging the survival of new plant varieties suggest another area of concern: the effects of intentionally introducing genetically engineered plants or their associated organisms into the environment. We will explore this prospect in the next chapter.

Background

To put all of these possibilities into perspective, it will be useful to consider the magnitude of the problem. The systematic domestication of plant species through scientific breeding and creation of hybrid crosses is no more than two hundred years old. Plant products currently constitute some 93 percent of the human diet, with some 3.75 billion metric tons produced in 1979. Some three thousand different species of plants have been used historically as foodstuffs for human populations.[9] Considering that there are at least three to five thousand varieties of potatoes alone, with about 10 percent of this number still in widespread use in Peru, it is clear that only a portion of the thousands of possible varieties and species is currently being exploited. Yet we are reducing the diversity of plant species rather than preserving it, and the consequences of such diminution in terms of productivity, pest resistance, and adaptability of essential food crops are now only dimly appreciated.

At present, the vast majority of the world's people rely on only twenty-nine basic food crop species, with eight species of cereals making up over half of the total amount.[10] Most of the recent progress in increasing the production figures for these key crops has centered on breeding techniques. According to Norman Borlaug, one of the pioneers in the effort to improve the genetic makeup of cereals, the key elements in the most successful programs have been (1) the intentional introduction and maintenance of genetic diversity through cross-pollination or the mating of diverse sources of germ plasm with complementary traits, and (2) the progressive selection of plants that are likely to carry the key genes that ensure uniformly high yields, disease resistance, and eventual agronomic uniformity.[11]

Borlaug and others document the dramatic success of these efforts beginning in 1961 with the introduction of leading varieties of high-yield semidwarf wheat that had strong resistance to wheat stem rust. Some, such as the variety Norin 10, produced yields twice as high as those of their predecessors. Similar successes were recorded with rice varieties, leading to the IR series of strains that now predominate world production. Borlaug points out that less spectacular benefits have accrued to maize crops, particularly in the developing world, since the need to have open-pollinated species with good drought tolerance and other factors especially suited to some Third World regions has not been fully met. Nonetheless, yields some 20–35 percent above the norm have become possible in these countries through the special selection of some seventy varieties of open-pollinated maize.

Recently, growers have come to rely on an ever-narrowing spectrum of crop varieties, each with special inbred characteristics. Reliance on these characteristics, such as male sterility, and on plant monocultures has sparked concern that we may be courting ecological disaster. Two eventualities in particular concern plant ecologists: the possibility of widespread epidemics of major diseases and the irrevocable loss of important genetic traits as the diversity of germ plasm is reduced. In 1970, whole fields of genetically homogeneous hybrid corn, representing some 17 percent of the U.S. corn crop, were devastated by a blight. According to a National Academy of Sciences report, "The losses in 1970 wiped out, for that year at least, some of the gain in efficiency in corn production acquired so laboriously during 50 years of research and its technological application."[12]

In spite of such ominous setbacks, genetic engineers believe the future lies with genetic control of plant epitypes. Some researchers, notably Kenneth Barton and Winston Brill of the Cetus Madison Corporation in Middleton, Wisconsin, believe that genetic engineering has the capability of generating an expanded diversity of genetic types among food crops.[13] Plant breeders, such as Norman Borlaug, are not nearly so sanguine. Borlaug believes that genetic engineering holds less promise than traditional breeding techniques of improving crop yields. Pointing to the success of genetic engineering in making insulin, he states that "there is no firm evidence that similar results will be obtained with higher plants. It will probably be many years before these [rDNA] techniques can be successfully used to breed superior crop varieties."[14]

The details of these intensive plant-breeding programs and some of the most spectacular successes are beyond the scope of this book. However, it is clear that the continued success of high-yielding food crops depends increasingly on massive use of nitrogen fertilizers, herbicides, and pesticides. Some of these applications and products leave undesirable residues in the environment that may be toxic in their own right.

Comparing the Old and the New

In addition to Borlaug, other researchers are skeptical about genetic engineering's potential for matching the achievements of traditional approaches. Certain plant characteristics may be beyond the capabilities of the gene-by-gene manipulations of most recombinant-DNA techniques. But the history of the "new" plant genetic engineering is extremely brief, beginning only in the late 1960s. Early discoveries, such as the ability to culture and regenerate entire plants from single cells and the fusion of "protoplasts" of plant cells (created by stripping the cell wall) to create plantlets with combined properties, do not adequately convey the opportunities offered by systematic genetic alterations. Within the last decade, plant molecular biologists have succeeded in isolating portions of the genome of higher plants in bacterial cells. (The details of this process are described in Appendix E.) By devising different ways to culture selectively the simplest plant cells such as yeasts, researchers have also begun to gain control over gene-directed products for possible commercial use from single-cell fermentation systems. Comparable successes in the agricultural area have been harder to come by, in part owing to the greater complexity of the genomes of higher plants.

The dearth of hard evidence that genetic engineering is the millennium for breeding food crops has not discouraged visionaries who see genetic engineering supplanting almost all other avenues of invention and control. In spite of only modest gains—and those only since 1983—in achieving the functional expression of foreign genes in tobacco and other only marginally valuable plants,[15] some observers remain extremely optimistic about the prospects for controlling plant properties through gene transfers across species lines. In mid-1983, one commentator on the genetic scene observed that "in principle the genetic resources of the entire biosphere are now available for crop improvement."[16]

The prospects for vast transformations of plant species understandably inspire awe and wonderment. But such potentialities also inspire an intense competitive spirit among entrepreneurs. There is danger in leaving the choices of types, varieties, and gene combinations solely to the corporate sector. One potential risk is that in the interest of pressing for short-term profit, we might ignore the long-term impacts of choices on genetic resources and composition of the species most important to human survival. In this light, it is not surprising that tobacco plants are among the most intensively studied varieties. Certainly, everything we have learned about the effects of our first depredations of the plant world (such as when we logged out whole sectors of the tropical rain forests or clear-cut soft-wood forests) suggests that we may not be ready to assume genetic stewardship of the planet.

We may have some time to contemplate these realities before we begin to engineer plants on a mass scale. Present capabilities for using rDNA to modify plants are still more theoretical than practical. Presently, only dicotyledonous plants—such as soy beans and most flowering species—can be genetically engineered. This means that the range for plant engineering presently excludes the phyla of greatest commercial and perhaps ecological interest—those that contain the monocotyledonous plants, including all of our major cereal crops such as rice and corn. Breakthroughs that will allow the construction of markers to permit the use of both single-leafed embryo plants (monocots) and broad-leafed ones (dicots) may come soon, but even this will not permit us to realize the large-scale application necessary to effect massive change.

Objectives

What, then, should our objective be in using our newfound prowess in plant engineering? Among the more obvious goals are larger yields and tolerance to drought, high salinity, and cold. But, as Mary-Dell Chilton, executive director for agricultural biotechnology for CIBA-Geigy's new experimental station in North Carolina has observed, "The trouble is that there is no known way to find genes controlling such traits, most of which are probably governed by a number of genes and perhaps by elaborate regulatory mechanisms."[17] And once we have controlled such traits we will still need to assess the risks of releasing such highly adaptive and resilient new crops into their respective ecosystems—a process still poorly understood by even the best minds in plant ecology.

In spite of these important limitations, several research groups have already embarked on ambitious genetic-engineering projects. In their November 1982 progress report on emerging biotechnologies in agriculture, the National Association of State Universities and Land Grant Colleges identified a group of major projects under way at the agricultural experiment stations at land-grant universities.

Some of the projects funded included the highly controversial ice-nucleation gene work at the University of California at Berkeley (see Chapter 7), use of pollen to carry genetically engineered DNA, and transfer of blight resistance to cotton plants. Reports of these scientifically spectacular but commercially rather modest projects were overshadowed by the agricultural industry's own sweeping projections of benefits to be reaped by wholesale production of new plant varieties.

The April 1983 issue of *Farm Chemistry* hailed genetic engineering as nothing less than a major revolution in plant breeding. According to this report, through precise genetic manipulation and nonseed propagation (i.e., cloning of plants in tissue culture), recombinant-DNA techniques would make it possible to reduce production time in improved crop varieties by 50 percent. By 1992, the editors of *Farm Journal* predict, new plant varieties generated by genetic techniques could constitute fully half of all commercial breeding lines in production.

Still more optimistic were the projections that appeared in the April 10, 1983, issue of the widely respected *Wall Street Journal*. In appraising the entry of major food producers such as Campbell and Heinz into the genetic-engineering field, the *Journal* cited a study by Arthur D. Little analyst D. Wheat (no pun intended), which declared that biotechnology could have more potential in agriculture than in medicine. According to Wheat, sales of bioengineered products could be in the range of $2–4 billion by 1990, echoing the *Farm Journal's* projection that genetically engineered plant varieties would equal those produced through more traditional means.[18]

The entry of Campbell into the genetic-engineering field was announced in a page one article in the business section of the *New York Times*.[19] The *Times* announced that Campbell had earmarked $75 million for development of some

100 products, an appreciable portion of which would be the fruits of genetic-engineering endeavors. As an example, the *Times* cited a squarish tomato being developed at Campbell's DNA Plant Technology Corporation that was being selected to grow on disease-resistant stock. Citing the high revenue generated by tomatoes at Campbell's (some $870 million), the *Times* writer took pains to highlight the new role that biotechnology will play in developing this "super" tomato. Given the limited success of introducing foreign genes into tomato plants and the social consequences to farm workers of putting in place more robust machine-harvestable crops, this prospect will not be an unmixed blessing.

Disease resistance appears to be an area where the prospects for engineering will be less likely to have adverse impacts and more value. The April 1983 issue of the *Farm Chemicals and Croplife*[20] contained a key trend-setting article on agricultural techniques. The editors of this influential journal predicted that traditional seed companies would be under considerable pressure over the entire decade of the 1980s to develop seeds that will not only require less production time and fertilizer than before but will be more resistant to pests or blights.

Making Plants
More Like Animals

The newest wave in agricultural research is to utilize plant tissues in the same manner as animal cells to produce valuable biological substances. According to a report in the trade journal *High Tech*, plant genetics leaders such as International Plant Research Institute (IPRI) and

Agrigenetics plan to conduct appreciable research and development using tissue-culture techniques to harvest plant-producing chemicals.[21] These companies have also invested significant capital in using genetic systems to improve food crops (Agrigenetics alone has $15 million earmarked for programs involving fifty different crop species), suggesting a strong commitment to the concept that new genetic techniques will indeed reap foreseeable benefits.

Of major importance to the Third World (see Chapter 10) is the fact that Agrigenetics is willing to concentrate a significant portion of this R & D money on cassava, a root crop that is a staple throughout much of the developing world. This isolated objective belies the industry trend, which is towards reinforcing already successful crops in the developed world through enhancing their efficiency and pesticide tolerance.

Needs

While investment activity has centered on making commercially valuable crops more valuable, food experts are quick to point out that even relatively simple genetic modifications of existing staple crops such as rice and wheat could have dramatic impacts on world nutrition. Most of the world's population—perhaps as much as 70 percent—depends on the seeds of these grasslike crops for their protein. The principal limitation of these plants as protein sources is that the amino acid composition of their storage proteins (called *zeins*) is usually deficient in terms of the balance needed for human nutrition. This deficiency centers on just two essential amino acids: lysine and tryptophan. Unfortunately, the technical difficulties inherent in enhancing the incorporation of these key amino acids has limited the likelihood of directly engineering the zein proteins.

Simple supplementation of the diet with lysine or tryptophan is a proven way of augmenting the human physiological utilization of wheat or rice proteins. In fact, major genetic-engineering efforts have been under way for several years in Japan for producing commercially usable lysine in bulk form. However, this successful program has been almost exclusively geared to the lucrative animal-feed market, where amino acid supplementation increases growth efficiency, and to the use of key amino acids as precursors to other commercially valuable products.

One such product, the nonnutritive sweetener aspartame, can be constructed from just two amino acids, aspartic acid and phenylalanine. Japan's Toyo Soda Ltd. uses these microorganisms to make aspartic acid, while Genex, a U.S. company, relies on monocultures of another to make phenylalanine. The resulting product (made by Searle) is commercially highly attractive, since it fills the void created by the prohibitions to cyclamates and the ill-tasting (and possibly carcinogenic) saccharin. The similarly lucrative animal-feed industry has attracted two Japanese firms highly experienced in fermentation technology, Ajinomoto and Suntory.

Skepticism

Despite evidence of considerable international interest in using plant genetic engineering on a large scale for pharmaceutical or agricultural purposes, some researchers and directors of product development have been privately skeptical about the actual promise of such ventures. One such person is Peter Carlson, an agronomist in charge of plant genetic engineering at Zoecon, a subsidiary of Sandoz. His remarks are significant because Sandoz has embarked on an ambitious program of seed development and marketing. In recent years, Sandoz has taken over three key national and international seed firms, Northrup, Rogers Brothers, and the Dutch firm Sluis & Groot—all leaders in seed production.

In Carlson's view, genetic engineering of plant cells constitutes an as yet untested tool with but few realized applications in the agricultural sector.[22] (Recall that traditional seed developers such as Norman Borlaug take an even more skeptical view of genetic engineering, pointing out that recombinant techniques will have to prove themselves in the marketplace against some remarkably successful and substantially less expensive breeding techniques.) Carlson's position in a corporation that is a world leader in seed development may in part explain his view that agricultural genetic-engineering activity "does not provide a tidal wave at all."[23]

To appreciate Carlson's view, it is worth remembering that major conceptual and experimental differences exist between genetic engineering and traditional methods of plant improvement. Genetic engineering relies on the reductionist view that all properties of plants that will be of commercial value can be linked to a single genetic locus. In all likelihood, as with major human attributes and traits, desirable characteristics of plants will also prove to be multifactorial and involve many different gene loci. This so-called polygenic inheritance is likely for properties such as yield, drought or salt resistance, or the size of the fully grown plant.

In their plant improvements, Borlaug and his contemporaries capitalized on identifying the strongest candidates for each of these phenomena and making suitable crosses. These pioneers achieved their success by joining plants having diverse characteristics into particularly robust hybrid varieties, or introducing whole blocks of genes through systematic back-crossing. These avenues are presently out of reach for rDNA technologies.

Benefits

One place where genetic engineering has a distinct advantage over traditional approaches, however, is in the intentional production and selection of mutants at a single-cell level. Such research is normally done in a coordinated program that involves including mutations in *haploid* cells (cells that have only a single set of chromosomes). With haploid cells, any new genetic change is expressed, permitting the researcher to produce a whole spectrum of discrete changes that can rapidly be assayed in tissue culture rather than awaiting a whole season for a new hybrid plant to "test out." Such advances also rely on the ability to induce mutations systematically and to produce protoplasts (cell-wall-lacking plant cells) that can be fused into viable cell clones. These clones in turn must be capable of being cultured in a medium that will encourage the regeneration of a complete plant. Such success has only recently been achieved, and then only for a few of the major food crops.

One of the potential gains of this research is in plant-disease control. Kenneth Barton and Winston Brill of Agricetus predict that genetic engineering will assist us by (1) increasing our understanding of the way plants become diseased; (2) allowing early identification of infecting agents; (3) providing ways to control pests and the symptoms of disease; and (4) enabling us to engineer crop varieties with heightened resistance.

Just two examples suggest how these accomplishments might be achieved in ways that would be harmonious with natural systems. A wide variety of substances produced as by-products of plants' metabolic activity are potent insecticides or repellents—the pyrethrins are classic examples. If we put the genes for producing these natural substances into valuable crop plants, we might dramatically augment the host plants' normally low resistance to certain pests without major perturbation of these crops' relationship to other plant species.

A second innovation would be to harness the ability of certain strains of bacteria (e.g., *Bacillus thuringiensis*) to produce short polypeptide insecticides with narrow host ranges. By putting the bacterial genetic sequences into the target plant species themselves rather than relying on expensive sprays, the agricultural specialist might succeed in encoding a natural protective system into valuable food crops. However, as I will suggest in the next chapter, even these ideal-sounding innovations are not without their risks.

Perhaps the single most sought-after benefit would be to improve the photosynthetic ability of plants. Although now almost entirely speculative, theoretically it is possible to encourage plants via genetics to use more efficient enzymes in one or more of the key pathways involved in photosynthesis. Similarly, genetic engineering might be used in efforts to decrease the fertilizer dependency of food crops.

A key limiting factor for the growth of agricultural crops is the availability of nitrogen. The nitrogen naturally produced in the soil is often inadequate to sustain the demands created by the intense cultivation carried out in most agrarian societies. Commonly, usable nitrogen in the soil is supplemented through the addition of ammonia, urea, or nitrate fertilizers.

"Naturally" fertilizing systems, such as the *Rhizobium* bacteria, which colonize the root systems of leguminous plants like soy beans and peanuts, rely on the ability of microorganisms to take atmospheric nitrogen and "fix" it into ammonia, which can be directly taken up by the roots. Most of these species, including alfalfa, peas, clover, and beans, get sufficient ammonia from their root-nodule bacteria to make nitrogenous fertilizers unnecessary. The genes responsible for this feat, called *Nif* genes, can be exchanged between such bacteria as *Klebsiella pneumoniae* and *E. coli,* which lack the ability to form complex symbiont relationships with legumes but can do so with natural symbiont bacteria. Recent developments have led to a better understanding and control of the complex genetic traits that allow plants to be colonized with bacteria having the special ability to do this nitrogen fixing.

Experiments with genetically selected soy beans have shown that crop yield can be increased through the intentional inoculation of peat-based legume seeds together with cultures of specially selected *Rhizobia*. Liquid cultures of *Rhizobia* readily colonize the roots of the resulting plants, giving them a higher productive capacity than traditionally sown legumes.

The *Rhizobia* themselves have proven surprisingly amenable to laboratory manipulation, suggesting that major improvements in utilizing atmospheric nitrogen and perhaps increasing their host range may be possible. For instance, genetic selection of bacteria that use more efficient nitrogenase (key nitrogen-fixing genes) has already been accomplished. The requirement for parallel genetic changes in host plants to ensure the existence of conditions encouraging colonization and nodule formation remains a major stumbling block to widespread success in effectively enhancing the species range of the *Rhizobia*.

For this and related reasons, some researchers believe that we are unlikely to achieve rapid success in providing fertilizer-dependent plants with nitrogen-fixing abilities through genetic engineering.[24] Others believe that genetic engineering of nitrogen fixation will neither be as efficient nor as ecologically desirable as traditional methods of increasing nitrogen fixation, such as inoculation of high-yielding indica rice paddies with special symbiont strains of a free-living blue-green algae and a water fern called azolla.[25]

Speaking in 1981 at the Fast Bio-Society Symposium on Biotechnology in Europe held at Oberursel, West Germany, Professor A. Puhler of the University of Bielefeld also pointed out the limitations of genetically engineering alternatives to fertilizers. Puhler observed that symbiont relationships, such as those between soy beans and *Rhizobium* species, are several times as efficient in delivering nitrogen as the application of nitrogen fertilizers.[26] But the intrinsic complexity of harnessing these systems means that several decades will pass before significant advances are made.

Some biotechnology firms obviously hold different views about the intrinsic worth of harnessing nitrogen fixation. In early January 1983, Allelix of Ontario, Canada, announced that it had struck a $2.2 million deal with McGillim of Canada to use *Rhizobium japonicum* to isolate and transfer nitrogen-fixation genes.[27] This report echoed one just two weeks earlier from Allied Chemical and Calgene of Davis, California, in which they announced a joint development venture for improving the nutrient efficiency of plants.[28] Obviously, both teams believe that genetic-engineering technologies afford an excellent prospect for harnessing the power of nitrogen fixation for commercial purposes.

Limitations

The key to effective genetic engineering of *Nif* genes in plants is understanding the complex interactions among plants, bacteria, and their environment. This has not always been accomplished. A case in point is the relatively poor groundwork that preceded the decision of some genetic-engineering companies (e.g., Calgene of Davis, California) to move the genes for nitrogen fixation into cereal crops. At the time, we knew little about the host genes needed for formation of the root nodules that contain the nitrogen-fixing bacteria.[29] Even now we know very little of the molecular genetics involved in plant biochemistry *generally*, relative to what we know of mammalian systems. Others share this interpretation. According to Agricetus scientists Kenneth Barton and Winston Brill, "before practical applications can be routinely expected, basic research is required in almost all areas of plant molecular biology."[30]

It is the nature of human invention to press beyond the bounds of present knowledge. In order to escape the limits of the more cumbersome breeding methods of the past, it is highly likely that some researchers will attempt to transfer foreign genes into new plant species before we fully appreciate the implications of their modifications.

To give some idea of how limited our knowledge is, consider the traits that have to be coordinated to ensure that bacterial/host symbionts fix nitrogen efficiently: (1) optimizing the degree of photosynthetic capacity and efficiency; (2) delaying the natural aging of the organisms (senescence); and (3) assuring efficient partitioning of the carbon and nitrogen cycles. As described by R. J. Rennie, each of these traits is physiologically complex and determined by diverse genetic systems.[31] Given such complexity, it is hubris to believe that success through genetic engineering is just around the corner.

Another major obstacle is the lack of sufficient "markers" that would allow the selection in tissue-culture systems of genetically altered plant cells in the same way that bacterial cells have been selected through the introduction of antibiotic-resistance genes. While some progress has been made, insufficient diversity and effectiveness of selection systems are still the rule. One step in the right direction is to move the genes for antibiotic resistance into plants, thereby facilitating selection in tissue culture. The April 25, 1983, issue of *Chemical and Engineering News* carried the announcement by Phytogen of Pasadena, California, that antibiotic resistance genes could be delivered to tobacco plants. (A similar report came out in the July issue of *Farm Chemicals and Croplife* of the same year. In this latter example, petunias were given genes for antibiotic resistance.) Similar successes with other plant systems have since been achieved, facilitating isolation and propagation of genetically engineered plants.

Optimism that these extremely preliminary findings will lead to successful development of crops with genetically engineered traits, such as resistance to herbicides or insecticides, is undercut by a key question: Will successfully introduced genes remain stable and be properly regulated as plants are propagated from modified clones or germ lines? And what about our ability to predict the long-range ecological consequences of such an approach?

Some companies are capitalizing on the herbicide dependence of many farming operations. Calgene has sought an enzyme variant for the target of a very potent and popular herbicide called Roundup®, or glyphosphate (phosphonomethylglycine). A mutant form of the targeted enzyme is protective because of its resistance to the toxic action of glyphosphate, making its successful introduction to valuable crop species a high priority. Such an event would be greeted with great enthusiasm by cotton farmers, according to the *Wall Street Journal,* since they expend upwards of $150 million per year on cotton seed only to see a large proportion of their crop displaced by fast-growing weeds. Presently, cotton farmers must apply potent herbicides such as glyphosphate sparingly, since it will kill cotton plants as well as weeds.[32]

A similar success in moving resistance genes across species barriers was achieved by Dr. Howard Goodman of the Massachusetts General Hospital. Reporting at the Thirty Years of DNA Conference held in Boston on September 19–21, 1983, Goodman described his success in transferring the genes for herbicide resistance into alfalfa. The successful reduction in crop susceptibility was due to a subsequent overproduction of the herbicide's target enzyme.[33] Such a feat is not truly genetic engineering, in that no new enzyme was introduced. Rather, the synthesis of an old gene was "amplified," or enhanced.

Rather than reducing dependence on chemical use, such advances actually encourage reliance on herbicides. And if glyphosphate performs like its chlorinated counterpart, 2, 4 dichlorophenoxy acetic acid (2, 4 D), and its salts, there is even the possibility that its use would encourage the proliferation of insect and pathogen pests, which in turn would require heavier treatment with other pesticides.

Future Applications

A more universally promising effort in plant engineering is to look for specific resistance genes, not to manufactured herbicides, but to viruses that cause substantial crop losses. The Rockefeller Foundation in New York made a major initial commitment to this end in granting 230,000 British pounds to two scientists at the Plant Breeding Institute, Cambridge, England. The grant is intended to encourage the investigation of how genetic engineering might be used to protect plants against tobacco rattle virus and cucumber mosaic virus, both of which cause substantial crop losses each year.

What is new about this grant is that it marks a major departure for the Rockefeller Foundation from its traditional emphasis on the genetic selection of food crops to one on engineering. Since funding its Agricultural Science Program in the 1940s, the Rockefeller Foundation has supported research expressly earmarked for improving food production in developing countries. As a result of this effort, recipients such as Norman Borlaug have participated in successful programs for developing wheat or rice strains that are now in widespread use worldwide. In this new program, Rockefeller will now budget one-third of its $7–8 million budget for specific research proposals that will utilize plant genetic-engineering techniques.[34]

Micropropagation

Perhaps surprisingly, it is a little known or poorly appreciated development in plant breeding that promises to open many of the most promising areas of research. Called *micropropagation,* this technique consists of growing genetically controlled plant embryos in culture and selectively planting them when they reach a suitable size. A typical experiment is shown in Figure 6.1. Individual cells taken from a surgically removed portion, or explant, of a leaf or even an entire plant embryo are cultured in special tubes where they produce thousands of cells. Through judicious control of the chemical composition of the medium, such a plant can be induced to form stems and leaves—and with further changes, even roots. In a compressed period (compared to a normal growth cycle), it is possible to generate a whole plant that can be planted

FIGURE 6.1 *(opposite)*
The micropropagation of a *Ti* plasmid-transformed
tobacco plant cell. (*Source:* Mary-Dell Chilton, "A
Vector for Introducing New Genes into Plants,"
Scientific American 248 [1983]. Copyright, W.H.
Freeman & Co. Used with permission.)

outdoors to become sexually mature and propagate itself.
Were some of the original cells to be genetically modified,
say, by a *Ti*-carried gene (see Appendix E), it is now possible
to produce a plant whose germ cells will in fact have the
genetic change expressed. In this way, whole new strains of
plants can be sexually propagated from a single successful
clone.

Even without starting with intentionally engineered cells,
it is possible to select and clone through micropropagation only those plants with the superior characteristics a
researcher wants to preserve. It is estimated that through
this technique yields from a single commercially important
species—the oil palm—have already increased 30 percent,
with comparable drops in production costs.[35]

According to this report in the second issue of the journal
Bio/Technology, these and similarly spectacular yields in production of the related date palms of North Africa and the
Middle East can be expected in the near future. Were these
techniques to extend to coconut palms, still greater benefits
might be realized. Even broader implications for these techniques are likely to ensue as cost-effective automated micropropagation systems are developed and extended to other
valuable crops.

As with many other developments in the agricultural
sector, there is no assurance that the criteria used to select
species for micropropagation will be based on factors other
than their commercial interest. Should this prove true—as

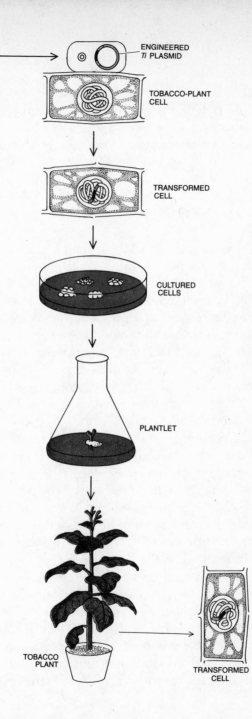

ENGINEERED
Ti PLASMID

TOBACCO-PLANT
CELL

TRANSFORMED
CELL

CULTURED
CELLS

PLANTLET

TOBACCO
PLANT

TRANSFORMED
CELL

seems to be the case for micropropagated timber species—
we may lose potentially valuable and endangered but economically unproductive plant species that might have been
given a selective advantage through micropropagation.

Advantages

Even considering these limitations, it is nonetheless clear that the new technology of genetic engineering
affords the plant researcher advantages not previously
enjoyed by the seed developer.[36] Traditional plant breeders
had to have large plots of land and large blocks of time for
testing varieties before they could be sure of a real success.
Besides saving space and time, genetic engineers can evaluate literally thousands of plantlets, each composed of 1–70
million cells, stored in a few laboratory shelves compared
with the hundreds of acres needed in achieving the same
end by conventional methods.

The unprecedented ability to alter the range and type of
genetic variability normally expressed in plant types is the
most challenging prospect of plant genetic engineering.
Plant engineers can now introduce totally novel properties
that previously had to be sought in rare and sometimes
remote varieties, and see them expressed in tissue-culture-
propagated plantlets. Such techniques would be particularly
valuable in plants like the perennial woody species, which
have long generation times and complex genetics.

In spite of these attractive alternatives, substantial risks
exist where researchers go into genetic-engineering ventures "blind" to possible ecological or social ramifications.
Some protesters believe that such risks are now being generated by the rapid development and release of genetically
engineered organisms into the environment. In fact, possi-

ble environmental effects of released organisms are now the focal point for the most intense debate in the recombinant-DNA revolution.

Notes

1. See. A. J. Faras and C. C. Muscopla, "Applying Genetic Engineering to Animal Health and Production," *Agri-Practice* 5 (1984): 13–19; and G. E. Seidel, "Production of Genetically Identical Sets of Mammals—Cloning," *Journal of Experimental Zoology* 228 (1983): 347–354.

2. Anonymous, "Impact of Biotechnology on Food Processing and Agriculture," *Strategic, Inc., Report* (New York, June 1982).

3. J. R. Murray, "1983 Financing for Health Applications Increases over Agriculture," *Bio/Technology* 2 (1984): 332–333.

4. Anonymous, "The NPGS: An Overview," *Diversity* (April 1982). The argument for free exchange of germ plasm was also put forward by representatives of the World Bank. See D. L. Plucknett, N. J. H. Smith, J. T. Williams, and N. Murthi Anishetty, "Crop Germplasm Conservation," *Science* 221 (1983): 414–415.

5. Telephone interview with Cary Fowler, January 20, 1984.

6. P. M. Boffey, "Judge Bars Outdoor Test of Genetic Engineering," *New York Times* (May 17, 1984), p. A20.

7. See T. M. Powledge, "Biotechnology Touches the Forest," *Bio/Technology* 2 (September 1984): 763–772 for a description of this still embryonic field.

8. Powledge, 772.

9. N. E. Borlaug, "Contributions of Conventional Plant Breeding to Food Production," *Science* 219 (1983): 689–693.

10. Borlaug, "Contributions," 689.

11. Borlaug, "Contributions," 689–690.

12. National Academy of Sciences, *Genetic Vulnerability of Major Crops* (Washington, D.C.: NAS, 1972), p. 9.

13. K. A. Barton and W. J. Brill, "Prospect in Plant Genetic Engineering," *Science* 219 (1983): 671–676.

14. Borlaug, "Contributions," 693.

15. A. Caplan, L. Herrera-Estrada, D. Inze, et al., "Introduction of Genetic Material into Plants," *Science* 222 (1983): 815–821.

16. M. Brummond, "Launching Genes Across Phylogenetic Barriers," *Nature* 303 (1983): 198–199.

17. M. D. Chilton, "A Vector for Introducing New Genes into Plants," *Scientific American* 298 (1983): 50–59.

18. D. Wheat, *Wall Street Journal* (May 10, 1983), p. 60.

19. P. G. Hollie, "Straining to Be More than Just Soup," *New York Times* (March 20, 1983), Sec. 3, p. 1.

20. *Farm Chemicals and Croplife* (April 1983): 39.

21. *High Tech* (October 1982): 74.

22. P. S. Carlson, "Plant Genetic Engineering," *Chemtech* 13 (December 1983): 744–746.

23. Peter Carlson, personal communication, January 25, 1984.

24. NAS, "Genetic Vulnerability."

25. M. S. Swaminiathan, "Rice," *Scientific American* 250 (1984): 81–93.

26. A. Puhler, "Genetic Engineering in Biological Nitrogen Fixation," *Proceedings of the Symposium on Biotechnology in Europe*, September 27–30, 1981, pp. 173–191.

27. *Chemical Engineering News* (Jan. 10, 1983): 19–20.

28. *Journal of Commerce* (December 24, 1982): 228.

29. Puhler, "Genetic Engineering."

30. Barton and Brill, "Prospects," p. 675.

31. R. J. Rennie, "Potential Use of Induced Mutations to Improve Symbioses of Crop Plants with Nitrogen Fixabacteria," in *Induced Mutations—A Tool in Plant Breeding* (Vienna: International Atomic Energy Agency, 1981), pp. 293–321.

32. *Wall Street Journal* (May 10, 1983), p. 60.

33. P. Newmark, "Thirty Years of DNA," *Nature* 305 (1984): 383–384.

34. T. Beardsley, "Rockefeller Seeks New Success," *Nature* 304 (1983): 479.

35. J. Aynsley, D. Diotz, and G. H. Kidd, "Micropropagation Enters Commercialization Phase," *Bio/Technology* 1 (1983): 166–169.

36. A major review of the spectrum of plant improvements possible through genetic engineering can be found in D. von Wettstein, "Genetic Engineering in the Adaptation of Plants to Evolving Human Needs," *Experientia* 39 (1983): 687–713.

CHAPTER 7

What Will Happen to the Environment?

In spite of our rapidly expanding knowledge of plant genetics, we are ill-prepared to anticipate what will—or will not—happen when the first genetically modified plants or microorganisms are actually released into the natural environment. What is clear is that virtually none of the major benefits of agricultural genetic engineering are likely to be achieved without such release. The pitched battle currently raging around the first deliberate introduction of a laboratory-modified microbe thus has tremendous symbolic importance as a barometer of the resistance—or absence thereof—that producers of genetically modified agricultural products can expect in the future.

As of 1984, regulatory agencies and the courts had given genetic engineers mixed messages about proceeding with engineered-organism releases. As we discussed in Chapter 1, in theory the NIH now permits the intentional release of genetically modified organisms into the environment on the condition that its Recombinant DNA Advisory Committee (RAC) and the institutional biohazard committees (IBCs) at the facility planning the release review and approve any proposed experiments. But even with such approval, routine environmental releases appear to be in trouble.

By mid-1983, the NIH had granted permission to three universities under its jurisdiction, a Stanford University proposal to modify corn plants, one from Cornell to improve tomato and tobacco plants, and a third, approved in June 1983, for U.C. Berkeley to release bacteria specifically modified to reduce frost damage. This last proposal included the experiment that the NIH considered least controversial and closest to readiness for trial.

Just before the approved test could be implemented, a consortium of environmental and consumer groups filed suit with the United States District Court in Washington, D.C., to enjoin the researchers from releasing the modified organisms. The issue before the court hinged on the demonstration that the first proposed release of genetically engineered bacteria could be done safely and with reasonable assurance of containment.

In mid-May 1984, Federal District Judge John J. Sirica found the NIH's environmental impact work flawed and declared the safety issue unresolved. Because of the importance of this finding he ordered NIH to suspend further authorization of experiments requiring environmental release and granted a delay in the first proposed outdoor experiment using genetically engineered organisms. According to the *New York Times*,[1] even this preliminary injunction casts a pall over future genetic-engineering experiments because it signals the need for detailed environmental impact statements (EISs) for all open-air testing of genetically modified organisms. As if heeding this prophetic interpretation, the Stanford University team has since also held back from its experiment with genetically modified corn.

The origins of this suit can be traced to experiments begun in 1982, when researchers in California first began to look for a way to reduce the likelihood of frost damage to crops.

"Ice-Minus" Bacteria

The science of the problem is fairly simple: "wild-type" strains of a common bacterium known as *Pseudomonas syringae* normally produce proteins on their cell surfaces that serve as nuclei for the formation of ice crystals. This effect is familiar to anyone who has made rock candy crystals from a concentrated or "supersaturated" sugar solution: the addition of a tiny grain of sugar on a stick starts a cascade of crystallization leading to the familiar geometric clumps of rock sugar. Apparently, widely distributed bacteria such as *P. syringae* serve as seeds for the formation of ice crystals from similarly supersaturated cold water. Their ability to "seed out" crystals of ice makes them a potent ice maker, both on the plants they colonize and in clouds.

The problem for growers is that by precipitating ice crystals on plants, the wild-type *P. syringae* allow frost to form at or near the freezing point of water. Plants that can be maintained free of the bacteria can survive without frost formation all the way down to 23° F, a substantial degree of protection. Given the USDA estimates that agricultural losses from frost damage will total at least $4–5 billion in the mid-1980s, any system that can marginally decrease the likelihood of freezing would be immensely valuable.

Presently, the methods being used rely on propagating mutant bacteria that lack the frost-producing capacity as a result of random mutations. One method is to expose the bacteria to chemical mutagens or ultraviolet light. But these "conventional" approaches have two drawbacks. Mutant bacteria are known to undergo *reversion,* changing back to their original wild-type form. Such an eventuality becomes likely when vast numbers of multiply mutated bacteria are released, as would be the case in any mass spraying program. Were this to happen in the course of applying bacteria to important food crops, the reverted bacteria could precipitate even worse frost damage.

A second, less likely eventuality is that the genetic changes induced by blind application of mutagens might render the bacteria pathogenic because of the inadvertent induction of toxin genes.

With these obstacles in mind, a research team on the West Coast began to use recombinant-DNA techniques to selectively modify the frost-inducing bacterium. Under contract with Advanced Genetic Sciences of Norwich, Connecticut, a scientific team headed by Dr. Steven E. Lindow and Nicholas J. Panopoulos, associate professors at the University of California, Berkeley, found a way to "disarm" *Pseudomonas syringae* of their frost-initiating capacity. The Berkeley team accomplished this feat by deleting a specific gene sequence needed to form the frost-inducing surface protein and returning the gene package to the bacterium.

According to Lindow, their work is probably safer than traditional approaches to reducing frost damage (e.g., widespread application of pesticides, induction of "blind" mutations through the use of UV light or mutagens), since it is exceedingly unlikely that their deleted gene sequence would be restored by chance.[2]

Following the announcement of their intent to release the bacteria in the summer of 1983,[3] the researchers finetuned their experimental design in expectation of trying out the bacteria at a test station at Tulelake in northeast California before the first fall frosts came. But at the end of September, the U.C. Berkeley team was stymied by a suit filed by Jeremy Rifkin of the Foundation on Economic

Trends, a long-time opponent of genetic engineering, and a consortium of public interest groups.[4]

Rifkin invoked the fifteen-year-old National Environmental Policy Act (NEPA). According to Rifkin, NEPA mandated that experiments of this kind be preceded by the submission of an environmental impact report. The Lin--dow team countered, claiming that they had in fact filed an acceptable report under the California Environmental Quality Act (CEQA), when what they had in fact filed was a request for an *exemption* from CEQA under a provision that allows putatively nonharmful projects to go forward without review.[5]

According to NIH's William Gartland, chairman of the Recombinant DNA Advisory Committee, NIH had also followed the environmental guidelines given by NEPA for this work. Rifkin's suit was nonetheless successful in forcing the Berkeley team to postpone their attempt to protect potato plants at Tulelake.[6]

In early January 1984, the Environmental Protection Agency reinforced Rifkin's position by putting an additional obstacle in the path of successful release. The agency declared that any newly constructed bacterium intended to prevent plant frost damage must be treated as a pesticide. The rationale for the agency's ruling was predicated on the observation that the wild-type bacterium damages crops. As such, it is thus technically a "pest," and anything that might prevent colonization by a wild-type bacterium is therefore a "pesticide." While industry spokespersons declared this conceptualization far-fetched,[7] it makes considerable sense to have the EPA involved in controlling the release of exotic or genetically modified organisms of any kind. (One of the most "chilling" ideas from an ecological standpoint is the intention of one genetic-engineering firm, Advanced Genetic Systems, to use wild-type *P. syringae* for snowmaking.[8])

Coming on the heels of its recently successful attempt to assert regulatory authority over genetically engineered organisms, the EPA general counsel's judgment of the legal equivalence of traditional chemicals and genetically modified DNA (another chemical) came as a surprise to industry representatives. Close observation of the evolution of the EPA's move to gain control over recombinant organisms could have foretold this kind of eventuality, since a highly detailed analysis of the legal rationale for the Environmental Protection Agency's proper hegemony over rDNA had been presented in the previous year.[9]

While it is easy to see Rifkin's concerns as short-sighted and self-serving examples of what James Watson called "political adventurism,"[10] the issues raised by Rifkin and his coplaintiffs go substantially beyond self-aggrandizement and the immediate questions of risk. They deserve close scrutiny if only because of Judge Sirica's ruling.[11] As such, the issues raised are precedent setting for establishing the kinds of review that will come to be expected of genetic engineers—and for the questions they raise about the second-order impacts of newly created organisms.

Concerns

The actual lawsuit filed with the U.S. District Court for the District of Columbia (Civil Action No. 83-2714) is much more far-reaching than the press has reported. In their complaint, the five plaintiffs (Rifkin, Fox, the Foundation on Economic Trends, Environmental Action, Inc., and the Environmental Task Force) enjoin Secretary of Health and Human Services Margaret Heckler, Director of the National Institute of Health James Wyngaarden, and Director of the National Institute of Allergy and Infectious Diseases Richard Krause against permitting any experiments involving the deliberate release into the environment of any organism containing recombinant DNA. In the complaint they also ask the court to declare the present version of the NIH Guidelines unlawful. The basis for this claim is that both the proposed experiments and the guidelines violate the National Environmental Policy Act (42 U.S.C. 4321 et seq.) and the Administrative Procedure Act (5 U.S.C. 551 et seq.).

Rifkin's suit[12] is based on the supposition that genetically altered microbes could disturb the environment in unanticipated and potentially serious ways. Among his claims is the assertion that Lindow's genetically altered *Pseudomonas* strains could spread from farm crops to wild plants and trees, where they could prolong the growing season and cause potential ecological perturbations. At the extreme, enhanced survival of species whose growing period is usually circumscribed by early frost could lead to depletion of soil nutrients. This could occur, according to Rifkin's affidavits, not only because frost-protected trees and shrubs might survive longer into each growing season, but because soil microbes would lack the usual interval to convert waste products from leaf fall into nutrients.

In Rifkin's estimation, such changes in the natural processes of growth and decay might even affect the rate of photosynthesis and thereby alter the balance of nitrogen and oxygen in the air. The coplaintiffs also put forward the possibility that the new form of *Pseudomonas* might be wafted skyward in sufficient numbers to displace the normal populations of ice-inducing bacteria that seed clouds. In the extreme, such a displacement could lead to a diminution of snowfall, with resulting perturbations in spring run-off.[13]

Affidavits filed in support of Rifkin's lawsuit add a further perspective on the ramifications of this first experiment projected by concerned scientists. Peter Raven, director of the Missouri Botanical Garden and author of a world-renowned textbook on botany, linked the possible unforeseen effects of this new organism with others that have wreaked havoc with the environment in the past. Raven (who later withdrew from the suit) cited the precedent of infestations of the gypsy moth, Japanese beetle, Dutch elm disease, chestnut blight, cacti, and rabbits in different parts of the world as testimony to the dangers of the uncontrolled release of genetically modified organisms.

Coplaintiff Michael Fox, a director of the Humane Society in Washington, D.C., observed that "the colonization of nondomesticated plants by this frost-inhibiting bacterium could likewise disrupt the seasonal cycles of a variety of frost-sensitive plants. . . . This in turn could have a multiplier effect . . ."[14] Fox envisioned a major perturbation involving explosive outbreaks of potentially disease-causing microorganisms that are kept in check by the frost-mediated killing of their hosts.

Given the limited biological characteristics of *P. syringae,* the target of this lawsuit, these claims seem far-fetched and extreme. At the same time, they raise issues deserving review for the more general case of environmental release.

As might be expected, the researchers took umbrage at what they considered the exaggerated claims of their opponents. They had chosen the "ice-minus" experimental system because they considered it the *least* likely of all contemplated recombinant-organism releases to create ecological problems or evoke public concern. In fact, the Berkeley group's spokesperson, plant ecologist Douglas Haefele, believes that the major research problems center on succeeding in even creating a strain of "ice-minus" bacteria that could compete in the wild for an ecological niche with the naturally occurring strains.[15] The group's director has asserted that extraordinary care will be taken to contain the bacteria within the test plot (a six-foot buffer of dirt will surround the half-acre site). In fact, Lindow has declared that "I don't think there's any possibility this project will have the dramatic effect some people say it will. . . . We just don't foresee this bacteria spreading at all."[16] According to Lindow, ultraviolet radiation is constantly creating analogous mutants of the same bacteria, so that their strain is no different from naturally occurring strains.

Had it been focused solely on the Tulelake experiments, the Rifkin suit would not have been sustained. It is highly unlikely that any claim of environmental disruption would have been sustained for ice-minus bacteria per se. What Judge Sirica did find, however, was that the environmental impact documents already filed were inadequate.

Regulatory Protections

Central to the overall problem of environmental release of genetically engineered organisms is the question of whether or not *existing* regulatory protections are adequate. As reviewed in Chapter 1, the environmental impact statement prepared to accompany the first set of NIH Guidelines of June 23, 1976, was not flawed, but expressly ignored the question of deliberate release of organisms, since that prospect had been expressly forbidden.[17] The currently operative guidelines of April 21, 1982, allow releases to be made after the RAC and the Institutional Biosafety Committees have been satisfied that the experiments are unlikely to cause environmental harm.[18] But given the present composition of these groups and their notable lack of qualified environmental and public health scientists, such evaluation is predictably incomplete.

On the issue of regulatory protections, the Rifkin suit is right to point to deficiencies in the overall scope of the present guidelines. In a letter dated November 7, 1983, Rifkin and his attorney Edward Lee Rogers filed a request on behalf of the coplaintiffs that the NIH amend its guidelines to focus on the broader issue of environmental harms rather than laboratory containment alone. Specifically, Rifkin asked that the guidelines themselves be accompanied by a "programmatic" environmental impact statement and that such a statement or an environmental assessment be filed for any research that involved the deliberate release into the environment of recombinant-DNA molecules.[19]

In support of this position, the Rifkin group declared an environmental-assessment requirement to be a minimum precondition to obviate any uncertainty that might surround the environmental consequences of a proposed experiment. As such, the Rifkin amendment restated the requirements of the National Environmental Policy Act and the subsequent regulations issued by the Council on Environmental Quality for implementing this law.[20]

In response to this lawsuit, Dr. Bernard Talbot, director of the National Institute of Allergy and Infectious Diseases, largely ignored the substantive concerns of the Rifkin group, stating instead that the issue lay outside the jurisdiction of the NIH and its committees that oversee the conduct of the NIH Guidelines,[21] thereby virtually inviting Judge Sirica's ruling.

Contributions

The original lawsuit filed by Rifkin and Rogers revealed a deep flaw in the current procedures. The core of Rifkin's contention is that the NIH neglected four discrete "risk components."[22] The first two embrace the possibilities that a genetically engineered organism will grow and survive in its new environment. The third, that such an organism will displace, compete with, or disrupt other organisms in the ecosystem. And the fourth considers the possible harmfulness of the release.

This construction is useful. Such risks should be evaluated prior to release of any organism with the capacity to disrupt ecosystems. A similar analysis applies to newly formed hybrid combinations or mutant varieties of cereal grains or other conventionally modified food crops. More particularly, such analyses would have been (and are now) particularly important in assessing the likely consequences of introducing genetic varieties of nonnative strains of grasses (such as the cheatgrass that presently covers most of the western United States up to the eastern slopes of the Sierra), kudzu vine (which occupies much of the southeastern United States), and other exotic species that were introduced without satisfying the fourfold risk criteria listed by Rifkin.

The irony is that it is extremely unlikely that the first recombinant-DNA-modified organisms or plants to be introduced into the environment will have been satisfactorily programmed to survive for long against the native competition. Ecological disturbances are still most likely to result from the unintentional or mistaken introduction of exotic wild species that have developed especially robust characteristics over the course of millennia of natural selection. This is not to say that highly adaptive strains of microorganisms or plants may not be designed in the near future. It implies only that the decision to focus on a relatively noncompetitive strain of microorganism (*Pseudomonas syringae*) is to miss the point of the legitimate concern over regulation.

An outside observer might consider experiments to enhance the likelihood of ice formation with bacterial particulates to be at least as compelling environmentally as those attempting to inhibit such formation. The fact that the Rifkin group's ecological concerns focused on the laboratory-engineered rather than "naturally" selected variants suggests that the Rifkin group was more concerned with the mode of construction than with the degree of environmental perturbation.

Were the issues of this case to be decided on the risks posed by *P. syringae* alone, there is little doubt that it would be dismissed out of hand. Precautions against spread are being taken. The organism is nonpathogenic. And natural variants with the same or related genetic changes have already been isolated from the environment where they have shown little if any selective advantage over their wild-type congeners.

Hence, this first case to present the more general issue of the environmental adequacy of the newest guidelines was a red herring. Concerns about the extent of any possible environmental disturbance per se are more valid than those about the technique (e.g., rDNA modification) used to achieve that end. Thus, the Rifkin attack was flawed, because it focused more on the *means* of gene modification than on the *ends*. The appropriate focus is the adequacy of the NIH's review system. The time and place to have challenged that system was at the point when the latest guidelines were released, not a year later on the pretext of the first experiment to be tried.

However flawed, the Rifkin suit has provoked governmental officials to take a fresh look at the present loopholes in the scope and intent of the guidelines. Dr. Bernard Talbot requested that the RAC meeting held on February 6, 1984, consider the present double bind that the committee has encountered in trying to regulate in the area of environmental release:

1. If the NIH continues to consider only laboratory research to be within its purview, it will automatically exclude proposals for environmental release.

2. If the NIH considers only those proposals that are strictly within its mandate (i.e., NIH or federally funded research in approved agencies), all industry work will go unexamined.

3. If the NIH opens all the RAC meetings to the public (as Karim Ahmed, of the Natural Resources Defense Council, requested earlier),[23] it would lose the ability to examine proprietary data.

4. If the NIH maintains its long-standing focus on biomedical research, it might overlook significant agricultural studies warranting its scrutiny.

Recommendations

Given the foregoing, there is little doubt that the NIH Guidelines and the accompanying review structure are presently weak. They are ill designed to anticipate adequately the full gamut of consequences to ecosystems that could ensue from environmental releases stemming from new experimentation or industrial applications. No experts in ecology, entomology, botany, population genetics, or infectious disease epidemiology are to be found among the RAC's twenty-five standing members. Also, the committee is limited by law to reviewing only NIH-funded research.

The EPA, while empowered by the Federal Insecticide,

Fungicide, and Rodenticide Act (FIFRA) to control field-scale tests of pesticides, generally exempts any experiment under ten acres. Likewise, EPA is charged under the Toxic Substances Control Act (TSCA) with regulating chemicals, but it cannot require researchers to notify EPA before laboratory testing. And the USDA's regulatory powers are even more uncertain.[24]

Thus, we lack the necessary apparatus to ensure an adequate process for anticipating the possible harm from rDNA research. For these reasons, Senator Albert Gore's subcommittee on investigations and oversight has recommended the formation of an oversight committee to sort out these jurisdictional problems.[25]

When a new structure is in place, lawmakers will find it insufficient simply to define harm in terms of the degree of displacement of indigenous species, since many newly engineered crop plants may be intended to do just that. Rather, a new sense of the balance among species in a circumscribed ecosystem may be needed. Such a view might consider the relative contribution of each species to the stability of the whole.

Ecosystems and rDNA-Modified Organisms

Certain environments are almost certainly less effectively "buffered" against intrusion than others. Island biota or rarefied communities such as those in sub-Arctic regions, for example, are less able to rebound from perturbations than those of more temperate climates. Such robustness need not be linked to species diversity alone, but may also depend on an ecosystem's vulnerability to niche occupation and its ability to regenerate through patterns of succession.

According to Spanish ecologist Ramòn Margalef,[26] we might find that tropical rain forests, with their great variety of species, are in fact the ecosystems most vulnerable to disruption. There, very few of the plant systems are adapted to the growth-and-crash cycles characteristic of some temperate climates. An example would be the fire-tolerant loblolly pine of the southeast United States, whose seeds are released from their cores after major burns. The tropics are characterized by limited regenerative abilities and poor soils and would potentially be the most hard hit by a major replacement of their diverse species by a limited number of genetically engineered plants. Temperate ecosystems, by comparison, are often adapted to regenerate stably through a series of stages known as succession.

Consideration of ecological impacts within these classic succession-dominated ecosystems would be critical prior to any widescale environmental release of an organism intended to integrate with the existing biomass. Similar assessments would be necessary regarding environmental impacts in other regions (e.g., the tropics). There, newly introduced species are likely to have different adverse effects than in temperate regions. Clearly, such assessments would have to be tailored to the limitations of the particular ecosystem as a whole to recover from potential perturbations.

What is evident from most accounts of the impact of genetically engineered organisms is that very little serious attention has been given to this type of analysis. As late as 1983, Professor Martin Alexander of the Cornell University Laboratory of Soil Microbiology observed that in terms of ecological consequences "the question of detrimental effects of genetic engineering has not been seriously addressed."[27] While Alexander clearly believes in the potential value of genetically engineered microorganisms in certain select environmental circumstances (pollution control is one example, discussed in the next chapter), he is chary about moving ahead full bore on environmental releases without carefully reviewing the likely consequences.

One very broad way to assess our ability to anticipate adverse effects from introducing new technologies is to chart our success in the past. In almost every case where we have introduced a technology on a scale requiring widespread application for its success, adverse consequences were realized. Typically, we achieve an initial period of remarkable success, followed by one in which natural systems adapt to the agent in question. Only after a sometimes protracted interval—in the case of DDT, perhaps thirty years—do the major perturbations in the affected ecosystem become evident. With regard to antibiotics, natural selection ensured that antibiotic-resistant genes carried on plasmids moved rapidly across species lines, leading to decreased sensitivities and new patterns of human epidemic disease. (A classic case in point has been the emergence and spread of penicillinase-producing *Neisseria gonorrheae*, or PPNG.[28])

Our blindness to the overuse of DDT, and more recently to the impact of the toxic wastes that have accompanied large-scale chemical production, do not bode well for a reasoned approach to the release of genetically engineered organisms. In the past, we allowed short-term gains to displace concerns about the longer-term consequences (as in the use of DDT against malarial mosquitoes). We permitted the profit motive to hold sway during the chemical revolution, largely ignoring the needs for costly removal and containment systems for the chemical industry's inevitable waste products.

Like many other concerned scientists and health policy experts, I am disturbed by these historical precedents. But analogies can only take us so far in the instance of recombinant-DNA-engineered organisms. Substantive differences exist between chemical agents and the live ones we are considering here. For one thing, in order for the released organisms to do their work in the environment, they will have to be suitably modified not only to perform their assigned tasks, but to grow, proliferate, and occupy old or previously unoccupied niches. This simple fact means that genetically modified organisms will in all likelihood require secondary modifications to assure their successful adaptation.

Such intentional "improvements" in survivability are the obverse side of the impairments we required of the first generation of host/vector systems. In producing organisms and genetic carrier systems for cloning DNA molecules or for producing proteins, researchers have been operating under relatively constant rules to reduce the likelihood that their modified organisms would survive outside the laboratory.

But with the need for environmental persistence, laboratory researchers are now designing entirely new organisms that can withstand environmental release. These new requirements will undoubtedly encourage a shift away from the attenuated strains and towards those with the greatest genetic robustness.

The hub of the dilemma is that on average the bulk of the genetic engineers doing this reverse genetic engineering know little or nothing of the intricacies of the environments in which they will be placing their organisms. With the notable exception of the group that has been designing the ice-minus bacterium for Tulelake (it includes a plant ecologist), very few teams have scientists with a good understanding of the ecological ramifications of their work. In Martin Alexander's words, "To the laboratory scientist, a natural ecosystem is, at best, an enigma."[29]

Risk assessors will have the almost impossible task of determining how likely these additional modifications are to have a deleterious impact on the local or extended ecosystem in which the genetically engineered organism will be placed. Experiments in controlled environments that simulate these situations will be difficult. Of primary concern will be the need to ensure containment of the modified organism while allowing a reasonably "natural" mix of native species.

According to Alexander, there are no illustrations yet of genetically engineered species causing harm. At the same time, he observes, meaningful tests of the probabilities for such eventualities have never been performed.[30] What is needed now, before recombinant DNA or other genetically modified organisms are released, are techniques to estimate the risks and procedures to assess any resulting deleterious effects.

Recommendations

While designing and hopefully testing various hypotheses of risk, much as Falkow's group did at the University of Washington (see Chapter 1), it is prudent to acknowledge the uncertainties involved and to behave appropriately.

The following guidelines might be useful in molding that behavior:

- Require simulation tests of the harmfulness, spread, and niche occupancy of genetically engineered organisms before release

- Ensure that newly introduced species contain genetically programmed devices for limited survival
- Assign a genetically fixed marker to the released population that will permit monitoring of the spread of an organism's genetic elements or of the organism as a whole
- Incorporate in the organism specific sensitivities to known therapeutic or other antagonistic agents (e.g., antibiotics, herbicides, or pesticides) so that any unanticipated or untoward spread could be contained
- Limit the initial release of microorganisms to ends that are balanced by the risks inherent in the means to achieve them

This last point requires the most explication and is likely to provoke the most heated debate. A good case study for reviewing this principle is the proposed uses of genetically engineered organisms for controlling or reducing the hazards of environmental pollutants, a subject we turn to in the following chapter.

Notes

1. P. M. Boffey, "Judge Bars Outdoor Test of Genetic Engineering," *New York Times* (May 17, 1984), p. A20.
2. H. M. Schmeck, Jr., "Gene-Splicers Plan Release of Bacteria to Aid Crops," *New York Times* (August 30, 1983), p. 17.
3. D. Perlman, "Berkeley Scientists' Frost-Fighting Bacteria," *San Francisco Chronicle* (August 11, 1983), p. 20.

4. D. Perlman, "An Attempt to Block U.C. Genes Tests," *San Francisco Chronicle* (September 15, 1983), p. 5.

5. David Doorstein, counsel for the University of California, personal communication, June 28, 1984.

6. Anonymous, "Scientists Delay Genetic Testing," *New York Times* (October 5, 1983), p. 14.

7. Daniel Adams, quoted in T. M. Powledge, "AGS Head Calls Frost Bug Ruling 'Far-Fetched'," *Bio/Technology* 2 (1984): 12–13.

8. Adams, in "AGS Head."

9. T. O. McGarity and K. O. Boyer, "Federal Regulation of Emerging Genetic Technology," *Vanderbilt Law Review* 36 (1983): 461–540.

10. James Watson, quoted in N. Heneson, "Genetic Engineering in Perspective," *New Scientist* (November 10, 1983): 424.

11. Boffey, "Judge Bars Outdoor Test."

12. *Foundation on Economic Trends et al.* v. *Heckler,* U.S. Dist. Ct. (District of Columbia) Civil Action No. 83-2714.

13. K. Schneider, "First-ever Release of Lab-created Life Form," *California Journal* (February 1984): 51–54.

14. Michael Fox, affidavit filed with Civil Action No. 83-2714.

15. Douglas Haefele, quoted in D. Perlman, *San Francisco Chronicle* (August 11, 1983), p. 4.

16. Steven E. Lindow, quoted in Schneider, "First-ever Release," p. 53.

17. See 41 *FR* 270-2 et seq., July 7, 1976.

18. See 48 *FR* 24557-58 L-II, 24580.

19. Quoted in the *Federal Register* (January 5, 1984): 697.

20. 47 U.S.C. 4332 and 40 *CFR* 1502.1-1520.25, respectively.

21. 49 *FR* 697, January 5, 1984.

22. *Foundation on Economic Trends et al.* v. *Heckler,* p. 15 at para. 21.

23. K. Ahmed, "Proprietory Interests and Biotechnology," *Science* 223 (1983): 440.

24. FIFRA (Federal Insecticide, Fungicide, and Rodenticide Act, As Amended, 1975, *Public Law* 92-516, 94-140) was intended to assure the safety of newly introduced pesticides. TSCA (Toxic Substances Control Act, 1976, *Public Law* 94-469, 15 USC 2601-2629) was intended to protect the public and environment from unsafe exposure to hazardous chemicals. The USDA position is discussed in K. C. Zoon, "Regulation of Recombinant DNA-derived Products and Syn-

thetic Peptides," *Food & Drug Cosmetic Law Journal* 37 (1982): 382–385.

25. A. Gore, "Regulation of Biotechnology," *Science* 225 (1984): 6–7; cf. the opposing view of Eli Lilly's Irving Johnson in the same issue. (Johnson would leave all scientific oversight to the RAC and have no new regulatory statutes or bodies.)

26. R. Margalef, *Perspectives in Ecological Theory* (Chicago: University of Chicago Press, 1968).

27. M. Alexander, "Ecological Constraints on Genetic Engineering," paper presented on July 30, 1983, Seattle, Washington, at the Conference of Genetic Control of Environmental Pollutants.

28. M. Lappé, *Germs That Won't Die: The Medical Consequences of the Misuse of Antibiotics* (Garden City, NY: Anchor/Doubleday, 1982).

29. Alexander, "Ecological Contraints," p. 17.

CHAPTER 8

Genetic Control of Environmental Pollutants

At first, the idea of using genes to control toxic substances seems to be a brilliant solution to an intractable and growing problem. Researchers have long relied on the special digestive (i.e., enzymatic) activities of bacteria for degrading and activating otherwise noxious sewage. And the idea of transplanting well-characterized genes from other species into bacteria for expanding this activity to toxic substances and metals is made eminently feasible by rDNA technology. As with all seemingly ideal solutions, however, there is a nagging doubt that the treatment may be worse than the cure. With properly engineered organisms, most researchers are confident that the solution will work—once the specifically tailored organism is found that can break down the toxic chemical in question. The remaining concern is simply this: How can we be sure the bug *stops* doing its job when we want it to?

Since the 1940s, industrial engineers have been modifying bacteria genetically to degrade unwanted chemical by-products and wastes of human and industrial origin. Before we can discuss treatments, we have to define the problem. The use of recombinant DNA to give microbes better ways of doing this work today has its origins in rather scatological beginnings.

Specially "engineered" microorganisms have been used since the beginning of this century to accelerate the biological breakdown of sewage. Initially, sanitary engineers used hit or miss methods to salvage "good" cultures of microorganisms that showed particular promise in detoxifying and activating sewage sludge. As early as 1914, researchers isolated bacterial strains that reduced the total organic matter and improved the efficiency with which sewage was oxidized or detoxified. As such, the original microbiology of sewage treatment was a relatively unscientific enterprise, relying on variable cultures of naturally occurring organisms for its success. Now researchers are engineering sewage-degrading organisms by adding plasmids with genes for enzymes that will catalyze key chemical reactions in the degradation process. According to Genex CEO J. Leslie Glick, the ambit of toxic substances that can be degraded is only limited by our ability to isolate the genes for the enzymes needed to break them down.[1] But experience tells us that such limitless optimism may need to be tempered by a dose of healthy skepticism.

Concerns

Environmentalists and health policy professionals have learned to be cautious about promises of unblemished environmental benefits. In the case of genetically engineered organisms, much of this concern hinges on three unanswered questions:

1. What are the potential consequences to the environment and public health of modifying microorganisms to control pollutants?

2. What happens to microbially controlled pollutants as they are broken down into presumably less toxic agents?

3. What happens to the genetically modified bacteria that degrade the pollutants themselves after the job is done?

The first question turns on the nature of the genetic changes needed to make otherwise innocuous bacteria avid metabolizers of toxic chemicals or metal contaminants. The key to converting bacteria to perform these functions has been to utilize their remarkable adaptability in utilizing diverse sources of nutrition. The genetic plasticity that makes such adaptations possible is the legacy of more than 3 billion years of evolution. This observation should give us pause before we attempt to modify bacterial genes to solve human-generated environmental woes.

From the viewpoint of the genetic engineer, all that is needed to encourage a particular bacterium to utilize a new energy source is a suitable set of enzymes. While simple in theory, achieving this goal in practice requires a highly refined understanding of the genetic basis for microbial metabolism. Bacteria, unlike nonbiological systems, work only within a narrow range of temperature and pH. In general, bacteria make up for any environmental fastidiousness by using an astonishing array of gene-directed enzymes to specify just which molecules will be attacked and how they will be modified. With the recent discovery of new heat-tolerant (thermophilic) bacteria near deep oceanic vents, the known range of conditions under which bacteria can operate will undoubtedly expand.

Some genetic mutations give bacteria the ability to make special enzymes that will recognize some of the most toxic chemicals, including aromatic chlorinated compounds such as the PCBs, some dioxins, and DDT. Two particular conditions seem to negate most environmental or public health concerns: (1) when the targeted chemicals are almost exclusively undesirable; and (2) when no natural (and desirable) analogs exist in biological systems that might be inadvertently degraded by the spread of enzyme-containing organisms. Where those circumstances obtain, it seems reasonable to conclude that the environmental release of genetically altered bacteria capable of degrading toxic chemicals is beneficial. But in fact almost every toxic chemical has a naturally occurring and potentially essential chemical cousin that might also be metabolized, and the question of impact is therefore very difficult to assess.

The adverse impact of environmentally released bacteria may also be enhanced by unanticipated by-products of detoxification. It is possible that during the course of digesting an undesirable pollutant, a bacterium will produce more dangerous chemicals than the parent molecule. Such an eventuality could occur if a relatively nontoxic chemical were activated into a more toxic form during the degradation process. An example would be the alteration that occurs during the metabolism or breakdown of some carcinogens. A case in point is benzo(a)pyrene, which can be activated by a general enzyme called aryl hydrocarbon hydroxylase (AHH). As one of the first steps in metabolism, AHH converts benzo(a)pyrene and structurally similar carcinogens into a much more potent form. Clearly, genetic engineers need to pay close attention to the metabolic pathways that are engineered into any pollutant-controlling bacteria.

Aftermaths

When the bacteria have finished their job of degrading the toxic substances, it is unlikely that they will simply go away or self-destruct. One of the key properties that may have to be genetically engineered into such bacteria is the ability to survive intermittent conditions of starvation. Residual microorganisms might persist indefinitely at a spent waste site or locale, as a kind of biological equivalent of long-lived nuclear wastes. In this eventuality, engineered organisms might have to be monitored for their ability to transfer genetic elements that reinforce survivability to less desirable organisms, such as those that cause human disease.

Environmentalists have also been inconsistent in ignoring the potential problems (and value) of using non-specifically modified bacteria to control oil spills or unwanted sewage by-products, while heavily critiquing proposed programs to achieve the same end with recombinant-DNA-produced bacterial systems.

A comparison of these two groups of organisms suggests that they are more similar than different. While rDNA-modified microorganisms can be engineered to contain multiple working copies of the needed genes by forcing plasmids to reproduce rapidly, they are not materially different from naturally occurring bacteria selected for the same properties. Ultimately, both bacteria, whether engineered or produced by mutation, will have similar genes that perform the desired task. The difference will be in quantity, not kind, of proteins produced. (The critiques of the Berkeley group's ice-minus bacterium, discussed in Chapter 7, reflect this misplaced distinction. Though on several occasions, Lindow and his group released radiation-produced ice-minus bacteria that had been randomly mutated, only the genetically engineered form, with its specific genetic deletions, provoked criticism.)

What is missing from both lines of attack is a focus on the long-term environmental implications of using genetic engineering to broaden the availability of "useful" microorganisms. Because the end point of the research—in this case, the control of a particularly noxious pollutant—may be perceived as an urgent and necessary good, researchers can lose sight of the consequences of rapid deployment. This is especially important in such cases as the ice-minus example, where critics saw a threat of literally billions of dollars of crop losses.

What is needed is a process of careful predeployment review of recombinant organisms, one similar to that currently in effect under federal statutes such as TSCA and FIFRA for environmental chemicals. Urgent conditions are generic to pollution control. Once pollutant-controlling bacteria are developed, the call for using recombinant organisms is likely to occur under emergency situations that may preclude a full environmental assessment. Under California's Environmental Quality Act (CEQA), an environmental impact report must be filed with any new project that generates significant controversy about adverse effects, but this process can be waived under a state of emergency declared by the governor. (This occurred in California in 1981 when malathion spraying was proposed to combat the Mediterranean fruit fly.)

Critical Inconsistency

In the past, environmentalists have been relatively short-sighted in their critiques of pollution-controlling microorganisms. One of their early targets was Ananda Chakrabarty, a staff scientist at General Electric's Research and Development Center at Schenectady, New York. When, in 1972, Chakrabarty applied for a patent for a strain of the *Pseudomonas* bacterium that could break down

the major components of crude oil, he was roundly criticized by environmentalists and other critics for what was
essentially a sound idea.

Another problem that continues to distract both critics
and proponents of environmental applications of rDNA is
the confusion between the propriety of patenting microorganisms per se and the desirability of using such organisms to degrade environmental contaminants. When
Ananda Chakrabarty announced his intention to obtain a
patent on an oil- and sludge-degrading microorganism, he
was criticized for attempting to patent a new life form—and
for potentially generating an ecological catastrophe.[2] The
resulting acrimonious debate may have sparked concern
within the industry over public opinion and put off its
further attempts to develop aggressive environmental uses
of microorganisms.

With the notable exception of Genex Corporation and a
handful of others,[3] few biotechnology firms have made
significant investments in environmental controls. This
point was underscored by biotechnology consultant Burke
Zimmerman, who pointed out in 1983 that pollution-con-
trol research was not identified as a high priority by most
genetic-engineering companies. Zimmerman professed
skepticism that many biotechnology firms were willing to
make such a commitment, saying instead that "most of that
work is going to have to be funded by large companies who
have a direct interest in controlling pollution."[4] If true, such
a conclusion suggests that the research most likely to be in
the public interest may be sidestepped as companies jockey
to develop safety systems directed at giving themselves legal
protection from environmental lawsuits. Such predicted
"defensive" development is likely to tap little of the great
potential of pollutant control through genetic engineering
and might sidestep some of the more critical ecological
issues.

These areas were among the potentialities covered in the

first conference on Genetic Control of Environmental Pollutants, held under the joint auspices of the Environmental Protection Agency and the University of Washington at Seattle, Washington, July 31–August 3, 1983. At the conference, a group of academic microbiologists and industry scientists identified potentially valuable uses of microorganisms. These uses included detoxifying and activating sewage sludge, enriching this sludge for possible use as fertilizer,[5] degrading specific compounds in industrial waste, and cleaning up environmentally hazardous spills of oil and other chemicals.

Industrial scientists in attendance clearly indicated their belief in the importance of genetic engineering to meet these pressing needs, but appeared to have considered neither the full range of obstacles to their success nor the possible adverse consequences of their initial attempts. These points have been exemplified by the continuing inability of existing methods to reduce the toxic fractions of oil and sludge from oil spills. Even the more common release of oil contaminants in ship ballast and wash water from oil tankers poses an unmet ecological hazard.

Researchers have isolated some naturally occurring bacteria that carry special genes that degrade these and related petroleum products. Amazingly, microorganisms such as *Pseudomonas putida* carry separate plasmids, each of which codes for a set of enzymes that digest hydrocarbons from different basic chemical groups: octane, hexane, and decane (common ingredients in gasoline and high-grade oils); xylene and toluene (often used as industrial solvents); and camphor and naphthalene (chemicals found in petroleum distillates).[6] (It was a combination of these different plasmids that Chakrabarty successfully engineered, and patented, to digest oil.)

Some environmentalists may be surprised to learn that a special strain of this bacterium developed by Flow Laboratory has already been used to eliminate petroleum residues in the water that the Queen Mary carried in her bilges when she was drydocked at Long Beach, California. (Such residues had presented an explosion hazard to the use of acetylene torches.) Six weeks after treatment, the bilge water was released into Long Beach harbor[7]—presumably with all of the reactive microbes intact—with nary a reaction from any environmental group. There is little doubt that had anyone raised the issue, an environmental impact report would have been legally required.

This graphic example underscores the likelihood that genetically modified bacteria that have been conventionally produced—that is, produced through the selection of new variants—have already been released into the environment. In his presentation to the Seattle conference, R. B. Grubb of Flow Laboratories identified other releases, including a 1969 episode involving the treatment of open-field sumps in Ventura and Santa Maria, California. In this latter instance, introduced bacteria successfully degraded 55,566 gallons of hydrocarbon mass. At a hazardous-waste site in Clearwater, Florida, 610,000 gallons of coal tar were similarly treated with suspensions of genetically modified bacteria.

Other large-scale uses of genetically defined bacteria have been in long-standing operation. One such site, at Bigham Canyon, Utah, uses rotating sprinklers to spray thousands of gallons of a solution of *Thiobacillus* bacteria to oxidize iron ore. Trillions of these bacteria are customarily used to convert iron ore from the ferrous to the ferric (oxidized) form. As many as 1 billion bacteria are used for each kilogram of iron extracted.[8] (The ferric iron is then used to extract copper by oxidizing copper-containing sulfide minerals to copper sulfate.)

What is remarkable in these examples is not so much the ingenious use of bacteria, but the almost total disregard of possible secondary impacts of the use of specially modified bacterial cultures. In the face of such blatant and massive releases of genetically modified microorganisms, it is amazing that no systematic studies of their environmental consequences have been done. Until such studies are performed, we are destined to remain in the dark about whether genetically engineered organisms are likely to produce problems that are qualitatively different from those produced by more conventional means.

Despite the notable lack of relevant studies, we can begin to answer this question by considering just what types of strains have been used. Most of the organisms in question are from the genus *Pseudomonas*, particularly the strains of *Pseudomonas putida* found in decaying animal matter. These bacteria are particularly attractive because many of their plasmid DNA sequences have been defined. These particular strains, if not modified too extensively, probably pose little hazard to people. They are nonpathogenic and have biochemical requirements that make them more adapted to external environments than those inside the body.

Other strains of *Pseudomonas* are not nearly so benign. *Pseudomonas aeruginosa* is the cause of often fatal blood poisoning and other systemic infections. As discussed in the following section, many of these strains have been found in association with hazardous-waste sites, making them ideal candidates for further modification as waste degraders. While the varieties used for most genetic-engineering experiments are not likely to include the genes that make *Pseudomonas aeruginosa* strains particularly dangerous in hospital settings,[9] they are nonetheless potentially hazardous to the people who work with them. The key to risk assessment of any *Pseudomonas* type is both its degree of disease-causing ability and the likelihood that disease-causing variants will persist following their use in the environment.

As a foil to the argument that such genetically altered organisms pose a risk to public health, microbiologists will argue that few if any organisms will persist once the toxic product is used up as a food substrate. But the environmental success of any genetically modified bacterium depends on the organism's ability to survive at very low levels of the substrates on which it feeds. Once the primary target chemical is depleted, the genetically modified organism may subsist on residues of related compounds.

Indeed, the targeted substrate will probably be toxic to other microorganisms, so that by the time the primary toxic chemical is gone, many of the bacterium's usual competitors will be too. In this way, a niche could be created that affords the modified bacterium an unusual advantage, allowing its population to expand. In the process, novel evolutionary possibilities may be created that select for still more variants, some of which could be detrimental to humans or their environment.

Given these and related possibilities, the claim that most genetically engineered bacteria will disappear—an argument used ineffectively by Lindow and his associates—must be tested on a case-by-case basis. One way to examine the likelihood of harm is to examine the histories of industries that have relied extensively on genetically modified organisms to produce a commodity. Antibiotic producers, for instance, are plagued by a high proportion of employees who develop hypersensitivity both to antibiotics themselves and to the fermentation organisms used to produce them. Elsewhere in the fermentation industry (e.g., in beer production) yeasts and other microorganisms have been used without evidence of major harm or disability.

The obverse side of the risk question is whether use of modified bacteria will ever be widespread enough to warrant concern about health or environmental impacts. Another speaker at the Seattle conference, Professor Martin Alexander, from Cornell's agronomy department, took a pessimistic view of the prospects for effective use of microorganisms in environmental control. Alexander pointed out that few of the researchers who test for microbial ability to digest pollutants operate with real-world assumptions as to the concentrations of the hazardous chemicals they would like to see controlled.

As Alexander noted, no microorganism has yet been found that will grow on a defined substrate containing the contaminants of greatest concern (e.g., dioxins or dibenzofurans) at realistic environmental levels (e.g., ten parts per billion). Much higher levels of other toxic chemicals have been found at or near hazardous-waste sites or storage facilities where concentrations of hazardous chemicals at the tens or hundreds of parts per million level are common. According to Alexander, if microbes will not grow consistently at such low pollutant concentrations, it is unlikely that they will survive in competition with existing organisms in the environment at large unless enormous numbers of the genetically engineered variety are introduced.[10] Alexander's solution to the dilemma of finding microorganisms to degrade low levels of environmental pollutants is to turn to novel species of bacteria that grow on dissolved organic carbon or use soil humus as their principal energy sources. But such species are not now being studied as hosts for recombinant DNA.

The point Alexander raises brings us back to the paradox posed by the ice-minus *Pseudomonas* strain. "Successful" introduction of genetically engineered bacteria in ecological terms would mean putting so many bacteria into the environment that the existing organisms are swamped. By their sheer mass, these extraordinary numbers, in turn, could create problems and inevitable genetic variation that are not foreseeable in small-scale pilot tests.

Other interventions using genetically modified bacteria may be equally risk-laden. For instance, "clearing" an ecosystem of competing forms before introducing the desired strain—an idea forwarded to improve the "take" of desired microbes—could create substantial perturbations in the final ecological balance as new populations of opportunistic organisms become reestablished following the intended degradation.

From an ecological perspective, the key to using microorganisms for useful purposes is thus a double-edged sword. To be successful in solving the problem it addresses, an organism must be given a "selective advantage" over naturally occurring ones such that the new forms will not only destroy the toxic substance (or better still, use it as their basic source of carbon for food), but will compete successfully against native species. But conferring that advantage to an otherwise poorly adapted microbe may mean increasing its ecological range, and in turn its negative impact on the environment. This possibility suggests that genetic control of pollutants carries a catch-22: should genetic engineers be successful in conferring adaptive traits on pollutant-destroying microorganisms, they are likely to displace the very organisms that are needed to assure ecological balance once the environment is pollutant-free.

Alexander suggests "starvation resistance" as an example of the type of ecological adaptation that microbiologists might consider desirable to engineer into bacteria. Microbes that would normally succumb after exhausting their substrate (i.e., after having digested all or most of the targeted environmental pollutant) would be given genes for survival. In this way, environments that might be expected to receive intermittent exposure to a contaminant, such as lakes or streams that receive industrial effluents, could be seeded with a starvation-resistant organism that would come out of dormancy in response to each fresh episode of pollution. According to unpublished studies by Alexander and his Cornell colleague J. L. Sinclair, extraordinary genetic changes may be necessary to ensure such behavior in nutrient-poor environments.[11] Of course, not introducing pollutants in the first place would be eminently more logical.

Other obstacles to the successful genetic engineering of pollutant-reducing microorganisms appear equally unyielding. The presence of predators such as protozoa that can devour genetically engineered bugs, physical barriers to dispersion in soils, and limited environmental tolerance to temperature, light, or toxic substances all combine to bedevil any genetically engineered organism.

Examples

One way to assess the likelihood of major environmental perturbations is to look at the actual microorganisms that have been applied to field conditions in which hazardous environmental pollutants have been found. Several research groups outside the United States have already developed genetically engineered organisms designed to be released into the environment. Given the selection of their genetic properties, these organisms may pose risks that go substantially beyond the ones that U.S. critics are now focusing on in the ice-minus bacteria at Tulelake, California. For example, a recently developed strain of pesticide-degrading bacterium was described in the Russian journal *Mikrobiologiya*.[12]

The technical details of this study are both illustrative of Russian methods likely to be used more widely and indicative of the lack of precision characterizing contemporary genetic engineering in the USSR. The Russians initially isolated a strain of *Pseudomonas aeruginosa* called 640X from apparently heavily DDT-contaminated soil in the Crimean region. Using crude genetic-engineering techniques, they then enhanced the strain's ability to degrade DDT through use of plasmids containing the genes for specific aromatic chlorine-degrading enzymes.

While it is unclear whether they have since tested this

highly effective organism in the environment, it is certain that the Russians successfully introduced new (and unknown) genetic material that improved the organism's ability to degrade organochlorine pesticides. Should these *Pseudomonas* strains be used to reduce the level of DDT contamination in the soil within the Crimea, it is equally unclear whether the Russians will attempt to monitor or control the possible entry of the organism into water supplies or other means of entering human habitations.

As important as these questions appear to be, they do not seem to have been addressed even in similar efforts performed in the United States. Starting from an abundance of environmental test sites created by the dumping activities of Hooker Chemical Company in New York State, scientists have isolated *Pseudomonas* bacteria from the harsh (pH 4) and toxic conditions of Hooker landfills at Love Canal as well as the Hyde Park site near Niagara Falls, the repository for some eighty thousand tons of chlorinated wastes.

These "natural" environmental sites provide intense conditions for selecting microorganisms with degradative activity. In the words of S. A. Sojka, the project leader at Hooker Chemical, "I view these land-fill sites as large chemostats. They have been around for twenty years and there has been a process of natural selection as organisms have adapted to their stressful environment."[13] In an after-the-fact spate of public concern, the Hooker people have claimed to be already testing *Pseudomonas* strains that appear to increase the degradative processes in sludges taken from these sites, and have set up a pilot plant at the Niagara Falls complex.

In their attempts to "improve" these wild-type strains, the Hooker staff have used genetic-engineering techniques to put the genes that control the degradation of particular chlorinated aromatic compounds in *Pseudomonas* into *E. coli.* Given their latest experiments to control the rate and specificity of the ability of these microbes to degrade wastes (in Sojka's words, "We want to control the microbe's taste for these organics"), there is little doubt that Hooker is earnestly seeking to develop a widely usable micro-organism.

The major difference between the Russian and American work is that the Russians clearly intended their organisms to be used in the wild where contamination of animal or human habitats might readily occur, while the Hooker group has limited its releases to contained test sites. It is also likely that Hooker will exert more genetic control over the end-product organisms than will the Russians.

New studies are progressing rapidly in at least three other companies, Sybron Biochemical, Polybac, and Flow Laboratories. All have programs for developing genetically altered organisms for degrading toxic chemicals. The general approach of these groups has involved putting in novel mutations to increase the rate by which the microbes degrade the wastes of greatest concern. One of these groups, under the direction of Dr. A. Kopecky, has developed techniques for isolating bacteria that allow organisms to be selected that do very well in the presence of otherwise toxic concentrations of metals. In terms of risks to the environment, Kopecky believes that microorganisms genetically engineered to degrade toxic chemicals lose their robustness as the substrate is consumed and remain confined to their sludge pits. But Kopecky and others appear to ignore the likelihood that many of these same chlorinated chemicals are potent mutagens in themselves. As a result of exposure, bacterial degraders of highly mutagenic toxic chemicals could be subject to further genetic change and thereby lose their predictable properties.

Finally, researchers will have to consider the ultimate toxicity of the by-products and residues of the microbially assisted degradation process itself. Once done with their degradation work, test bacteria leave residues that themselves can contain toxic substances.

Comment

From much of the material presented at Seattle, it is evident that major corporations such as Hooker have not restrained themselves from testing their genetically modified organisms on pilot plants or models out in the environment. To be sure, they are not bound by the NIH Guidelines, but at least in New York State they are required to abide by the same terms and conditions that bind university researchers. Presumably, this includes RAC review before intentional release into the environment.

It is plausible that the risks are limited to the immediate vicinity of the substrate being attacked, but only when the testing ground is an environmentally isolated sump or waste pit. The experience at many toxic-waste sites is that chemical wastes are rarely limited to their initial sites of deposition. As amazing as it may seem, many waste-pit liners have only recently been tested for their resistance to permeation by the chemicals being used to fill them. And the history of outmigration of wastes from sites such as the one at Stringfellow Quarry in California and that at Hyde Park, New York, are anything but reassuring.

If the wastes from these sites can migrate, so will some of the microbes used to digest them. Moreover, as the microbes are subjected to subsequent selection pressures, it is highly likely that new variants will be produced, just as antibiotics have propelled new resistant varieties of pathogens into hospital environments. While industry commentators such as R. S. Grubbs may be right that "biotechnology offers some exciting possibilities in making spaceship earth more habitable . . . ,"[14] it is also likely that we will make some mistakes if we listen uncritically to his plea to get on with the work.

Clearly, great caution—and wisdom—are needed if this seemingly promising field is going to evolve safely with the greatest proportion of public good to risk.

As observed by the President's Commission for the Study of Ethical Problems in Medicine and Biomedical and Behavioral Research, "Any realistic assessment of the potential consequences of the new technology must be founded upon a sober recognition of human fallibility and ignorance."[15] With respect to pollutant control, we are likely to be tempted to try unproven remedies by the urgent need to detoxify chemicals before we completely understand the second-order consequences of our interventions. This dilemma will be particularly acute where we believe that widespread application in open environments is the only solution to thwart pending disaster—for example, where the oil spill from the *Torrey Canyon* threatened an entire coastal ecosystem off the southwest coast of England and the Normandy coast of France in 1967. In that case, the detergents used to disperse the oil probably did more damage to living organisms than the oil itself would have. In such circumstances of extreme peril in particular we must heed the admonition to acknowledge the limits of human understanding and foresight. And for now we should take the time to test fully the ramifications of releasing genetically modified organisms into the environment, and not be stampeded into pursuing the expedient but potentially foolish course.

Notes

1. Leslie Glick, personal communication, January 25, 1984.
2. See Jeremy Rifkin, Amicus curiae brief, in *Diamond* v. *Chakrabarty*, U.S. Department of Commerce, PTA, sec. 2105, 1980. This landmark Supreme Court patent decision is ably discussed in S. Krimsky, "Patents for Life Forms *sui generis:* Some New Questions for Science, Law, and Society," *Recombinant DNA Technical Bulletin* 4 (April 1981): 11–15.

3. Examples cited in the 1984 *International Dictionary of Biotechnology* include Koppers Company, Petroleum Fermentation, Cytox, all U.S. firms, and WBE of Ireland.

4. B. Zimmerman, discussion session, Conference on Genetic Control of Environmental Pollutants, Seattle, Washington, July 31–August 3, 1983.

5. A major obstacle to widescale use of this process—namely, the presence of toxic heavy metals such as cadmium—has been largely resolved through the addition of steps that precipitate these elements.

6. D. A. Hopwood, "The Genetic Programming of Industrial Microorganisms," *Scientific American* 245 (1981): 91–102.

7. R. B. Grubbs, "Environmental Applications of Biotechnology: The Current State of the Art," paper presented at the Conference on Genetic Control of Environmental Pollutants, Seattle, Washington, July 31–August 3, 1983.

8. A. L. Demain and N. A. Solomon, "Industrial Microbiology," *Scientific American* 245 (1981): 67–75.

9. See Chapter 9 in M. Lappé, *Germs That Won't Die: Medical Consequences of the Misuse of Antibiotics* (Garden City, NY: Anchor/Doubleday, 1982), pp. 105–122.

10. M. Alexander, "Ecological Constraints on Genetic Engineering," paper presented at the Conference on Genetic Control of Environmental Pollutants, Seattle, Washington, July 31–August 3, 1983.

11. J. L. Sinclair and M. Alexander, unpublished studies, cited in Alexander, ibid.

12. L. A. Golobelva et al., "Degradation of Polychloroaromatic Insecticides by *Pseudomonas aeroginosa* Containing Degradation Plasmids," *Mikrobiologiya* 51 (1982): 973–978 (translated by Plenum Publishing, Acquisition No. UDC 576.851.132.095, 1983).

13. S. A. Sojka, discussion session, Seattle conference, August 2, 1983.

14. R. B. Grubbs, "Environmental Applications," p. 4.

15. President's Commission for the Study of Ethical Problems in Medicine and Biomedical and Behavioral Research, *Splicing Life: A Report on the Social and Ethical Issues of Genetic Engineering with Human Beings* (Washington, D.C.: U.S. Government Printing Office, 1982).

CHAPTER 9

Nefarious Uses

It is one of the more disturbing paradoxes of the recombinant-DNA debate that critics have paid more attention to inadvertently produced biohazards than to intentionally generated ones. This reluctance to consider the more directly injurious possibilities of rDNA research can be traced to the early days of the debate.

The possibility that rDNA technologies could be used for biological warfare was considered fully three months before the February 1975 Asilomar conference. During this period when I worked with Richard Roblin, cochairman of the Genetics Research Group of the Institute of Society, Ethics and Life Sciences, at Hastings-on-Hudson, New York, I proposed a paragraph on biological warfare uses for a draft of the Singer-Söll letter (see Chapter 1). The proposed paragraph declared, in part, "that as scientists, we are concerned that recombinant DNA could be used for the express purpose of constructing hazardous organisms with biological warfare capabilities."[1]

On reading this suggested addition, Roblin and members of the NAS group that was composing this letter rejected the inclusion of any reference to biological warfare. Roblin believed then that it would be a mistake to draw attention to an issue that would only confuse the public, noting that the recently signed Convention on Biological Weapons[2] made this concern hypothetical and largely moot. Subsequent events and discoveries were to prove this view to be an overly optimistic reading of history.

The core question was whether rDNA technologies might be so useful to the military that they would be subject to misuse, even in the face of existing treaty commitments. The disdain of most molecular biologists to the military attractiveness of their technology is in marked distinction to that of the early nuclear physicists and organophosphate pesticide chemists. In both instances, scientists who played key roles in developing the basic science were aware of the potential of their new knowledge to greatly change the conduct of warfare. While the story of the atomic physicists is now widely appreciated (see the biography of Oppenheimer written by Alice Kimball Smith and Charles Weiner of MIT for a particularly probing account[3]), that for chemical warfare is less well known.

The basic science for an organophosphorous pesticide was developed by Gerhard Schrader at Germany's I.G. Farbenin Industrie in the early days of World War II. Schrader recognized the potential of this chemical to inhibit aceytlcholinesterase, the key enzyme needed to break down the otherwise nerve-blocking accumulations of acetylcholine at the junctions of the nerves and muscle cells. Schrader knew that with such properties, an organophosphate pesticide could be a potent weapon of war, and he made it available to the German high command. Under Eichmann's direction, nerve gases such as Sarin and Tabun were used to gas Jews at such concentration camps as Buchenwald and Auschwitz.

Ironically, these agents continue to be studied—and some believe stockpiled—by governments. They have proven to be among the most potent cholinesterase-inhibiting chemicals ever known.

Social Responsibility

As we have seen, it can be claimed that recombinant-DNA researchers took a diametrically different course from Schrader's once they uncovered experimental designs that could generate novel health hazards. They called public attention to their work and risked substantial delays in recommending safeguards for the protection of the public. But from the outset of the recombinant-DNA debate, researchers kept the biological-warfare issue distinct from the question of research-related biohazards. On the former, their position was clear: as stated by Paul Berg at a Stanford conference in 1977, any agent can be used for good or evil purposes, and certainly recombinant-DNA scientists should not be held responsible for what others might do with their research.[4]

Berg and other scientists appear to believe that rDNA should be regarded as a neutral teclogical tool. Whether it is used for good or ill depends on the vagaries of political morality, a force, they believe, that is outside the control of the scientific community.

Similar arguments were put forward at about the same time by Soviet scientists who derived the fear that genetic engineering might be misused. I have argued that some rDNA technologies, such as those involving the earliest organophosphate pesticides, *intrinsically* lend themselves to misuse and therefore deserve the closest scrutiny. Where the research leads to great possibilities of harm, control seems justified. Until now, our uncertainty regarding the inevitability of harm has kept us from asking that some research not be done. In 1976, Soviet science policy spokesman Aleksandr Bayev declared that "we in the Soviet Union have no fear of the future, nor of some powerful and blind forces being capable of misleading science into doing evil."[5]

Philosopher Carl Cohen, writing in the *New England Journal of Medicine*,[6] identified principles that would warrant a consideration of a blanket prohibition on rDNA research. He argued that research might be prohibited when there is a high probability that the knowledge developed will be used with very injurious consequences. This claim, according to Cohen, requires that the advocates of any ban demonstrate the likelihood of such consequences.

A thorough review of the conditions under which military-directed recombinant-DNA research is being conducted, the treaties in place to limit nefarious use, and a documentation of the uses that pose the greatest potential for misuse are the minimum needed to assess the application of this first principle.

Toxin Studies

The area of rDNA research that warrants the closest scrutiny is the isolation and cloning of genes that code for potent biological toxins. Recombinant-DNA-based technologies such as DNA probes and gene-isolation techniques have greatly facilitated the ease with which genes for highly toxic substances can be cloned and their products collected for study and/or application. The volume of such research has recently expanded greatly, as a result of the relaxation of the guidelines governing toxin studies.

From 1976 to early 1982, the isolation of gene sequences coding for toxins that would be lethal for vertebrates at doses of less than 100 nanograms (billionths of a gram) for each kilogram of body weight were expressely proscribed. However, in the version of the NIH Guidelines published in April 1982, research on such toxins (including botulinum toxins, tetanus and diphtheria toxins, and the neurotoxin of *Shigella* dysentery) was allowed provided that the Recombinant DNA Advisory Committee reviewed the proposals and the NIH and Institutional Biosafety Committee approved of their safeguards.[7]

The lifting of this regulatory floodgate has led to extensive study of biological toxins. Such an expansive research program, much of it conducted under the aegis of the military, raises serious questions about the ultimate purposes served. The policy dilemma is that some of this research can be justified on the basis of its critical need for securing public health benefits. Ironically, the same work can lead to military preparedness by demonstrating the limits—or strengths—of offensive preparations for warfare use and the effectiveness of possible countermeasures (e.g., immunization).

The key to resolving the dilemma is learning how to distinguish between research that is intrinsically harmful and that which is beneficial. Sometimes, as I will show below, it may be impossible to control presumptively nefarious uses without compromising some benevolent ones.

By 1983, laboratories had isolated at least ten classes of naturally occurring toxins that could be applied to one or more military situations. These included various aflatoxins, lecithinase, aspergillic acid, diphtheria and cholera toxins, diethylarsine, cytochalasins, ochratoxins, sporidesmin, T-2 toxin, ricin, tremorgen and other tricothecene toxins.[8]

Another intractable dilemma rests in the duality of purpose to which almost all of these products can be directed. Some of the same toxins that lend themselves to biological-warfare applications have medical uses. Recombinants that produce ricin or diphtheria toxins (types A or B) produce molecules that can be linked to specially designed anti-bodies, thereby creating "immunotoxins" with potential use in cancer therapy and the treatment of autoimmune dis-ease. Other antibodies, in turn, can be used as reagents for further purifying the toxin molecules themselves.

Even after assembly into antibody/toxin combinations, a toxic agent can be used for either therapeutic or military purposes. Depending on whether it is used to selectively deliver the toxic substance to a malignant or other un-wanted cell or to a normal one, it may either eliminate a cancer cell or destroy an organ. An example of the more beneficial uses contemplated for immunotoxins include their application to strip bone marrow of immunologically aggressive cells (responsible for the "graft-versus-host" re-action) that limit the success of marrow transplants or to seek out and destroy metastatic breast cancer cells. This latter research, being developed at Cetus in Emeryville, California, entails linking the A or B chain of diphtheria toxin with tumor-specific antibodies. Another, more ex-perimental use of such systems involves linking the A chain of the ricin toxin to antibodies to abolish certain undesirable cell lines elsewhere in the body. A recent experiment suc-cessfully used this system to suppress the autoimmune reac-tion characteristic of Hashimoto's thyroiditis.[9]

On the other end of the spectrum, some researchers have hypothesized that toxins could be linked to antibodies di-rected against antigens that occur exclusively or predomi-nantly in the cellular makeup of a targeted ethnic population, thereby giving the agent especially attractive military characteristics in conflicts with distant populations. Such a hypothetical scenario was played out in the pre-rDNA era in an article in the November 1970 issue of *Military Review*. This military journal projected the development of race-specific biological or so-called "ethnic weapons" that could be developed to exploit the existence of distinguishing genetic polymorphisms among human populations. While no evidence has surfaced that suggests that this eventuality has occurred, the very existence of speculation (and some would consider it irresponsible speculation, in the face of current potentialities) is disturbing. One person's imaginary scenario is another's recipe for terrorism.

The ultimate problem is the ambiguity inherent in the system itself. A toxin linked to an antibody directed against a tumor antigen becomes a "magic bullet" for cancer; the *same* toxin directed towards a different cellular component, such as the surface characteristics of specialized nerve cells, becomes a potent biological-warfare agent.

The possibilities for producing both direct and indirect biological-warfare agents are largely a matter of imagination. What is the likelihood of any of these scenarios actually occurring?

James W. Larrick, a senior scientist at Cetus's Immune Research Laboratories in Palo Alto, California, expressed his concerns about research directed at isolating toxin genes. In a letter to *Nature*, Larrick described the expanding toxin-cloning program as "a potential Pandora's box." He went on to write that "it is my fear that these toxins could be used for military purposes. Just 10 micrograms or less can kill a 70 kg human being . . ." Ken Coleman, of the Harvard Medical School, replied three months later, greatly downplaying any special risks from cloned toxins as compared to those occurring naturally in bacteria.[10]

Much of what passes for toxin research is thus arguably of military benefit, even as it is directed toward public health ends. One example is the research that has yielded the successful isolation of the genes responsible for expression of "virulence" antigens in bacteria that infect the intestinal tract. These antigens, along with molecules that permit their transfer across the intestinal wall, give these organisms the ability to cause diarrhea and a resultant dehydration that can be fatal. So a vaccine directed against these toxins has great potential for ameliorating such major public health threats as cholera and other enteric diseases.

Not surprisingly, such research appeals to the military. The high concentrations of troops in foreign countries where enteric disease is endemic make it an attractive candidate for study. At the same time, knowing which of the more potent enterotoxins can be isolated—and developing defenses against them—is good military strategy to offset (or initiate) any foreign biological-warfare effort.

Just such a project is being conducted at the Walter Reed Institute of Research in Washington, D.C. It is intended to create a vaccine that can neutralize the toxin responsible for the ability of *Citrobacter* and *Salmonella* bacteria to produce serious gastrointestinal illness.[11]

Analogous research done at the University of Maryland was first reported at the Sixth Mid-Atlantic Regional Extrachromosomal Genetic Elements Conference held November 12–14, 1982, in Virginia Beach, Virginia. A group of researchers at the Center for Vaccine Development headed by Dr. James B. Kaper successfully cloned the cholera toxin gene, thereby providing the basis for effective vaccination with an attenuated *Vibrio cholerae* strain.[12] Subsequently, Kaper demonstrated how to weaken the cholera strain by deleting a portion of its toxin gene, leaving an active portion that could still generate an immune response.[13]

A third research project is not nearly so clearly in the public interest. Both salmonellosis and cholera are urgent public health problems. And with the new oral cholera vaccine, this scourge of many developing nations now appears headed for control. It was therefore surprising when, in mid-1983, Dr. Alison O'Brien and Randall Holmes of the Army's Uniformed Services University of the Health Sciences petitioned the RAC to allow their group to clone the *Shiga*-like toxin expressed in virulent cholera and some enterotoxigenic *E. coli*. This toxin is found only in some cholera strains, and is much more toxic than are the previously isolated toxin molecules. So much so, that initial review had indicated that the work had to take place in a highly protected and contained "P-4" facility. This prospect would seemingly pose little obstacle to O'Brien, since he was already conducting the research at the Fort Detrick containment facility, which has the only operational P-4 center in the nation. O'Brien nonetheless petitioned the RAC to allow the *Shiga*-like toxin to be cloned in a K-12 strain of *E. coli* under the less restrictive containment condition of a P-3 facility.

According to O'Brien's arguments, if this "desirable public health related work" was to proceed at a reasonable pace, some relaxation of the present safeguards would be mandatory. His views were seconded by the U.S. Cholera Panel of the National Institute of Allergy and Infectious Disease, at the RAC meeting on October 16, 1983, where it was declared that as long as these strict requirements existed, they would prevent most laboratories from deleting the *Shiga* toxin gene, a necessary condition for making an attenuated *Vibrio cholerae* and enterotoxigenic *E. coli* vaccine strain.[14] Alternatively, the isolated toxin itself, if suitably inactivated, could be used as part of a vaccine.

At the February 6, 1984, meeting of the recombinant-DNA Advisory Committee, this seemingly health-directed research was reviewed. Seven protesters, including Jeremy Rifkin and Paul Warnke, former Arms Control and Disarmament Agency chief, attacked the proposed study on the ground that it opened the door to biological-warfare research.[15] Warnke's counterproposal was that the experiment be postponed until the arms control agency and the Department of Defense provided an "arms control impact statement," as required under the Arms Control and Disarmament Act. This act requires that any program involving technology with potential military applications be subject to such review.

After reviewing evidence, the RAC voted nine to five with four abstentions, to allow the research to go forward. The lack of unanimity of RAC members clearly impressed the responsible federal officials. In early May 1984, Richard Krause, director of the National Institute of Allergy and Infectious Disease, turned down the majority recommendation, citing the absence of a consensus on a particularly critical issue.[16]

The question of whether or not such work would lend itself to future abuse remained on the minds of at least some of the participants. During the debate, Jeremy Rifkin invoked the concept of collective responsibility in chiding RAC members that they would be liable for future biological-warfare applications of this toxin. According to Rifkin, "In authorizing the *Shiga* experiment and other similar experiments, the RAC becomes an active participant in the final uses to which the work is put. . . ."[17] In spite of the fact that *Shiga* toxin is an unlikely candidate for warfare purposes, Rifkin's point raises the larger issue of the responsibility for current inocuous work that can lead to more hazardous applications.

Some contemporary studies appear much more likely to be misused. Some of the research going foward on *Yersinia pestis,* the organism that causes plague, is much less unequivocally health-directed. This bacterium has been a candidate for biological-warfare work in the past. Two groups of Russian and European researchers are actively seeking to identify the genetic basis for the virulence of the plague

bacillus.[18] If successful, control of the plasmids that determine this potent toxin could be used to provide other bacterial strains with similar virulence without being detectable
as plague bacteria.

Even these studies inevitably fall into a grey area of
uncertainty, since their results can be used for both military
and public health purposes. It is difficult accurately to predict the ultimate ends of either of these projects without
second-guessing the motives of the researchers. But given
the rarity of plague in continental Europe (it is endemic in
pockets of the western United States and Southeast Asia),
the scale tends to tip towards a greater military than health
interest, particularly in the Soviet Union. By some accounts,
this superpower has a burgeoning biological-warfare program although other observers, like Susan Wright of the
University of Michigan and Richard P. Novick of New York
State's Public Health Research Institute, have questioned
whether this impression has been deliberately created by
U.S. intelligence agencies to justify further American biological-warfare work.[19]

Soviet Biological-Warfare Capabilities

While detailed assessments of warfare capabilities
are more the province of the CIA than of this book, a sense
of the Soviet Union's interest in and commitment to biological warfare can be gleaned from the published literature. To
avoid appearing to be in violation of the 1972 Convention
on Biological Weapons, the Soviet Union relies on the clas-
sification of biologically produced toxins as chemical-war-
fare agents.

The 1977 version of the East German *Textbook of Military Chemistry* (the standard text for all Soviet block armies) declares that "toxins are not living substances. They thus differ from biological organisms, so that they can be included among chemical warfare agents. When they are used in combat, the atmosphere can be contaminated over relatively large areas."[20]

Like the Japanese, the Soviet Union has had an interest in biological-weapons systems that antedates World War II. As early as 1919, Lenin established a bacteriological weapons institute, and evidence suggests that Russia has pursued a biological-warfare program uninterrupted since then.

The reality of this commitment was brought home by reports by Soviet dissident Zhores Medvedev that an explosion in 1979 at a Soviet biological-weapons facility in Sverdlovsk blew *Anthrax* spores into the atmosphere resulting in the infection of thousands of citizens and military, and killing at least a thousand people.

If we put aside for the moment the controversial and still questionable use of tricothecene toxins in Southeast Asia, we can still view the Soviet Union as bent on achieving an offensive capability in toxin-based biological warfare. According to the most recent edition of its *Military Encyclopedia,* the Russians believe that "achievements in biology and related sciences . . . have led to an increase in the effectiveness of biological agents as a means of conducting warfare. Improved methods of obtaining and using them have resulted in a qualitative reexamination of the very concept of 'biological weapons.'"[21] This commitment has proven so convincing that Secretary of Defense Caspar Weinberger issued a report on April 10, 1984, stating in part that "Soviet research efforts in the area of genetic engineering may also have a connection with their biological warfare program. . . ."[22] That the Soviets have an increasingly powerful basic genetic-engineering-science program has now been documented by Raymond Zilinskas.[23]

What we are apparently seeing, according to Weinberger, is a sustained effort to transfer technological know-how from the civilian to the military sector. Soviet doctrine has long accepted the notion that biological weapons can legitimately be considered part of the strategic arsenal arrayed against the West. More recently, biologically derived weapons have apparently been insinuated into their terrorist weaponry. The surface manifestations of this program suggest a much larger and more insidious strategy in operation in the underground terrorist cells that operate out of Eastern Europe. The most notorious example of the Soviet program was the infamous "umbrella assassination" in 1978 by lethal injection of ricin toxin into Bulgarian dissident Georgi Markov on a busy London street.

According to interviews with Russian expatriots and emigrés conducted during a controversial seven-month investigation by the *Wall Street Journal*,[24] Russian scientists are actively pursuing studies that would expand their ability to use neurotoxins as agents of war. William Kucewicz of the *Journal* uncovered evidence that venom-producing genes from cobra snakes were being introduced to viruses with the ability to infect human hosts. In principle, such a vector could ensure that an enemy agent could surreptitiously introduce paralytic cobra neurotoxin into human targets. By the same token, this toxin research, like dozens of other studies, may be nothing more than an innocuous investigation into basic biology. Kucewicz has also documented research activities at the scientific research complex called Academe City, about thirty kilometers southeast of Novosibirsk, directed at using the common flu virus to make neurotoxins.[25]

Further investigations of the published literature reveal

more than three dozen related studies involving bee toxin, Bulgarian viper venom, scorpion poisons, tetrodotoxin from puffer fish, and saxitoxin from marine algae. Like the plague toxin studies mentioned earlier, some, all, or none of this work could be directly linked to biological-warfare applications. The proof assembled by Kucewicz that the Russians have gathered and used at least some of these toxins in actual biological weapons suggests that nefarious use is uppermost on the mind of some Soviet military leaders.

This use is all the more questionable in light of the Soviet commitment (along with 110 other nations) to abide by the terms of the Biological Weapons Convention. This document, as we have seen,[26] expressly includes biological toxins among the prohibited biological weapons, banning both their manufacture and possession in anything but microscopic quantities for research purposes. A closer examination of the legal basis for these prohibitions and the United States's own interpretation of its commitments is revealing.

Limitations
of Legal Protections

Theoretically, we are insulated from the most egregious possibilities by common agreement of developed nations not to develop biological-warfare agents. In principle, the United States is party to two separate treaties that expressly outlaw the development of biological weapons of war. The first is the Geneva Protocols of 1925, which expressly forbid the use of either chemical or biological weapons during wartime. Initially, when the member nations were asked to ratify this treaty, all *but* the United States signed. The U.S. Senate belatedly ratified the protocols in 1975. In their final form, the Geneva Protocols ban the use of most chemical and all biological weapons except when nonsignatory nations use such weapons first.

In 1969, President Richard Nixon formally renounced the use of biological-warfare weaponry and pledged to dispose of any stockpiles of those weapons. Three years later, he signed the *Convention on the Prohibition of the Development, Production and Stockpiling of Bacteriological (Biological) and Toxin Weapons.*[27] This treaty forbids any signatory from stockpiling or even possessing quantities of agents sufficient for mounting a biological-warfare program.

However, the treaty does allow a signatory to maintain biological agents that are intended for "prophylactic or protective" purposes, leaving to each nation the determination of the nature of the materials and the amounts needed to achieve these objectives. The convention also permits a signatory to conduct research on *potential* weapons—but only for the presumptive purposes of developing defensive capabilities. (As will be clear in the more detailed study of this provision below, this clause was clearly intended to permit the development of only laboratory quantities of agents or toxins, and *not* to permit the country in question to develop a "deterrent" capability.)

Although recombinant-DNA technologies were not anticipated in the 1972 draft, the language and subsequent interpretation of the treaty clearly indicate that rDNA is embraced by the convention. The treaty does not limit rDNA research per se, even where it could clearly lead to development of new materials or agents that lend themselves to military applications. The limiting condition appears to hinge on the interpretation of when research moves into its development state. It is only here that the convention expressly forbids significant activity.

Military Interpretations

Given the ambiguities implicit in the convention itself, it is not surprising to find military spokespersons who are ambiguous regarding the nature of our commitment under the 1972 treaty. In 1976, John Allen, a Department of Defense spokesperson in Research and Advanced Technology, declared that the "DoD is prohibited from developing biological agents by international treaty. As a result of the approval of the treaty, *all work* [emphasis added] involving recombinant DNA experimentation [in the U.S.] has been terminated."[28]

Clearly, something has changed over the ensuing six years. In 1982, Dr. William Beisel, Deputy for Science at the Army Medical Research for Infectious Diseases, in Maryland, declared, "There is no offensive biological warfare work going on in this country; there are no plans for such work, and, very categorically, there are no plans for anything dealing with recombinant DNA work in regard to an offensive program."[29] This transition from "no research" to "no offensive research" signals a major shift in American policy.

With the assistance of writer Charles Piller of the University of California at San Francisco, I have documented the burgeoning number of studies and contracts for recombinant-DNA work funded by the military. This compilation, shown in Table 9.1, suggests that the key escape clause for the military is the focus on "no offensive" programs.

As early as 1976, Defense Department spokespeople were balking at the NIH ban on toxin research. The department's John Allen provided the justification for future plans: "Other advanced technical countries could conduct such work secretly. This could result in a major technical surprise for the United States. . . . In today's international climate, we see our task as one of preparing to prevent or

Table 9.1

Recombinant-DNA Research Projects via Contracts
Funded by the Department of Defense*

Investigators	Project
1. Dr. M. I. Simon at University of California, San Diego (ONR)	Molecular basis of marine bio-fouling
2. Dr. A. Purchino, Dr. J. S. Salstrom, D. F. Pass, and Dr. A. J. Faras at Molecular Genetics, Inc., Minnetonka, Minnesota (USAMRDC)	Cloning of M-segment antigen gene of Rift Valley fever virus for vaccine development
3. Dr. H. V. Aposhian at University of Arizona (USAMRDC)	Cloning of the acetyl-cholinesterase gene for study and possible use in therapy
4. Dr. R. H. Singer at University of Massachusetts (USAMRDC)	Cloning of the acetyl-cholinesterase gene for study and possible use in therapy
5. Dr. J. D. Baxter at University of California, San Francisco (USAMRDC)	Cloning of the acetyl-cholinesterase gene for study and possible use in therapy
6. Dr. J. W. Patrick at Salk Institute, San Diego (USAMRDC)	Cloning of the acetyl-cholinesterase gene for study and possible use in therapy
7. Dr. H. Soreq at Weizmann Institute, Israel (USAMRDC)	Cloning of the acetyl-cholinesterase gene for study and possible use in therapy
8. Dr. W. J. Harris at Inveresk Research International, Scotland (USAMRDC)	Cloning of the acetyl-cholinesterase gene for study and possible use in therapy
9. Dr. R. K. Padmanabhan at University of Kansas (USAMRDC)	Cloning of dengue-2 virus surface protein gene for vaccine development

*As of September 8, 1983.
Abbreviations: USAMRDC: U.S. Army Medical Research Defense Command; DARCOM-ARO: Defense Army Command-Army Research Office; ONR: Office of Naval Research.

Table 9.1 *(continued)*

Investigators	Project
10. Dr. F. C. G. Hoskin and Dr. D. J. Cork at Illinois Institute of Technology, Chicago (DARCOM-ARO)	Cloning of squid gene for the enzyme diisopropyl phosphorofluoride hydrolase (DPPase) for organophosphorus detoxification
11. Dr. H. G. Khorana at Massachusetts Institute of Technology (ONR)	Cloning of rhodopsin and other visual photoreceptor proteins
12. Dr. M. J. Fournier and Dr. Thomas L. Mason at University of Massachusetts (USAMRDC)	Cloning of V3 surface proteins of Flaviviruses (Japanese encephalitis and dengue-1 viruses) for use as vaccines (done in collaboration with the Salk Institute)
13. Dr. J. Kraut at Agouron Institute, La Jolla, California (ONR)	Generation of catalytic enzymes for decontamination of chemical-warfare agents
14. Dr. J. H. Richards at California Institute of Technology (ONR)	Generation of enzymes to catalyze the hydrolysis of organophosphates
15. Dr. D. T. Kingsburry at University of California, Berkeley (ONR)	a. With Dr. S. Falkow: creation of species-specific hybridization probes for rapid identification of pathogenic organisms b. With Dr. A. E. Karu: studies of *recA* protein function and regulation in *E. coli* c. With S. Tracy: studies of RNA:cDNA cloning systems in *E. coli K12*
16. Dr. J. L. Ingraham et al. at University of California, Davis (DARCOM-ARO)	Training grant for graduate students in biogenic engineering of *Pseudomonas* denitrification enzymes
17. Dr. R. Lester at University of Kentucky (DARCOM-ARO)	Training grant for graduate students in biochemistry of enzyme cloning

Table 9.1 *(continued)*

Investigators	Project
18. Dr. W. Magee at University of Idaho (DARCOM-ARO)	Traning grant for graduate students in biogenic engineering for cloning of bacterial enzymes
19. Dr. G. Blobel at the Rockefeller University (DARCOM-ARO)	University Research Instrumentation Program
20. Dr. R. H. Singer at University of Massachusetts Medical Center (DARCOM-ARO)	University Research Instrumentation Program
21. Dr. T. M. Lohman at Texas A & M University (DARCOM-ARO)	University Research Instrumentation Program
22. Dr. P. Setlow at University of Connecticut (DARCOM-ARO)	University Research Instrumentation Program. The equipment will support recombinant-DNA research in each location
23. Dr. P. Setlow at University of Connecticut (DARCOM-ARO)	Study of a spore protease of *B. megatherium*
24. Dr. J. B. Kaper at University of Maryland School of Medicine (ONR)	Study of gene transfer in marine microorganisms
25. Dr. D. J. Moore at Purdue University	Support for an international forum on three-dimensional structure of antibody combining sites
26. Dr. J. E. Donaldson at Iowa University	Characterization of antigens expressed by *Trypanosoma brucei* during the metacyclic stage for vaccine purposes
27. Dr. K. Stewart at Issaquah Health Research Institute, WA	Characterize the surface glycoproteins of African trypanosomes for vaccine development

Abbreviations: USAMRDC: U.S. Army Medical Research Defense Command; DARCOM-ARO: Defense Army Command-Army Research Office; ONR: Office of Naval Research.

minimize such a surprise. To do this, the DoD must draw upon the research results and technology in this field that is being conducted in the civilian research community. Therefore, we judge the continuation or reimposition of a research ban [as had been in effect for cloning of toxin genes under the NIH guidelines] to be counterproductive for us."[30]

Certainly by 1982, the DoD had perceived Russian recombinant-DNA research as a "new threat" for increasing the selectivity, lethality, and stability of microorganisms. With this rationale in view, the DoD expanded its program to "provide a better understanding of the disease mechanisms of bacterial and rickettsial organisms that pose a potential BW threat, with or without genetic manipulation."[31]

An identical defensive rationale was used in the early 1950s to justify our own offensively oriented chemical- and biological-warfare program, which lasted at least through 1969. It too was designed "to anticipate the capabilities of potentially hostile nations," and to develop defenses against putative weapons systems. At that time, our intelligence identified several bacterial diseases such as tularemia and plague, and rickettsial diseases such as Rocky Mountain spotted fever (or its Russian counterpart, winter-spring fever) as the targets of our development effort. Less well known were our research projects in developing weapons designed to decimate key food crops in Russia or, secondarily, in China.[32]

Some observers of our contemporary programs believe that the DoD is in fact conducting clandestine offensive research under the guise of "defensive" research. In the words of one correspondent, even this so-called defensive work "could give the U.S. military the capability to wage biological war. The results of that research could send the arms race off on another dangerous spiral."[33]

Invidious Distinctions

It is now clear from explanations by Dr. Robert Mikulak, of the Arms Control and Disarmament Agency, to the RAC that from a treaty perspective no distinction between "offensive" and "defensive" weapons exists. Both types of research are proscribed by the 1972 Biological Weapons Convention.[34] It was in part a concern for Army and Navy development of "defensive biological weapons systems" that prompted Professor Richard Goldstein of Harvard Medical School and Richard Novick to urge the NIH to consider an amendment to their guidelines that would ban the construction of biological weapons through recombinant-DNA techniques.

The specific amendment, circulated to members of the academic community on June 8, 1982, stipulated in part that "the construction of biological weapons by molecular cloning" be added to the proscribed list of experiments. In soliciting this support, Goldstein pointed out that such a restriction had been expressly omitted from the latest version of the NIH Guidelines, ostensibly owing to the existence of the 1972 convention. According to Goldstein, this omission left out "the most serious biohazard imaginable for this [rDNA] technology. . . . The construction of biological weapons constitutes an egregious misuse of scientific knowledge."[35]

According to Novick and Goldstein, their proposed amendment would do three things: (1) provide a public declaration of support for the scientific community's non-cooperation in the development of rDNA-mediated weapons; (2) convince governments that the 1972 prohibition should apply to laboratory studies leading up to full-scale development as well as to that development itself; and (3) encourage a much broader base of support for the existing prohibitions against biological warfare.

At the climactic meeting of the Recombinant DNA Advisory Committee on June 28, 1982, Karim Ahmed of the Natural Resources Defense Council emerged as the key supporter of the Novick-Goldstein amendment. Ahmed pointed out that the language of the 1972 convention failed to encompass *research* directed at developing or stockpiling weapons. Ahmed then asked the Department of Defense representative at the RAC meeting whether he agreed with his interpretation.

Dr. Robert Mikulak indicated that his agency did not object to the NIH's incorporating language that dealt with biological weapons, but asked that any language be amended to be consistent with the 1972 convention. Dr. William Beisel, from the Department of Defense, reiterated his department's official stance that the DoD was not involved in research on biological weapons, only in what he termed "medical defensive" research. This research, which is "entirely unclassified," focuses on diseases that could threaten military or civilian populations. All this research, according to Beisel, "is of a public health nature."[36] An examination of the DoD funded research listed in Table 9.1 shows that much of the work bears only a remote relation to public health.

After a heated discussion and the defeat of language that would have modified the original Goldstein-Novick amendment, Dr. Ahmed moved that the original language be incorporated into the guidelines. Dr. David Baltimore, of the Massachusetts Institute of Technology, stated that Dr. Ahmed's recommendation was dangerous in that it might undermine the Biological Weapons Convention obligations of the United States. With no further dialogue, the vote was taken, and the Goldstein-Novick amendment to prohibit construction of biological weapons by molecular cloning was defeated seventeen to two with one abstention.

Dr. David Martin, of the University of California at San

Francisco (now vice president for Research at Genentech), proposed a compromise amendment that would allow the RAC to introduce a statement of concern but that would still be consistent with our treaty obligations. Under Martin's amendment, *no* language would appear in the NIH Guidelines themselves. His statement would simply advise the director of NIH that the terms of the existing treaty "includes the prohibition on the use of recombinant DNA methodology for development of microbial or other biological agents, or toxins of types or in quantities that have no justification for prophylactic, protective or peaceful purposes."[37] This proposal passed by a vote of fifteen to five.

This last "sense" amendment left the existing ambiguities of the Biological Weapons Convention intact, opening the gate for recombinant-DNA research directed at defensive purposes. The failure of the RAC to take a positioned stand on biological-warfare uses—and their research antecedents—is all the more inexplicable in light of a letter sent three weeks earlier to William J. Gartland, Jr., director of ORDA (Office of Recombinant DNA Research), from James L. George, assistant director of Multilateral Affairs of the U.S. Arms Control and Disarmament Agency. This letter was a response to Gartland's request for comments on the question of whether or not laboratory research involving recombinant-DNA organisms for "defensive" (deterrent) research was in fact proscribed by the 1972 Biological Weapons Convention. George gave explicit guidance to the RAC members, pointing out that the convention expressly limited any development or use of biological weapons that could aid or abet the conduct of war. Citing a report by the Secretary of State dated June 21, 1972, and transmitted to the U.S. Senate as part of the ratification process, George pointed out that "the terms 'prophylactic' and 'protective' are not intended to convey any broader meaning which would in any way permit possession of biological agents or toxins for weapons purposes on the theory that such weapons were for defensive warfare, retaliation or deterrence."[38]

Despite the fact that the actual language invited opportunists to skew interpretations given to the convention, Dr. David Baltimore declared that it was extremely important that any action taken by the RAC "raise no suggestion that the treaty is insufficient."[39] This "don't rock the boat" view prevailed with the other RAC members, with the notable exception of the five who voted against the acceptance of the government's position. It is clear that we are bound by the Biological Weapons Convention not to conduct any work even in the name of deterrence or defense. How rigorously is the U.S. military adhering to this strict policy of pursuing only the most peaceful aspects of rDNA research?

What Is Being Done

The Department of Defense released a partial listing of its unclassified research in September 1983. By its own description, these twenty-eight studies included thirteen directed at developing vaccines, six at developing a possible therapeutic approach to cholinesterase poisoning (nerve gas), two at decontaminating chemical weapons, and other individual projects at decreasing the detectability of potential biological-weapons systems (see Table 9.2).

Some of these studies, like those directed at isolating plasmids that can carry toxin genes, are clearly double-edged swords of the kind discussed above. A full look at the unclassified summaries that accompany this listing supports the DoD's contention that vaccine production is indeed its principal research objective. Several research projects are in fact being directed at major human diseases, such as African leishmania, typanosomiasis, malaria, and some bacterial enteric diseases. It is unclear, however, why the army finds

Table 9.2
Recombinant-DNA Research Projects Done in In-House
Laboratories Funded by the Department of Defense*

Investigators	Project
1. Dr. G. Knudson, CPT Mikesell, and Dr. M. Vodkin at USAMRIID	Cloning of protective antigen genes of *Bacillus anthracis* for vaccine usage
2. Dr. P. Olenick at WRAIR	Cloning of varient-specific glycoprotein gene of African leishmania and trypanosomes for vaccine usage
3. Dr. D. Kopecko at WRAIR	Cloning of cell-wall genes of *R. tsutsugamushi* and *R. conorii* of the O-side chain genes of *S. flexneri* and of surface-antigen genes of *N. gonorrhea,* all for vaccine usage
4. Dr. G. A. Dasch and Dr. M. D. Dobson at NMRI	Cloning of rickettsial antigen genes for vaccine usage
5. Dr. R. L. Beaudoin, Dr. W. Zolg, and Dr. T. T. Palmer at NMRI	Cloning of surface-antigen genes of *P. falciparum* for vaccine usage
6. Dr. C. S. Schmaljohn and Dr. J. M. Dalrymple at USAMRIID	Cloning of V3 surface proteins of Flaviviruses (Japanese encephalitis and Dengue-2 viruses) for use as vaccines
7. Dr. E. C. Lee at NMRI	Cloning of *Campylobacter* surface-antigen genes for use as a vaccine against enteric infections
8. Dr. O. R. Pavlovskis, Lt. R. C. Hedstrom, and Lt. D. R. Galloway at NMRI	Cloning of *Pseudomonas* gene for Exotoxin A to produce a protective toxoid
9. Dr. R. K. Holmes and Dr. S. L. Welkos at USUHS	Control of bacterial toxins by viruses and plasmids

*As of September 8, 1983.
Abbreviations: USAMRIID—U.S. Army Medical Research Institute of Infectious Diseases; WRAIR—Walter Reed Army Institute for Research; USUHS—Uniformed Services University of the Health Sciences; NMRI—Naval Medical Research Institute.

it desirable to control work that has such broad public health importance.

Charles Piller has pointed out that the Federal Emergency Management Agency (FEMA) and the Department of Health and Human Services are both more logical and more appropriate centers of defensive, health-protective work than is the Department of Defense.[40] Yet neither agency has requested that the DoD integrate its work with its own programs. In fact, Dr. William Beisel of the DoD has publicly declared that all its research at the U.S. Army Medical Research Institute of Infectious Diseases is of a public health nature. The army itself admits that its research "does not and will not involve research to create and screen 'new' organisms as potential biological warfare agents. Our research is, and will continue to be, limited to developing protective measures to recognized agents that pose a biological warfare hazard."[41]

However, some of the research that the DoD has sponsored at USAMRIID laboratories includes studies that would clearly have to be classified as militarily oriented. Among these are two that involve research to assess the potential of biological agents for creating military threats. One is a study being done under the leadership of Dr. K. W. Hedlund to assess and characterize the virulence factors, growth requirements, and pathogenesis of both well-recognized and newly discovered pathogens "with acknowledged BW potential." This work will involve anthrax bacillus, *Coxiella burnetti*, the Q fever agent, and the bacterium that causes Legionnaire's disease. Anthrax and Q fever are hardly public health threats in the United States.

The second study, under the direction of Dr. J. M. Dalrymple, of the Virology Division of USAMRIID, involves a relatively obscure group of organisms. Dalrymple is studying toga and bunya viruses that cause disease primarily in Asia. Even less well justified from a public health perspective is the research directed at finding antidotes to nerve gas.

The DoD has also publicly admitted that it is reviewing the toxicity of one group of fungal toxins. As part of this work, it has let a contract with a genetic-engineering firm to devise sensitive tests for identifying tricothecene toxins, the fungal by-products found in the so-called "yellow rain." Were it not for the sensationalized accounts of Russian use of such agents in Southeast Asia,[42] such a project would appear to be more appropriately sponsored by the Department of Agriculture. (Tricothecene toxins, like aflatoxins, are a major problem of contaminated and poorly stored grains.)

In fact, much of the available evidence suggests that the tricothecene toxins occur more commonly in the natural world than in any presumptive uses of yellow rain for warfare purposes. According to the widely respected view of Harvard's Matthew Messelsohn, most of the samples of yellow rain taken following reports of biological warfare are nothing more than bee feces!

In spite of such confusion over the toxins' origins, NAS's National Research Council (NRC) sponsored a major conference on protection against trichothecene mycotoxins "as a result of the growing concern about the possible use of trichothecenes in warfare." As a measure of the seriousness with which the army takes the prospect of biological warfare using such agents—and without visible attention to the misgivings of the research community—it asked the NRC to form a special Committee on Protection Against Mycotoxins. This committee was to study the effects of yellow rain on civilians and military personnel who might be exposed to high concentrations of these substances. The NRC agreed, but only after extracting an agreement from DoD to allow the findings to be published.

In 1983, the results of these deliberations were published

as a book, *Protection Against Trichothecene Mycotoxins,* by the National Academy Press in Washington, D.C. The book deals with both military and civilian aspects of contamination with these toxins, including long-term environmental effects of their use and strategies for prevention and treatment.

All this attention belies the fact that *any* use of tricothecene toxins is expressly forbidden by the Biological Weapons Convention. Hence, if any exposure has occurred, these toxins should be the subject of a political and diplomatic offensive. That no such offensive has been mounted argues poorly for effective limitation of other uses of rDNA for biological-warfare purposes.

Corporate Involvements

Two problems related to DoD-sponsored recombinant-DNA research are profitability and notoriety. The Department of Defense has been notably unsuccessful in soliciting large commercial recombinant-DNA companies, such as Cetus Corporation, to cooperate in joint ventures. According to confidential sources, some companies are so afraid of the resulting negative publicity that they have prohibited their employees from mentioning such contacts or even from speaking generally on the topic of biological warfare.

One successful link forged by the DoD is that with Molecular Genetics of Minnetonka, Minnesota. Under the direction of Anthony Purchio, the Molecular Genetics project is designed to develop an immunogenic protein from the Rift Valley fever virus suitable for use as a vaccine to protect American military personnel in northern Africa or Asia. In spite of the language in the $343,715 contract, Purchio and his colleagues apparently also intend to market the vaccine for protecting agricultural livestock.[43]

From the Rift Valley fever and other microbiological research being sponsored, it is clear that much of the army's work centers on cloning the coat proteins of exotic micro-organisms. The final vaccines in such research could be used as suspensions delivered as aerosols, thereby facilitating the mass vaccination of troops or civilians against the agents in question. But aerosols are also the most likely vehicle for delivering biological-warfare weapons on a large scale. As such, aerosol vaccines, even with attenuated organisms or dead cell products, carry a deterrent force not achievable by rattling a test tube.

This deterrence policy was presented to me at the Naval Bioscience Laboratory in Oakland, California, in 1969 as the primary justification for conducting aerosol research on bacterial pathogens. (These studies included the ill-fated experiment with *Serratia marcescens* in the late 1950s, which exposed several thousand people to an agent previously thought to be nonpathogenic, but by the late 1960s known to be capable of producing pneumonia.) The army described its current aerosol-vaccination research in its *Annual Report on Chemical Warfare and Biological Research Programs* as part of broadly based public health attempts to protect military personnel against infectious agents. However, the suspicion that something else is afoot is reinforced by the military's checkered history as well as its weak explanation for this approach. From the army's perspective, an aerosol vaccine increases "the local resistance of mucosal surfaces" in the throat, nose, and lungs to the agents in question as well as conferring lasting immunity to the body as a whole. The idea that an aerosol will cause "local stimulation" is unsupported by classical immunology theory. In fact, as demonstrated by the success of the Legionnaire's disease bacterium, *Legionnela pneumophila*, in penetrating the lung's defenses, the aerosol route is better suited to *overcoming* host defenses than strengthening them.

But is aerosol recombinant-DNA research outlawed by the convention? According to military spokespersons, the use of any recombinant-DNA-based technology is expressly limited to that which "is *directly related* to the development and means and methods for the prevention, diagnosis, or treatment of disease"[44] (emphasis added). By this token, vaccine development is technically permissible.

But the convention lacks the iron-clad assurance against offensive military uses. In the same letter that defines the limitations, the DoD representative suggests that *indirect* uses of recombinant DNA to assist the military effort might also be condoned. These ancillary uses—as in dealing with marine fouling problems, for example, or in materials and polymer engineering or fuel and lubricant development— raise serious questions as to the sharpness of the distinction between "direct" and "indirect" use of recombinant-DNA technology to assist the military, but they are nevertheless clearly outside the domain of disease prevention.

The current dilemma grows out of the fact that the Convention on Biological Weapons never considered the possibility that microorganisms might be used to aid and abet the conduct of war, only that they or their by-products might be used as agents of war themselves. Little question now remains that military planners are capitalizing on new capabilities afforded by recombinant-DNA technology to augment existing warfare programs. Among the targets for recombinant-DNA technology are submarine warfare work, naval efficiency, chemical warfare, and special explosives.

The submarine work builds on research conducted at the Navy Biological Laboratory in Oakland, California, over the last twenty years. In addition to using recombinant technologies for increasing the efficiency of surveillance of air-flow systems to exclude or identify potential air-borne pathogens, the navy will probably develop and use mono-clonal antibody kits for rapid detection of potential infec-tious diseases that could spread in explosive fashion in the confines of a nuclear submarine. Several unclassified stud-ies are already under way to develop vaccines for enteric (diarrheal) diseases and to isolate the toxin responsible for much of the morbidity associated with burn-wound infec-tion from *Pseudomonas* bacteria.

Similar research has been contracted out to Biotech Research Laboratories, a Rockville, Maryland, genetic-engi-neering firm. Under its contract with DoD, this company will develop extremely sensitive biological detecting systems based on monoclonal antibodies. Biotech's initial contract is with the Defense Advanced Research Projects Agency, and according to its President, Thomas M. Li, the research should be worth some $600 million in the military sector alone.[45]

The navy also hopes to use recombinant-DNA-derived products to reduce the fouling of ships and allow sub-marines to work at greater efficiencies and speeds while submerged. This work is being undertaken by Professor M. I. Simon at the University of California at San Diego's Center for Developmental Biology.

There is substantial evidence as well that rDNA is being used to facilitate chemical warfare. All six unclassified con-tracts awarded for isolating the gene that codes for a key enzyme in the regeneration of nerve conductivity have gone to respected university professors (see Figure 9.1). By identifying the gene that codes for acetylcholinesterase, the army could be on its way to developing an antidote to the major targets of the nerve gases presently in use.

The army has also contracted with Professors F. C. G. Hoskin and D. J. Cork at the Illinois Institute of Technology in Chicago to isolate a key enzyme from squids. Known as diisopropyl phosphorofluoride hydrolase (DPPase), it is the most potent detoxifying enzyme yet identified for organophosphorus intoxication of the kind likely to occur from chemical-weapons systems. While not "offensive" work, this research is also clearly not directed toward preventing normally occurring disease, since it has virtually no likelihood of being used to offset organophosphate- or carbamate-pesticide-produced cholinesterase depression.

Recombinant organisms are also apparently being used in classified work to augment the development of special explosives. By improving the characteristics of the slurries to make these products, the highly sensitive reaction mixtures needed to produce quantities of high explosives safely could be improved.

Singly and together, these projects suggest the scope and prospect of recombinant-DNA technologies to be used to augment military preparedness or offensive capabilities. Even if legally justified by existing loopholes, the moral acceptability of using a technique developed with public health funds to assist nonhealth-related military functions is surely questionable. But both the legal and moral issue of using recombinant DNA to reinforce or create offensive weapons or capabilities is clear: it is impermissible.

Article I of the Convention on Biological Weapons declares that the *only* acceptable uses of toxins or biological agents (including rDNA-produced agents) are those that are purely peaceful in purpose. The exact language reads,

Each party . . . undertakes never in any circumstance to develop, produce, stockpile or otherwise acquire or retain: (1) Microbial or other biological agents or toxins, whatever their origin or method of production, of types and in quantities that have no justification for prophylactic, protective or other peaceful purposes.[46]

In affirming the positive uses of biological agents or products, this language simultaneously excludes any adjunctive use that is not peaceful. The convention would exclude developing a recombinant-DNA organism or product whose only purpose was to make it easier to make explosives. In spite of this concern, there is no indication to date that the DoD believes it has to justify its expansion of this technology into either primary "defensive" research or these secondary military applications. No one has questioned this use—and no one appears ready to challenge it.

In early November 1984, the *New York Times* reported that the army had requested $250 million to make just such an expansion at its Dugway, Utah chemical and biological warfare proving grounds.[47] These plans include $1.4 million for a maximum security "aerosol test lab" intended to allow "maximum containment for working with substantial volumes of toxic biological aerosol agents." Another $7 million was earmarked for additional "toxic agent test support" chambers. From the dimensions of this undertaking, it is highly unlikely that the quantities of agents involved or the "defensive" anticipatory research proposed jibe with the language and intent of the Biological Weapons Convention.

Capping the Spread of Weapons

While the early debates on the safety of recombinant-DNA organisms were raging in the mid-1970s, several events occurred that should have suggested a more direct threat. In the December 2, 1976, issue of *Nature,* an ad appeared under the headline "Bacteria by the Kilogram."

This ad, placed by the Microbiological Research Establishment, which has a laboratory in Porton, some sixty miles south of London, advertised the availability of purified microbial products, "especially enzymes and toxic proteins." Even more ominous was the offer to ship these toxins "to any destination." The *New York Times* picked up the issue with the banner headline "British Group's Sale of Bacteria Stirs Fear of Use by Terrorists."[48] But journalistic vigilance is not enough.

The penultimate conclusion is that it will be impossible to limit recombinant-DNA research simply on the grounds that broad categories of research (e.g., isolation of toxin genes) are intrinsically subject to nefarious use. What is possible is the demand that we pursue only peaceful or health-directed use of such agents.

As long as we fail to reinforce our commitment to the Biological Weapons Convention, we will continue to be severely handicapped in our ability to rein in biological-warfare research. But without substantial strengthening, the convention is likely to continue to be abused.[49] As far as the military is concerned, existing conventions are shot through with loopholes. For many public health officials, distinctions between military and civilian uses of research-derived information are blurred. Some substantial portion of the RAC membership and many government officials either cannot or care not to see any distinction between basic rDNA research that lends itself to military uses and that having a clear public health content. And too many researchers disdain the likelihood of biological-warfare applications, especially in covert operations, in spite of overwhelming evidence to the contrary. This latter view is exemplified by the statement of Johns Hopkins University Professor Gary Ketner, who declared, "My attitude about the whole notion [of biological warfare] is that it's ludicrous, as there are undoubtedly easier ways to make all of the things you can make by recombinant DNA. I don't think rDNA could fundamentally change the way which we conduct warfare."[50]

This state of affairs will remain with us until five things happen:

1. Public health is given a specific priority in all recombinant DNA research.

2. Congress withholds funds from any rDNA study that is not directed to health or peace, in keeping with our treaty commitments.

3. Disincentives are created for research that serves a mix of health and military objectives in favor of projects that are purely health related.

4. The public sector research community refuses to take on classified contracts under the aegis of the Department of Defense.

5. All investigators and their parent organizations and companies decline to enter into Defense Department contracts for work that involves recombinant DNA for augmenting any military capability in violation of convention or law.

The rationale for the first position is fairly simple: scientists performing publicly supported research have what Maxine Singer has termed a basic "responsibility to the public . . . that the results will have a significant positive impact on society."[51] Her view was echoed by an Eastern block counterpart, Professor J. Riman of the Institute of Molecular Genetics and member of the Czech Academy of Science in Prague. Riman declared at a conference celebrating the First Century of Modern Biology that "it is up to us to endeavor in genetics . . . that all practical applications serve solely the peace and prosperity of mankind."[52]

The second and third points are supported by the contention that all the research that has as its primary objective public health, be it the health of civilians or military personnel, is most properly conducted under the auspices of the Department of Health and Human Services. In contrast with the Department of Defense, this agency alone is fully accountable to the public. Thus, as of 1982, the DoD was the only one of twenty-one governmental agencies that had not fully adopted the protocols that protect human subjects against experimental abuse.

With respect to the fourth point, if one wishes to protect against the likelihood of scientific knowledge being misused, open publication of results is mandatory. For work done under the aegis of the NIH and such universities as those in the University of California system, the first step has already been taken: findings from any experiments contracted under the auspices of DoD have to be published in the open literature.

The commitment required by the fifth point—that all recombinant-DNA biologists refuse to engage in classified research—would move those researchers closer to the scientific and medical ideal of doing no intentional harm. (Language to effect this end, although defeated, was presented as a policy statement to the American Society of Microbiology in 1969, during the height of concern about military misuse of scientific research.)

Finally, if major biotechnology firms agreed to refuse Defense Department contracts (a phenomenon now limited to a small number of companies), their stockholders and the public at large might well support such a move. (Were they to do so, it would not necessarily be out of concern for the integrity of science or with the military, but, I suspect, for the much more pragmatic likelihood that any profits would be substantially circumscribed by the Defense Department's traditional low cost-reimbursement programs for vaccines and related products.) In the end, it will be the scientists conducting rDNA research who will carry the moral weight for constraining their activities and channeling them towards greater, rather than lesser, human ends.

Notes

1. Draft letter from M. Lappé to R. Roblin, December 5, 1975.
2. *Convention on the Prohibition of the Development, Production, and Stockpiling of Bacteriological (Biological) and Toxin Weapons and on Their Destruction*, United Nations Treaties in International Agreement Series, TIAS No. 8062 (New York, 1972).
3. Alice Kimball Smith and Charles Weiner, *Robert Oppenheimer: Letters and Recollections* (Cambridge, Mass.: Harvard University Press, 1980).
4. Paul Berg, statements made at a Stanford Conference on Recombinant DNA, April 14, 1977.
5. A. Bayev, "Genetic Engineering and Ethics: Science Is as Science Does," *Development Forum* (September–October 1976): 5.
6. C. Cohen, "When May Research Be Stopped?" *New England Journal of Medicine* 296 (1977): 1203–1210.
7. 47 *Federal Register* 77 at 17186, April 21, 1982.
8. B. Athenson and F. Mavilona Maiituna, eds., *Biochemical Engineering and Biotechnology Handbook* (London: Nature Press, 1983), p. 45.
9. D. P. Rennie et al., "An Immunotoxin of Ricin: *A* Chain Conjugated to Thyroglobulin Selectively Suppresses the Anti-thyroglobulin Auto-antibody Response," *Lancet* II (1983): 1338–1340.
10. J. Larrick, "Beware Cloned Toxins," *Nature* 301 (1983): 651; and K. Coleman, "Toxin Gene Cloning," *Nature* 302 (1983): 649.
11. D. J. Kopecko, L. S. Baron, and K. F. Noon, "Cloning of the Determinants Responsible for Reversible Expression of the Virlence (*Vi*) Antigen of *Citro-bacter freundii*," *Plasmid* 10 (1983): 207.

12. J. B. Kaper et al., "Cloning of Cholera Toxin and Development of a Live Oral Cholera Vaccine," *Plasmid* 10 (1983): 207.

13. J. B. Kaper, H. Lockman, M. M. Baldini, and M. M. Levine, "A Recombinant Live Oral Cholera Vaccine," *Bio/Technology* 2 (1984): 345–349.

14. 49 *Federal Register* 698, January 5, 1984.

15. V. Cohn and P. J. Hills, "Genetic Experiment by Military Approved," *Washington Post* (February 7, 1984), p. 1.

16. Jeffrey L. Fox, "NIH Rejects Modified Plan to Clone *Shiga* Toxin," *Science* 224 (1984): 582.

17. "*Shiga* Toxin: No Smoking," *Science* 223 (1984): 799.

18. O. A. Protsenko et al., "Detection and Characterization of *Yersinia* Pests Plasmides Determining Pesticin I," *Genetika* (Moskva) 19 (1983): 1081–1090; and R. Babour, Y. Laroche, and G. Cornelis, "Study of the Incompatibility and Replication of the 70 kb Virulence Plasmid of *Yersinia*," *Plasmid* 10 (1983): 279–289.

19. Anonymous, "Experts Question Soviet Biowar Build-up," *Bio/Technology* 2 (September 1984): 749.

20. *Textbook of Military Chemistry* (East Germany, 1977), cited in A. Santoli, "How the Soviets Use Chemicals to Wage War," *Parade* (June 26, 1983): 5.

21. W. Kucewicz, "Soviets Search for Eerie New Weapons," *Wall Street Journal* (April 23, 1984), editorial page.

22. "Soviet Military Power," cited by Kucewicz, ibid.

23. R. Zilinskas, "Biotechnology in the USSR," Part I, *Bio/Technology* 2 (July 1984), 610–616.

24. See *Wall Street Journal* for April 23, 25, 27, and May 1 and 3, 1984.

25. W. Kucewicz, "Surveying the Lethal Literature," *Wall Street Journal* (April 27, 1984), editorial page.

26. *Convention on Prohibition,* United Nations Treaties.

27. Ibid.

28. Letter from John L. Allen, deputy director, Research and Advanced Technology, Department of Defense, to L. Douglas DeNike, Ph.D., September 22, 1976.

29. William Beisel, quoted in H. Zochlinski, "Army DNA Researchers Try to Shed Bio-Warrior Image," *Genetic Engineering News* 2 (September/October 1982): 33.

30. Allen, Letter.

31. *Department of Defense Annual Report on Chemical Warfare and Biological Research Programs,* Fy 1981, Section 2, p. 16 (Washington, D.C.: Government Printing Office, December 30, 1981).

32. See M. Lappé, "Biological Warfare," in *The Social Responsibility of the Scientist,* Martin Brown, ed. (New York: The Free Press, 1970).

33. C. Piller, "DNA—Key to Biological Warfare?" *The Nation* (December 10, 1983): 595, 597–601.

34. Robert Mikulak, statement appearing in the minutes of the June 28, 1982, meeting of the RAC, *Recombinant DNA Research,* vol. 7 (Washington, D.C.: Government Printing Office, 1982), p. 464.

35. Letter from Richard Goldstein to Marc Lappé, June 8, 1982.

36. Minutes of the June 28, 1982, RAC meeting, *Recombinant DNA Research,* vol. 7, p. 464.

37. Ibid., p. 466.

38. Cited in James L. George, letter to William J. Gartland, Jr., June 8, 1982.

39. David Baltimore, minutes of June 28, 1982, RAC meeting, *Recombinant DNA Research,* vol. 7, p. 462.

40. Piller, "DNA—Key."

41. See the statement from the U.S. Arms Control and Disarmament Agency as reported in *Nature* 297 (June 24, 1982): 615–616.

42. See, for example, Al Santoli, "How the Soviets Use Chemicals," pp. 5–8.

43. H. Zochlinski, "Biotechnology in Military R&D: Two Firms Look for Future Profits in Joint Projects," *Genetic Engineering News* (March/April 1983): 28.

44. Letter from William R. Beisel to William J. Gartland, Jr., June 9, 1982, *Recombinant DNA Research,* vol. 7, pp. 788–789.

45. Cited in *Genetic Engineering News* (March/April 1983): 29.

46. *Convention on Prohibition,* United Nations Treaties.

47. W. Biddle, "Army Is Requesting $250 Million for Utah Chemical Warfare Unit," *New York Times* (November 2, 1984), p. 10.

48. *New York Times* (February 11, 1977).

49. Susan Wright of the University of Michigan and Robert Sinsheimer, Chancellor of the University of California, Santa Cruz, have argued forcefully for the strengthening of the Biological Weapons Convention, particularly on research and verification to prevent the application of rDNA techniques to weapons development. See S.

Wright and R. L. Sinsheimer, "Recombinant DNA and Biological Warfare," *Bulletin of the Atomic Scientists* (November 1983), p. 28; and the letters, "On Recombinant DNA Technology of Biological Warfare," *Bulletin of the Atomic Scientists* (February 1984): 14, 59–63.

50. Gary Ketner, quoted by H. Zochlinski, "Army DNA Researchers Try to Shed Bio-Warrior Image."

51. Maxine Singer, congressional testimony quoted in *Recombinant DNA Research,* vol. 7, p. 245.

52. J. Riman, "From Mendel to Molecular Genetics and Biotechnologies," *Folia Biologica* (Prague) 29 (1983): 1–8.

CHAPTER 10

Priorities

In spite of industry protestations to the contrary, the potential environmental problems, treaty obligations, and federal regulations have not impeded the development of recombinant-DNA-based technologies in the United States. The evolution of this field has been heavily capitalized and fueled by an extraordinarily broad base of rapid medical and scientific advances. It was the novelty and intellectual challenge of many of these advances that generated the entrepreneurial excitement and enthusiasm for many of the new biotechnology firms. Some of these inventions, such as cell fusion, directed mutations, and cloning of plants and animals, still hold immense potential. Others, such as "single-cell protein" derived from oil as feedstocks or fine chemicals produced from sucrose as a raw material, have fallen by the wayside.[1] Increasing numbers of recombinant-DNA-produced molecules are finding uses in chemical and physical catalytic systems. Future possibilities point-to applications in electronics and space technology. Indeed, wherever microminiaturization, high resolution, and biological specificity are needed, biotechnology offers potential solutions not found elsewhere.

But as J. Coombs, editor of *The International Biotechnology Directory*, has pointed out, "These discoveries can only have an impact where the biological aspects are limiting. At present, the limitations [in achieving these goals] are frequently educational, political or economic. It is a pity if concentration on biotechnology, and the more novel aspects in particular, diverts resources from other more pressing priorities."[2]

Priority setting is only now being recognized as a crucial element of the biotechnology revolution. Just what kinds of forces actually drive the selection of priorities in the biotechnology industry are difficult to discern. But at least some of the major features are evident from discussions with industry leaders.

For some executives, such as J. Leslie Glick of Genex Corporation, the forces are self-evident: profitability, projected market shares, proportionate risks, and potential for growth.[3] In Glick's view, the existence of heavy regulation in areas such as pharmaceuticals serves as a strong disincentive for development. According to Glick, Genex's almost unique concentration on specialty chemicals for use in waste and water treatment, food processing and agricultural products, and mold removal stems from a priority-setting scheme that tends to minimize potential legal pitfalls as well as competition. Genex's priorities are based on three considerations: (1) exclusion of heavily regulated areas; (2) accurate estimation of the size of the market; and (3) projection of the likely competition and hence, Genex's "edge." Obviously, if all research and development in biotechnology took this perspective, we would not see any significant investment in the drug and medical-devices areas. All the same, it is likely that purely financial considerations do play the key determining factors regarding the future of biotechnology—if for no other reason than most of that future is concentrated in the private sector.

For these and related reasons, it is evident that the forces that shape the choices of the private sector will not necessarily select for biotechnological products that have the greatest human benefit. In fact, some observers have noted (not without some irony) the recent emergence of a "junk biotechnology" industry in which manufacturers of snacks, food additives and fragrances, and other nonessential commodities are seizing on rDNA-based products to facilitate production. Companies in this new field emphasize the high profitability of relatively scarce and expensive ("high tech") and small-volume commodities such as flavors, fragrances, and perfumes. The 1984 *International Biotechnology Directory* lists sixty-three firms worldwide, including such major pharmaceutical houses as Hoffman-La Roche and A. H. Robins, as offering such products.

Similarly, major food producers and processors such as Campbell (see Chapter 3) and General Foods have made strong investments in new processes that can increase their efficiency in marketing such new mass products. Nabisco and other major producers of bakery products see a particularly rich opportunity in using rDNA to make artificial fragrances that mimic the smell of fresh baked goods.[4]

Other companies have devised schemes for exploiting biotechnological capabilities in even more marginal areas relative to their ability to meet fundamental human needs. As an example, Frito-Lay Corporation developed what seems now to be an ill-fated idea to use genetic engineering to short-cut major production problems. In the early 1980s, Frito-Lay's management attempted to launch a program to genetically engineer potatoes so that they would contain up to 50 percent less water. Such a transformation had an unusual objective. It was not, as you might think, to make a more nutritive source of carbohydrate and protein. Rather, the Frito-Lay consultants had decided that the principal cost factor in their potato chip division was the transportation of the potatoes themselves. The high weight-per-volume ratio of the potato and the subsequent need for processing to remove unwanted water were the major impediments for efficient production. The Frito-Lay management believed that genetic engineering could reduce the water content of potatoes by half.

The project went on the rocks—and another genetic engineer became a job seeker—when the company's principal scientist suggested that it might not be possible to engineer genetic systems over the short run that could accomplish this major plant-engineering feat. According to my informant (who has asked to remain anonymous), no one ever asked whether or not such an objective was consonant with human nutritional needs. Nor did he think it necessarily should have been. After all, he opined, since when do we hold the food industry in general, and the junk food industry in particular, accountable for the human impact of their production choices?

Goals of the Industry

Recombinant-DNA-based biotechnology industries, like most other innovative new enterprises, are obviously not under any binding convenants directing what they will produce or where they will market their products. Given the universal limits of the antimonopoly and price-fixing statutes, in theory they are as free as any industry to charge "what the market will bear." Indeed, as with many other investments sponsored by venture capitalists, it is predictable that a significant portion of recombinant research will spin off into areas of less than essential but nonetheless lucrative projects. Such projects, like those in the junk biotechnology field, might be vapid but innocuous accidents of supply and demand—or they could represent more ominous diversions of badly needed resources.

The development of hopefully safe nonnutritive sweeteners such as aspartame, and of other genetically engineered ersatz foodstuffs, has spawned an entirely new diet industry. At least three companies listed in the *International Biotechnology Directory*—the Cambridge Plan, Diasan AG of Switzerland, and Anton Hubner KG of West Germany—are currently in the business of using rDNA to make "slimming products." How can one criticize their free choice in an openly competitive market, where consumers are the ultimate arbiter of what sells and what does not?

From a purely ethical perspective, one can argue that where the risks to public welfare from developing products are minimal, the economy has and can tolerate the generation of commodities, such as those listed above, that may be devoid of any intrinsic value beyond their appeal to consumer tastes. Thus, while most of us are mildly annoyed (or amused) at the advent of sugarless nonsticking bubble gum, few would question the propriety of allowing a corporation to develop and promote it.

But we may draw the line where a product is made on such a vast scale that it can only be produced at the expense of other, more essential uses of certain basic resources. Were all fermentation plants being used to make nonessential feedstocks or precursors to products like aspartame, this objection might hold. The more general case, in which companies diversify their products, proves more difficult to assess. A case in point would be the selective investment of genetic-engineering companies into animal hormones or other polypeptides for treating rare human disorders or deficiencies rather than in products that would benefit a broad cross section of humanity.

Malaria Vaccine:
An Example

As shown earlier, the advent of recombinant-DNA technology has offered a relatively safe and sure way to generate vaccines with minimal risks of contamination or infection. A malaria vaccine holds out the greatest promise to relieve human suffering of all those currently being considered. (Malarial parasites cause illness in some 200 million people worldwide, and kill a million children in Africa alone.) For the last 19 years, an answer has been sought under the aegis of the U.S. Agency for International Development, which has doubled its investment in malaria vaccine research from $11.9 million to $22.7 million over the years 1983–1985.

While developing a vaccine has proven problematic (as we discussed in Chapters 3 and 4) owing to the different forms the parasite assumes, scientists in Australia, England, and the United States have now isolated the antigens from at least two of its stages (sporozoite and gametocyte). In particular, the work of husband and wife team Drs. Victor and Ruth Nussenzweig of New York University has brought us to the threshold of technical feasibility for making an effective vaccine.[5]

It is against this backdrop that New York University and the World Health Organization approached Genentech to assist in actually marketing a vaccine prototype. One of WHO's conditions was that the public have access to any research it would sponsor. Genentech wanted exclusive rights to the vaccine to protect its investment. According to published accounts, this impasse led to Genentech's withdrawal from the project.[6] But the actual story is more complex.

In early 1984, Genentech's vice president for research, David W. Martin, Jr., gave the Committee on Issues and Priorities for New Vaccine Development of the Institute of Medicine, a study committee of the NAS, an explanation of his company's reasons for declining.[7]

Martin highlighted three main points in his position statement:

1. The company was young and inexperienced.
2. It was underfinanced.
3. It could not afford to take risks.

Martin pointed out that the products that Genentech intends to manufacture had been carefully selected to provide their stockholders with a significant return on investment. He described Genentech as a "young and small" company. (In fact, it is among the three largest genetic-engineering companies in the world—and according to its 1982 annual report, capitalized with at least $85 million of shareholder's equity.) In spite of Genentech's substantial capitalization, Martin argued that the firm "has insufficient discretionary resources to provide for the development and manufacture of products for which the market is ill-defined, diffuse and dependent upon governmental sponsorship or advertising."[8] The market for a malaria vaccine covers at least 200 million people in the developing world and is very well defined in both WHO and CDC publications.[9]

Genentech addressed the "humanitarian" side of the argument in its corporate decision-making process by comparing different societal goals. According to Martin, "Clearly there is the humanitarian issue, but it was concluded that the necessity to displace other potential products (also having humanitarian value) from our development and manufacturing resources might jeopardize the future of the Company, including the malaria vaccine itself."[10] (He had presented a more candid rationale on the previous page: "we are forced at this stage of our corporate development to compare vaccines with other opportunities. The Company does not have the resources such that it can afford to take extraordinary risks.")

But Genentech clearly took such a risk with its Factor VIII project. What was the difference? One clue can be seen in their board of director's annual report of 1982. As stated on page 3 of this report, "Genentech's goal is to obtain the highest return on its substantial research investment by manufacturing and marketing the products it develops. Toward this end, the Company has focused on products that will allow early market entry."[11]

The annual report also highlighted American Association for the Advancement of Science (AAAS) President Phillip Abelson's controversial endorsement of Genentech's "judicious choice of projects to tackle."[12] The company's priority-setting scheme clearly did not include the choice of a malaria vaccine—in part, according to Martin, because the market for such a vaccine was too "diffuse and global." Martin cited Genentech's "limited familiarity with regulation, marketing and distribution in foreign countries," although this has not been an obstacle to Genentech's collaborative development (with Eli Lilly) of insulin in the world market. Some of Genentech's motives with malaria were alleged to be self-protective, since Martin implied a malaria project might bankrupt the company.

Martin's paper concluded with a clear-cut statement of preference. The bottom line, in Martin's candid monograph, was simple: "Thus it seemed apparent that the development of a malaria vaccine would not be compatible with Genentech's business strategy."[13]

So here was a clear instance where the world may have been denied—in the short run, at least[14]—a critical commodity from a company that had its roots in public investments in basic scientific research.

Dislocation

Priority schemes for rDNA projects that rely on this type of "business necessity" argument also raise the question of how much the issue of social dislocation is considered by biotechnology firms. Some critics have cautioned that major investments in rDNA industries can cause social disruptions in less-developed economies. The introduction of hybrid seeds by companies under the control of a few multinational corporations can make small farmers dependent on outside corporate interests at the expense of self-sufficiency and can displace ecologically important traditional seed varieties.[15]

The displacement of traditional sugar commodities by biotechnology-assisted production of high-fructose corn sugars constitutes a second example of potentially adverse social dislocation. Using immobilized enzymes and the conversion of sucrose to fructose through direct bioengineering—as yet unsuccessful in full—the rDNA industry has augmented the displacement of sugars that have been largely produced by less developed countries. Because high-fructose corn syrups are capital intensive rather than labor intensive, they are more commonly produced in developed countries. Given import quotas and the traditional volatility of the sugar market, the United States is acting in ways that further displace cane and other Third World sugar crops with high-fructose corn sweeteners produced under industrial conditions. The possibility that such displacement may also increase the frequency of certain diet-dependent diseases such as diabetes[16] and coronary artery disease (a point discussed in Chapter 11) further reinforces the argument against allowing such major transistions to occur without close public scrutiny.

Public Involvement

If the selection of rDNA products were found to supplant more valuable uses of essential basic resources, this confirmation would constitute another reason for allowing public inspection of the industry. Such a phenomenon may be occurring with the current expansion of the fermentation industry's production plans to convert grains into alcohol and single amino acids into animal feed supplements or feedstocks for chemical reactions. Some of these amino acids, such as lysine and methionine, are intrinsically valuable as human as well as animal nutritional additives, since they supplement the major amino acid deficiencies of cereal grains. Others, such as the phenylalanine and aspartic acid used to make the nonnutritive sugar aspartame, are valuable substrates for pharmaceutical products or building blocks for small, pharmacologically active polypeptides.

The fact that the major producers of these commodities, by pursuing their efforts, divert significant resources away from their more traditional fermentation products also deserves comment.

Ajinomoto and Suntory, the major producers of these amino acids in Japan, have historically been among Japan's natural resources—developing fermentation systems for soy and rice products. In contrast to their more recent ventures (e.g., Suntory's whiskey-production work), the conversion of soy beans into a high-protein paste (tofu) has provided a mainstay of the nutritional base for a large percentage of the Japanese population.

In the absence of public input regarding the priorities that industry should follow, it is highly likely that investments will continue to be made that are proportional to economic gains and not necessarily to public benefit. As Sheldon Krimsky has pointed out, "If social priorities are not set for the use of rDNA technology, then the public will miss out on important applications which private markets will not find profitable to pursue."[17] Krimsky cites the example of "orphan drugs" that have stood by the wayside, waiting for a more profitable picture to assure their development.

One solution has been suggested by the influential scientific planner Carl-Goran Hédèn, of the Karolinska Institute in Stockholm. Hédèn has declared that rDNA technologies should be given an important role in stimulating the development of novel sources of fuel, fertilizer, food, and fodder for the developing countries. Writing in 1981 for the United Nations' Industrial Development Organization (UNIDO),[18] Hédèn proposed that biotechnology could serve the public good most by harnessing natural systems that could provide direct benefits to people in underdeveloped nations. This view of biotechnology is at variance with the commercial view, since it requires investments in basic science as well as start-up costs—and promises very little return.

But in a world of supply and demand, in which market forces are allowed to shape the distribution and sales of even so basic a commodity as wheat, how can the claim be made that rDNA-based investments or processes warrant a closer scrutiny? From a public policy perspective, researchers Diana Dutton and Halstead Holman of Stanford have argued that priority setting for any innovation that has massive potential for good or evil warrants public involvement. They also argue that rDNA in particular warrants this public involvement, because the science in question is publicly financed and uses other publicly supported knowledge to generate new technologies. Under these conditions, Dutton and Holman maintain that "the fruits of science are a public possession and their distribution a matter of public concern."[19]

A case in point has been the evolution of controls of the nuclear energy industry. Once entirely within the military sector, the shift first to a civilian control agency (the Atomic Energy Commission) and ten to a presumptively publicly responsive agency (the Nuclear Regulatory Commission) has been predicated in part on the congressional perception of the need for public oversight. This oversight, at least in the civilian uses of nuclear energy, has been instrumental in assuring at least a modicum of rationality in the controlled evolution of this technology.

Such oversight is particularly important in critical industries like biotechnology, where the diversion of critically needed resources and the usurpation of others contribute to potentially large opportunity costs. When one of the major biotechnology companies decides not to pursue certain objectives (e.g., the development of a malaria vaccine), other smaller companies shy away from related projects. Though firms may justify their decisions not to pursue beneficial courses by citing their need to avoid risk and minimize capital outlays, this is a weak rationale indeed for deflecting current activities away from needed long-term objectives.

If only those rDNA products that could be rapidly developed with minimal regulatory oversight were pursued, major advances in medicine would stagnate. Biotechnology firms might do well to heed *Science* correspondent and author Nicholas Wade: "The proponents of genetic engineering should not let near-term goals, such as profits and research goals, outweigh long-term risks if they wish their craft to enjoy a long run."[20]

Arguments for Priority Setting

At root, two arguments for moving away from the present laissez-faire regulation philosophy, which allows the biotechnology industry to be controlled primarily by market forces, appear cogent and justified. Both evoke the principle of equity. The first hinges on a growing consensus that equity should be a major determinant in the distribution of the results of any new medical research. This view was underscored by the President's Commission when it wrote of the imperative to assure to all groups in society equal access to the benefits of medical research.[21] The basis for a similar assertion in the instance of recombinant-DNA-based technologies turns on something more than a simple restatement of the investment principle: that because public funds were used to develop this technology, the public at large, as much as any late-comer entrepreneur, deserves a portion of the proceeds and benefits. The additional argument is that recombinant-DNA-based research may often be the *only* vehicle to solving life-threatening probs involving major diseases, resources, or energy availability— all of which are unequally distributed among the poor and Third World nations.

A second argument turns on the legitimacy of the assertion that the biotechnology industry has a special obligation to recognize the distributional aspects of human need when determining its internal priorities. These aspects are linked more firmly to the degree of need than to the ability to pay. When considering the possibility that biotechnology would someday modify the course of human genetic disease, for example, the President's Commission argued that we have a fundamental obligation to use genetic technologies to protect or improve the health of children consistent with "an adequate minimum of health care" as measured across the needs of the population as a whole.[22]

Ultimately, the acceptance of a comparable principle of equity in the distribution of the broad spectrum of technological benefits that might come from rDNA research depends on society's commitment to distributional justice. But where does the locus of responsibility for effecting such ends lie? Sheldon Krimsky asserts that it is government's responsibility "to guide the benefits so that they are at least shared equitably and at most shared in a manner that narrows distributional gaps." Among the examples he cites are the need to ensure that small farmers are not disadvantaged by being denied access to new strains of genetically engineered seed stocks, that consumers get better quality products at more reasonable prices, and that environmental health is not traded off for higher rates of return to the producer.[23]

These observations suggest the existence of a hierarchy of principles that can guide the priority-setting process. One such hierarchy I have advocated[24] is based on a schema developed by ethicist William Frankena. In his book *Ethics,* Frankena lists in descending order four priorities for actions that potentially effect the well-being of others: (1) avoid the imposition of harm; (2) reduce the likelihood of harmful consequences; (3) mitigate harmful effects; and (4) do good.[25] In the context of priorities for rDNA technology, these ideals would appear to have been partially

met: attempts to ensure the safe development of the field
have been made, and tests to assure that adverse consequences—for example, from environmental release—
have now, it appears, at least been required. But this rank-
ing does not go far enough to provide positive guidance
about what should be done with the benefits of the research.

Whether the benefits of rDNA technology reduce or
exacerbate existing inequities in the distribution of essential
world resources depends on a complex mix of political and
economic realities. A more radical construction would require the benefits of rDNA technology to be shaped to
fundamental social and ethical ends. These ends would
include uses that contribute to (1) a basic minimum of
health and well-being among the world community; (2)
more equitable control and distribution of production of
essential commodities and resources; and (3) a redress of
the inequalities of distribution of basic foodstuffs and medicines that now characterize much of the developing world.

Of course, it is beyond the ability of any single technology
to achieve these ideals itself. But it appears reasonable to ask
that a technology largely developed with public funds and in
the domain of critical medical innovation choose its ends
with the public weal in view. These observations reinforce
the desirability of public oversight like the Gore committee
(see below) and involvement (e.g., through such organizations as APHA and AAAS, with their broad public mem-
berships). And certainly it is reasonable to ask that a new
technological development not exacerbate existing inequalities.

We can examine a list of possible interventions to determine where rDNA technology can be responsive to inequalities. A major step in this direction was taken at a
workshop called "Priorities in Biotechnology Research for
International Development" held in Washington, D.C., and

Berkeley Springs, West Virginia, from July 26 to 30, 1982. While participants at this workshop came from developed as well as developing countries, the specific objectives they identified reflect a common commitment to priorities that meet the needs of Third World countries. They gave highest priority to developing vaccines against human diseases, such as dengue, bacterial respiratory and enteric diseases, malaria, and leishmaniasis, which are most common in the underdeveloped world. The animal diseases were likewise those that caused the greatest depredations of livestock in developing countries. An examination of the rDNA research priorities identified in the Smithsonian Science Information Exchange (SSIE) for 1979–1981 suggests that the workshop's objectives and those of the rDNA research community do not jibe. Out of 1,529 public sector rDNA-related research programs cited by SSIE, only 16 (1 percent) dealt with vaccine development of which 4 were veterinary and 12 human. Three of these 12 were DoD-sponsored projects.[26]

The agricultural priorities for crop plants named at the workshop reflected a concern that development-assistance agencies provide mechanisms to ensure the equitable distribution of rDNA-related developments. For instance, among their overall recommendations, the participants advised that funding agencies give "highest priority to proposals that include provisions ensuring that the products of tissue culture technology reach farmers and consumers" in the developing countries.[27]

But we have good reason and better evidence to suggest that the immediate benefits from recombinant-DNA technologies in both the health and agricultural sectors (with the notable exception of a cholera vaccine that may be rapidly marketed) are unlikely to trickle down to Third World countries during the 1980s. Martin Kenney, of Cornell University, believes that this eventuality is highly unlikely, based on his Marxist economic analysis of biotechnology developments. According to Kenney, biotechnology is most likely to be used to "strengthen control over farmers and workers"[28] rather than to provide benefits to the people of Third World countries.

Recently, two groups met to determine the priorities that would be the most desirable for Third World countries were biotechnology to be expanded to centers outside the United States, Europe, and Russia. The Council on International and Public Affairs in conjunction with the International Center for Law in Development proposed four objectives for such a study:

1. To increase the equitable access of developing countries to the fruits of biotechnology;

2. To reduce external dependency on utilizing biotechnological advances to meet indigenous needs of food, energy, and related fields;

3. To keep close watch on the social and economic consequences for the poor that flow from the introduction of these new technologies;

4. To enlarge the scope of public participation in decision making about biotechnology, particularly for communities that are now disenfranchised by their position in the marketplace.[29]

The objectives of this joint work suggest a common recognition of at least two of the themes stressed in this book: the claim for equity and the interest in increasing the scope of public involvement in oversight and decision making.

Solutions to Oversight

Now such an oversight committee appears within reach. Under the authorship of Senator Albert Gore (D-Tennessee), a special commission is planned that will review the ethical implications of recombinant-DNA-based applications. Its purview is likely to be limited to medical applications and interventions for human genetic disease, or screening for genetically based predisposition to disease, but it will have the potential for overseeing a much wider swathe of biotechnology. Senator Gore invoked the past history of nuclear energy regulation in arguing the merits of this commission.[30]

But rDNA is not nuclear energy. The degree of hazard posed by uncontrolled use is nowhere near that posed by even the "peaceful" uses of the atom. And the benefits of this technology, like those from its near cousin the fermentation industry, will flow towards *some* publicly valued end whether so shaped or not. The immensely successful development of antibiotic-producing cultures of microorganisms that has provided the backbone of the pharmaceutical industry for decades is a case in point. Under public oversight we would not rein in fermentation systems simply because they are used to make beer!

These limitations notwithstanding, I would endorse the President's Commission conclusion that continuing public involvement is not only desirable but necessary to ensure that the industry is responsive to public needs and that its evolution occurs in public view. In concluding its 1982 report, the commission declared, "Assuming that [rDNA] research will continue somewhere, it seems more prudent to encourage its development and control under the sophisticated and responsive regulatory arrangements of this country, subject to the scrutiny of a free press and within the general framework of democratic institutions."[31]

Solutions

Clearly, something beyond passive oversight is needed to ensure that "enlightened self-interest" does not blindly direct all major policy decisions. One solution is to change the market conditions themselves to favor those investments that would best serve the public interest. Some have suggested that such priority-facilitating schemes could be patterned after the Orphan Drug Act, which gave pharmaceutical giants incentives to develop commodities with limited market potential.[32]

If the unwillingness of Genentech to pursue broad public health goals like the malaria vaccine is representative of a general phenomenon, marketing incentives may be needed to allow small biotechnology companies to devote a significant portion of their limited resources to products with major long-term public health values. Biotechnological products have the potential of affecting the health of every major population group on earth. But as long as biotechnology companies "must" opt for financial security, this opportunity will be lost.

The federal government clearly has the power to assist in providing support for biotechnology firms, perhaps by giving special incentives for investment. International cooperation may also be needed, as when WHO strategy made possible the eradication of smallpox. Given the unique origins and sometimes exclusive values of recombinant-DNA-based biotechnology, powerful moral arguments exist to encourage these developments.

Notes

1. See in particular the report of the failure of the large-scale British Imperial Chemical Industries (ICI) effort to produce single-cell protein cited in Martin Sherwood, "The Money-Hungry Microbe," *Bio/Technology* 2 (July 1984): 606–609.

2. J. Coombs, editor "Overview," *The International Biotechnology Directory* (London, New York: Nature Press, 1984), p. 3.

3. Telephone interview with J. Leslie Glick, CEO, Genex Corporation, February 10, 1984.

4. Burke Zimmerman, personal communication, January 23, 1984.

5. Other major investigators include Dr. Sidney Cohen of Guy's Hospital, London; Drs. J. B. Darbe and T. T. McCathan, NIH and NIADID, Bethesda, Maryland; and Drs. A. Kilejean and S. Chem of the Public Health Research Institute, New York.

6. See "Genetic Engineering Makes Malaria Vaccine Possible," *Cincinatti Enquirer* (July 3, 1984), pp. A-1, A-8.

7. D. W. Martin, Jr., "Issues in Vaccine Development from the Perspective of a 'New Biotechnology Based Company,'" paper presented to the Committee on Issues and Priorities for New Vaccine Development, Institute of Medicine, NAS, Washington, D.C., 1984.

8. Ibid., p. 4.

9. See in particular, vol. 29 of the *American Journal of Tropical Medicine and Hygiene* (1980), which presents a symposium on "DNA Technology and Parasites." For discussion of the WHO Special Program for Research and Training in Targetted Diseases of the Third World, see *Tropical Diseases Today—The Challenge and the Opportunity* (Geneva: WHO, 1975); and *Transactions of the Royal Society of Tropical Medicine and Hygiene* 73 (1979): 147–149.

10. Martin, "Issues," p. 5.

11. Genentech, Inc., *Annual Report* (South San Francisco, Calif.: 1983), p. 3.

12. P. H. Abelson, "New Biotechnology Companies," *Science* 219 (1983): 609.

13. Martin, "Issues," p. 6.

14. Martin states on p. 6 that Genentech would continue to assist the Nussenzweigs "informally" so that a vaccine might be developed "at another institution."

15. C. Fowler, "Sowing the Seeds of Destruction," *Science for the People* (September/October 1980): 8–10.

16. This possibility is suggested by A. M. Cohen, A. Teitelbaum, and E. Rosenmann, "Diabetes Following a High Fructose Diet," *Metabolism* 26 (1977): 17–21.

17. S. Krimsky, "Biotechnology and Unnatural Selection: The Social

Control of Genes," in *Technology and Social Change in Rural Areas,* Gene F. Summers, ed. (Boulder, Colo.: Westview Press, 1983).

18. Carl-Goran Hédèn, United Nations Industrial Development Organization (UNIDO), Report No. 261, New York, November 27, 1981.

19. H. R. Holman and D. B. Dutton, "A Case for Public Participation in Science Policy Formation and Practice," *Southern California Law Review* 51 (1978): 1520.

20. N. Wade, "The Question of Genetic Tinkering," *Technology Illustrated* 6 (November 1983): 67.

21. President's Commission for the Study of Ethical Problems in Medicine and Biomedical and Behavioral Research, *Splicing Life* (Washington, D.C.: U.S. Government Printing Office, 1982), pp. 51 ff.

22. Ibid., p. 66.

23. Krimsky, "Biotechnology and Unnatural Selection," p. 57.

24. M. Lappé, "Values and Public Health: Value Considerations in Setting Health Policy," *Theoretical Medicine* 4 (1983): 71–92.

25. William Frankena, *Ethics* (Englewood Cliffs, N.J.: Prentice-Hall, 1973).

26. *Smithsonian Science Information Exchange,* Smithsonian Institute (Washington, DC, 1982.)

27. *Priorities in Biotechnology: Research for International Development* (Washington, D.C.: National Academy Press, 1982), p. 17.

28. M. Kenney, "Is Biotechnology a Blessing for the Less Developed Nations?" *Monthly Review* 34 (1983): 10–19.

29. International Center for Law in Development and Council on International and Public Affairs, "Work on Biotechnology and the Third World," undated publication distributed by the Council on International and Public Affairs, 777 United Nations Plaza, New York, NY 10017.

30. A. Gore (D-Tenn.), "Regulation of Biotechnology," *Science* 225 (1984): 6.

31. President's Commission, *Splicing Life,* p. 78.

32. See, for example, "Gene-Splicing Protein to Have Orphan Drug Status," *Science* 223 (1984): 914, for a report of the first such application of this act to an rDNA technology.

CHAPTER 11

Ethical Issues

The biotechnology industry has come to see its major ethical problem as diffusing the public's concerns for the impact of its work. According to biotechnology industry representative Harvey Price, director of the Industrial Biotechnology Association, the future success of the industry as a whole depends on winning public acceptance for its programs.[1] That Price's concern is real is documented by a Yankelovich poll. Sponsored by an unnamed consortium of biotechnology and other high-tech companies, the pollsters found that nearly two-thirds (62 percent) of the people sampled believed that American society should proceed cautiously in encouraging biotechnological innovations, with almost a third (31 percent) expressing concern that the risks of biotechnology may outweigh its benefits.[2]

Some of the public's concern focuses on what Dr. Williard Gaylin, president of the Hastings Center, a bioethics think tank in Hastings-on-Hudson, New York, calls "the Frankenstein factor."[3] For many people, the dominant ethical issues are the possibility that recombinant DNA will be used to modify human beings and inevitably subvert our basic social institutions by shifting us towards accepting genetic modification of people.

These views are fueled by a growing literature that portrays scientists as "playing God" and manipulating or distorting nature through genetic techniques.[4] But the public is equally concerned with the more imminent (and more likely) applications of biotechnology. Yankelovich found that the majority of his sample understood that the most important application of biotechnology was the development of health products. But many such applications raise major questions of their own. What are the most appropriate uses of new recombinant-DNA diagnostic techniques in prenatal tests? How should we guide the development of predictive tests that can be used to define our genetic legacy to our children or our physical qualifications for health insurance or employment? As we saw in the preceding chapter, the President's Commission has raised the legitimate claim of the underprivileged and the poor for an equal share of the fruits of biotechnological research. Other questions include how we are to assess the different priorities that might be pursued in agriculture, medicine, and energy generally.

At its most basic level, biotechnology raises questions of freedom of inquiry, the balance of benefits to risks, costs to the public as a whole, public participation and involvement in decision making, and the legitimacy and scope of governmental regulation. Each of these issues is important on its own, and each has been prominent during various phases of the recombinant-DNA debate. For the mid-1980s through the end of the century, the ethical issues of greatest moment will turn on the answers to three interrelated questions:

> 1. In what way, if any, can the biotechnology industry be said to have a special obligation to serve the public beyond that created

through the delivery of products
manufactured in response to market forces?

2. Does the biotechnology industry have any
   special duty to enhance the advancement of
   freedom of inquiry specifically and scientific
   knowledge generally?

3. Does the biotechnology industry have a
   particular obligation to anticipate and offset
   large-scale adverse effects of its
   developments that escape existing oversight
   or controls?

Implicit in each of these inquiries is the suggestion that
companies or entrepreneurs that rely on recombinant-DNA
technology should be held to a different—and higher—
standard than the rest of the technical world. The coun-
terclaim to this view is simply that existing federal and state
statutes in conjunction with the NIH Guidelines provide
more than an equitable and adequate safeguard for regulating the industry. It has been argued that to apply a more
stringent standard to recombinant-DNA enterprises is
intrinsically unfair, since the rest of the corporate world is
limited only by existing laws governing antitrust, product
safety, and environmental impact.

Why should we apply a special standard to recombinant-
DNA entrepreneurs? We can find the answer easily in the
social history of the field, its present state of development,
and the special qualities of the products it produces.

Social History

The principal developments that made the entire
field of applied rDNA technology feasible evolved under
the aegis of public funding agencies. This fact was under-

scored in conversations I held early in 1977 with Dr. David Martin, professor of medicine (with a joint appointment in biochemistry and biophysics) at the University of California, San Francisco. At that time, Martin was seriously concerned about the movement of cultures of plasmid-containing organisms from a UCSF laboratory to the then fledgling biotechnology firm Genentech. For Martin, who at the time was director of the local biosafety committee, this transfer raised troubling questions, because the material had been developed under the aegis of an NIH grant. The matter was resolved "internally" with UCSF accepting a settlement from Genentech.

Other examples of concern center on the propriety of allowing nonprofit institutions such as universities to profit from inventions made under the auspices of federal grant support. The tenor of this concern can be found in correspondence between the NIH and key genetic-engineering firms. On September 7, 1976, Donald Fredrickson, M.D., the director of NIH, wrote to Ronald Cape, president of Cetus Corporation, about the knotty question of how to encourage development of biotechnology while respecting the special requirements for safety and public accountability.[5] Fredrickson's letter solicited Cape's views on the question of handling patent rights. According to Fredrickson, the unique origins of recombinant DNA had forced the NIH to reconsider its usual policy of allocating invention rights to its grantees.

In the patent application from Stanford University and the University of California on the process for creating DNA recombinants, Fredrickson observed that "this invention was generated in performance of an NIH grant" and implied that direct patenting with exclusive royalty rights going to Stanford would be unacceptable. Fredrickson asked Cape to provide him with comments on the present and proposed institutional policy that would encourage more equity in the distribution of rDNA patent benefits.

Fredrickson pointed out that under NIH rules a non-profit institution may enhance its "technology transfer capability" by entering into an Institutional Patent Agreement. Under the terms of this agreement, the institution is entitled to ownership of its inventions as long as it meets several key conditions. Among the most important are (1) that it provide the government and any agency or institution that functions under its aegis a royalty-free license to practice the invention; (2) that it sign a limited-term agreement for exclusive licensing; (3) that it allow for NIH's prerogative to withdraw specified grants from the agreement; and (4) that it allow NIH or other federal departments to regain its ownership of the patent en bloc if such were deemed to be in the public interest. Ironically, the federal government has never activated this last provision, in spite of increasing evidence of the public interest in controlling at least some of the applications of biotechnology.

The major public value of patents, according to Fredrickson, was that the ensured that uniform—and presumably safe—recombinant-DNA procedures would be used. Fredrickson pointed out that the NIH Guidelines envisioned a "delicate balance between (the) need for rapid exchange of information unhampered by undue concern for patent rights and a potential for achieving uniformity in safety practices through conditions of licensure under patent agreement."[6] In light of the special public interest in the fruits of this research—and in its safe undertaking—Fredrickson proposed the following five types of patenting:

1. No patents on rDNA work, relying instead on publication to cut off all possible competing ("adverse") patent claims.

2. File patents, but dedicate all issued patents to the public.

3. Assign all inventions (and by inference the patent rights to them) to the federal government.

4. Permit institutions to patent under the conditions of an Institutional Patent Agreement (see the four points outlined above), but with conditions to be set by the department.

5. Same as in 4, but with the permission for exclusive licenses to the institution.

From these itemized conditions, and the bulk of the remainder of Fredrickson's letter, it is clear that the NIH recognized that almost all the facilitating techniques for allowing the first recombinant DNAs to be produced were developed with public support. This fact justified the NIH's proposal to the industry to return some or all of the controls and rights to these inventions to the public. Any of the first four options would have accomplished this goal. But it was the fifth that the NIH finally agreed to.

On March 2, 1978, Fredrickson confirmed Stanford's exclusive right to a patent on the Cohen-Boyer technique to persons or corporations that are in accord with the NIH Guidelines.[7] While the NIH apparently abdicated its position on public control via patents, many of its officers, like Fredrickson, did not believe they were relinquishing the public's right to receive returns from the fruits of biotechnology research. But even a generous interpretation of subsequent events suggests that in 1985 the public is still far from receiving the full benefits of rDNA research.

Serving the Public Good

The proposition that the rDNA industry has a special obligation to serve the public good depends on the special nature of the research and its origins. Sheldon Krimsky, author of *Genetic Alchemy*, has argued that the public has a right to a say in the selection of priorities for rDNA research. This obligation itself hinges on the fact that public monies were the principal source of funds for the development of rDNA methods. A corollary to this position is that the public is entitled to a just return on its investment.[8]

A second argument for the special moral position of the biotechnology industry is that rDNA-based work creates an unprecedented opportunity for benefiting humanity. We have seen that recombinant DNA now offers an extraordinarily broad array of novel innovations to assist humanity. As suggested by the Genentech malaria decision, much research and product development now proceeds without serious consideration of the broadest possible social goals they could serve. Disregard or de-emphasis of humanitarian concerns allows potentially large portions of biotechnology resources to be channeled away from difficult areas such as vaccine development and to areas that serve a smaller portion of the public (e.g., hemophiliacs) but offer greater returns on investment.

A third argument for the special status of recombinant-DNA-based biotechnology involves simple promise keeping. In the early days of the rDNA debate (circa 1973–1977), some of the advocates, and later benefactors, of this technology testified that their work was developed to serve the public good. In the hearings that I organized in California in early 1977, when asked if recombinant-DNA technologies would be likely to generate significant public health benefits, key scientists such as Maxine Singer, Paul

Berg, and Genentech founder Herbert Boyer answered in the affirmative (and, I should add, they were right). Boyer, in particular, averred that he saw this end as being facilitated by allowing the free transfer of ideas from the public to the private sector.

Proponents of biotechnology argued that allowing the free evolution of this technology without the fetters of extra regulation was the only way to assure public benefits. State Assemblyman Barry Keene (D) accepted this rationale as a bona fide reason for holding back on additional controls, such as requiring industry compliance with the NIH Guidelines for state licensure or establishing a watchdog committee to oversee the industry as a whole. These and related claims of the linkage between limiting research restrictions and optimizing public benefits were repeated in publications and in testimony given in both federal and state proceedings by many recombinant-DNA scientists, including codiscoverer of the recombinant-DNA process Stanley Cohen.[9]

It is probably unreasonable to hold these spokespersons accountable for the subsequent performance of an entire industry. But we could justifiably ask the major biotechnology firms now to provide evidence of good faith by assigning a portion of their patent royalties or a small percentage of their profits to a public corporation or appropriate nonprofit institution. (In fact, Stanford University has done just that in asking for $10,000 for limited license rights to the Cohen-Boyer patent, and another 0.1 percent of corporate profits from its application in a commercial process.) Even biotechnology supporter David Baltimore admits that "it seems grossly unfair that a small number of people benefit enormously from the development of this technology, never mind whether it was funded privately or publicly."[10]

Such beneficence from biotechnology is not an impossibility. At least one biotechnology firm, New England Bio-labs of Beverly, Massachusetts, under the leadership of Don Coomb, already gives a substantial portion of its profits to fund research and conferences on Third World diseases. According to Coomb, thirteen of its seventy employees presently work full or part time on projects related to malaria or filiariasis, two of the most significant causes of morbidity in the Third World.[11] And, to be fair, such companies as Chiron of Emeryville that championed the successful development of the first hepatitis B vaccines have done so in the public interest. But there is no way to ensure the continuation of this fledgling and underrepresented trend without public input into the priorities of the biotechnology industry as a whole.

Impediments Posed by the Business Ethic

Part of the dilemma in implementing such an idealistic scheme is that the public no longer has the leverage it once had when the NIH was the only game in town. Now it is universities such as Columbia (which has the Axel, Silverstein, and Wigler patent that uses a two-step process to assist in isolation of rDNA clones[12]) and Stanford (which has the Cohen-Boyer patent on both the psc101 plasmid and, more recently, the process of creating rDNA vectors) that hold the cards. According to Senator Albert Gore, "arrangements that are being made by contract, between private corporations and the universities, present the problem that corporations may be receiving the fruits of public investments, and then selling the public those breakthroughs back again. So the public pays twice."[13]

The immense infusion of private capital into rDNA technology poses a major ethical dilemma. As we saw in the last chapter, the conditions of the marketplace are to a greater or lesser degree the limiting factors in the priority-setting regimes of many, if not most, of the major genetic-technology firms. As Biogen's Walter Gilbert put it, "The role of the [biotechnology] company is to move a technology from the laboratory . . . out into production and exploitation of the world. The work we do in the company has to be something that has direct social value next year, or three years from now, not something of social value twenty years from now, we cannot take that long time-frame; we have to focus on the immediate."[14]

While such a reality is certainly common to the entrepreneurial mode, it is certainly neither a universal rule nor even the best way to conduct a successful business venture (witness Mitsubishi and GM, both of which have ten- and twenty-year plans). It is likely that regulatory requirements and economic factors constitute forces of natural selection that drive a portion of investments away from those sectors that are in the public interest. This is because the areas of greatest regulation are almost always those of greatest public concern for their efficacy and safety. Pharmaceutical agents, medical devices, and foods are all areas in which the American public traditionally has had a large stake. Biotechnology firms' increasingly common tendency to test and develop their products abroad violates the spirit and intent (if not the letter) of our food and drug regulations and thereby undercuts part of this public charge.

Similarly, while many successful pharmaceutical agents serve a public need, the most profitable products for any given year are almost always those used to treat the diseases of advanced societies (e.g., Tagamet, an anti-ulcer medication; Valium, a tranquilizer; and Naprosyn, an anti-inflammatory agent). Not coincidentally, those recombinant-DNA companies that have major pharmaceutical programs have tailored their product development to drugs with the greatest markets, not the greatest need. This dichotomy nonetheless reflects a problem for society in assuring the fair and equitable development of critically important drugs based on some formula of need. In turn, the absence of incentives for the innovation of drugs and vaccines of major health importance constitutes a major regulatory failure on the part of the federal government. (While some progress in underwriting "orphan drugs" may be occurring in the biotechnology industry, the support is barely sufficient to warrant enthusiasm.[15])

Members of the scientific community as a whole have begun to recognize the need for a broader, more coordinated program. The National Academy of Sciences, under the direction of Dr. Roy Widdus, has prepared a document that addresses the question of innovation in vaccine development with an eye to improving the investment picture for the biotechnology industry as a whole.[16]

A related argument for the special standing of this industry is that some biotechnology products (e.g., cellulose-degrading enzymes) can only be made through the use of a certain technical capability or—in some cases—the specific patented invention, held by a member of the biotechnology community. But it is in the nature of the things that rDNA can produce that many commodities will be valuable and often irreplaceable substances that cannot be made by other means (e.g., a detoxified *Vibrio cholerae* vaccine). Other substances, though isolatable by other means, are now too dangerous or expensive to be isolated (e.g., Factor VIII, the clotting factor for hemophiliacs that may be seriously compromised by the risk of AIDS). This observation suggests that rDNA-based technology firms have a special obligation to the public.

The theory of special obligation also rests on the premise

that the material being manipulated is in some fundamental sense the "property" of all of the organisms that share a common genome. Thus, a patent on the production of recombinant-DNA probes that use the human insulin gene relies on the novel use of a set of base sequences that can be said to be the common property of all persons. As MIT's Jonathan King has said, "We are all one species, we are all interfertile. And I am very, very uncomfortable with the thought of any aspect of human DNA . . . becoming private or corporate institutional property. They are part of the heritage of the whole species."[17]

Unanticipated Adverse Effects

Present loopholes in the regulation of the private sector as well as the economic imperatives that drive the industry create a climate in which unanticipated adverse effects are almost inevitable. As embodied in the congressional intent of the various acts protecting the physical and natural environment (such as TSCA, FIFRA, the Clean Air and Water Acts, etc.), the public is entitled to strong protections against malfeasance or negligent though unintended harm stemming from product defects, unsafe drugs, or environmental contamination.

There is a common myth that these statutes provide ample legal protections to ensure that rDNA developments will proceed safely. The gradual relaxation of the NIH Guidelines, many point out, was predicated on the demonstration of safety in the laboratory procedures needed to handle rDNA organisms. But few have expressed concern about long-term adverse effects that might stem from the widespread use of these same organisms or, as we saw in Chapter 8, from their intentional release into the environment.

While presently not directly regulated, the biotechnology industry is nonetheless held to the common standards of practice that dictate behavior in other sectors of the economy. Thus, while the NIH Guidelines do not directly apply to industry (except by statute, and then only weakly in New York and Maryland), they nonetheless set the standard for product development to which the industry as a whole will be held accountable. However, the absence of direct regulation means that some of the products being developed could generate novel problems that would remain undetected by the present review system.

A case in point would be new genetically engineered crop lines used to supplant lineages of key cereal plants. The indirect consequences of such developments in the past have included the depletion of the diversity of germ lines and the increased risk of disease (as with the introduction of male sterility factor in corn). While it is true that past adverse effects are not inevitable, the absence of a forum for public discussion (as would be present if environmental impact assessments were routinely required) augurs badly for our ability to attract public input adequate to allow us to *anticipate*, and hopefully avoid, such problems.

Freedom of Inquiry

Many observers of the rDNA scene have expressed concern that the intense concentration of research in the private sector threatens freedom of inquiry in a basic way. University/corporate arrangements are now commonplace (see Appendix B), with varying degrees of restriction on the activities of institutions or its researchers. Some key industry spokespersons claim that these relationships have not compromised the free exchange of ideas and that they are unlikely to undercut free inquiry in this critical area of science.

Dr. David Martin, Jr., vice president and director of research at Genentech Corporation, stated that Genentech's university relations continued to be strong. Citing weekly seminars and a special university/industry liaison program, Martin believes that Genentech continues to serve the academic sector in an ongoing manner.[18]

Similarly, J. Leslie Glick, president of Genex Corporation, believes that the concentration of rDNA researchers in the private sector is unlikely to have an adverse effect on the free transfer of ideas. Except in those rare instances where covenants are drawn that include protection of research data as proprietary, or where extremely large grants are involved, Glick believes that none of the present arrangements impede the rapid expansion of knowledge in the rDNA field. As an example of a contractual arrangement favorable to the free flow of ideas, Glick cites the Hoechst arrangement with Massachusetts General Hospital (see below). Characterizing it as a bad business arrangement for Hoechst, Glick points out that except for the stipulation that some data be seen early, no impediments to the free publication of research ideas were likely.[19] Furthermore, the Hoechst arrangement for patenting and exclusive licensure were to be done in a manner that gave the university free use of any materials.

But even the seemingly innocuous requirement of an early look over the shoulder of a researcher, and prepublication review rights by the parent company, can have a chilling effect on free inquiry. Scientists have long relished the ability to study and challenge ideas freely. With the prospect of a "big brother" examination of research findings in advance of publication some of that freedom is inevitably lost. Would a Harvard scientist who had a choice between looking at the genotoxic effects of a Hoechst chemical and that of a competitor's really be free in his choice? And what if he wanted to discuss the findings with a colleague in advance of publication? Clearly, the one-to-three-month gag rule imposed by funding giants could stifle the free exchange of ideas so integral to scientific inquiry. Finally, who is to say that corporate interests will not be insinuated into the very choices of the research community for basic areas of research. Certainly, the reward for doing "relevant" work is implied by the extraordinarily "generous" grant in the first place. Hence the very choice of a problem could become skewed to match real or imagined corporate needs.

University/Corporate Relations

A closer look at the nature of this and other arrangements made between the corporate sector and academic institutions suggests a different picture. The Hoechst agreement with Massachusetts General Hospital and Harvard University was announced on May 21, 1981. Amounting to some $70 million, it made the front page that day of both the *New York Times* and the *Boston Globe*. Under the subsequent agreement, Hoechst was to give Massachusetts General Hospital $50 million for a ten-year research and development program in exchange for licensure to use all patents—and to train up to four Hoechst scientists at Harvard each year. As shown in Appendix B, it is the issue of patents that poses the most significant trade-off in these arrangements.

Ironically, it is precisely in the area of patenting where

the free flow of information is likely to be impeded. While the intent behind patenting inventions has always been to make the fruits of others' creative activities available to the public at large, the incentive to protect ideas as property has also prevailed.

An inventor has a one-year period of grace after research results are published in which to file for a United States patent. But certain peculiar aspects of patent law act to limit freedom of inquiry to a substantial degree. This is acutely true in obtaining patents under foreign laws. In a number of jurisdictions, patents must be filed *before* any formal publication is made. As Burke Zimmerman pointed out in his recent book, *Biofuture*,[20] biotechnology scientists are often frustrated in their wishes to exchange information freely at scientific meetings because of the constraints imposed by the rules of filing patents abroad.

In marked contrast to the public-spirited tone of NIH Director Don Fredrickson (see his correspondence with Cape, discussed above), the answer to this dilemma reached by the NIH was to facilitate rDNA patent applications without imposing an "undue burden on disclosure." In the *Federal Register* of January 13, 1977, the Commission of Patents and Trademarks issued a declaration of the intent to offer accelerated processing of patent applications for inventions in the rDNA field. Noting the "exceptional" importance of recombinant DNA and the desirability of prompt disclosure of developments, the assistant secretary for Science and Technology asked the patent commissioner to accord "special" status to patent applications involving recombinant DNA. By so doing, the NIH was encouraging the early publication of ideas while assuring their protection under foreign patenting conventions.

If the normal interval between initial filing and official recognition were collapsed, inventors could meet the requirement to make all inventions freely available to the public at the time their patent is issued without losing their proprietary rights in the product. At least this was the theory. In practice, patenting of rDNA-related inventions has had a different impact. In the period between 1976 and 1980, Fredrickson and other government officials expressed their concern over the intrinsic importance of assuring the rapid dissemination of research results. But by the time the fundamental issue of patenting new forms of life was resolved, the initial idealism of freedom of inquiry had been replaced by the realism of the marketplace.

Commenting on the traditional scientific incentive of "publish or perish," Roman Saliwanchik notes that the resulting peer recognition "is an ego trip that cannot be denied." For this reason, patent attorney Saliwanchik cautions "this very act of publishing rapidly can result in the irretrievable loss of valuable property rights" to both the scientist and employer.[21] In the legalisms of the trade, if an invention is published in a form that is an "enabling disclosure"—one that permits the reader to learn the process in question or to practice the invention—the secrecy of the invention is destroyed.

The possibility that scientists might inadvertently "destroy the secrecy of their ideas" (a strange way to think of the consequences of promulgating scientific ideas) leaves the inventor with few desirable options. According to Saliwanchik, the scientist may file for a patent in the United States within a year of publication of his results, but major foreign patent protection, as we have seen, is lost if publication precedes filing. This catch-22 leaves inventors who wish to protect their property rights with what Saliwanchik calls "some hard decisions early on." What advice does he give? In a phrase: hide the new information.

If the invention is one that the employer or scientist recognizes as a trade secret, Saliwanchik urges his readers not to publish their findings at all. If the invention lends itself to effective patenting, then the application should be filed before the invention is published.

This requirement, if widely followed, would slow the advance of science to a snail's pace, since almost every major biotechnological process is patentable. Thus, the extent to which scientists as a whole will see the work will depend in large part on where they practice their art. Increasing numbers are moving from the university to the private sector. And increasing numbers of universities are forging contracts with major corporations. In practical terms, this transition will lead to the very privatization of scientific ideas and research innovations decried by scientists around the world.[22] The movement of scientific knowledge from the public to the private sector may thus be detrimental in terms of the accessibility and accountability of scientific knowledge.

The answer to this unfortunate trend is clear. Reverse the decision to allow patenting of recombinant life forms and help make scientists aware of the potential conflicts they run when they contract with the private sector. As science correspondent Nicholas Wade so eloquently put it, "This journey of discovery can only be undertaken once, and it would be better undertaken by people who have no interest in anything other than discovering the truth, whose hands are clean, whose motives can never be criticized. . . . And if commercialization . . . ever starts to influence the scientist's primary goal . . . then the scientists themselves, I hope they will have the sense to put a halt to it."[23]

Secondary Effects

It is a truism that little is known about the secondary impacts of using this or any other new technology, particularly on a mass scale. Current public protections for new drugs or medical devices assure only that their development does not injure or harm the subjects of the *initial trials* to determine their safety and efficacy. This process expressly excludes review of second-order effects of development. The NIH Guidelines for Protection of Subjects of Biomedical Research proscribes research review committees from considering consequences to the public at large from widescale application of the invention or treatment modality under question.

Institutional Review Boards (IRBs) may *not* consider the secondary effects of a project on social, political, or other institutions. This means in practice that such committees must confine their considerations of risk and benefits to the human subjects in the immediate purview of the experimenter.[24] Take, for example, an experiment designed to test a recombinant-DNA-produced "immunotoxin" containing a potent toxic agent that simultaneously affords some promise of therapeutic benefit to a group of terminally ill patients and a risk for nefarious use. The committee might well approve it for the proximal use without being able to consider the long-term biological-warfare implications of its development. It appears that such a circumstance occurred during the course of IRB reviews of a Department of Defense project on the use of lethal radiation for terminally ill cancer patients at a Cincinnati hospital in 1974–1975. It seems that the DoD had an ulterior purpose—to study the effects of lethal radiation on the human body—but these aspects of the study were apparently not reflected in the materials reviewed by the IRB.

By the same token, implementation of some rDNA applications, even when they do not directly involve human subjects for their development, may lead to major environmental or public health sequelae. Under existing regulations, many such projects can be done without prior review if they are planned by the private sector or any non-NIH-affiliated university.

A case in point is the possibility generated by widescale

development of fructose as a sweetener in place of sucrose. Animal studies suggest that the wholesale substitution of fructose could plausibly accelerate the development of diabetes or diseases of arteries and arterioles.[25] Just such a massive project was begun by SoCal (Standard Oil of California) and Cetus, only to be abandoned some two years later because of financial considerations. Had it been successful, the Cetus project to produce pure fructose could have further displaced traditional reliance on other high-fructose corn sweeteners. Loss of beet-sugar refineries, such as the plant in Salinas, California, is a second-order effect of this technological invention.

In the Salinas instance, loss of the refinery led to disruption of social institutions, financial collapse of key support industries, and out-migration of many local inhabitants.

Given the literature cited above that suggests adverse effects of fructose in animals, it is possible that substantial inroads on human health could result from implementing a large-scale project to displace our reliance on varied carbohydrates. In fact, continuing interest in this project suggests that such second-order eventualities are still not being considered. However, there is an up side to this analysis.

As a result of Judge Sirica's ruling on the University of California at Berkeley's planned release of the ice-minus bacterium, it is now likely that the second-order effects of novel recombinant-DNA organisms released into the environment will begin to be considered. Bringing these discussions into more open forums is a necessary but not sufficient first step for ensuring that researchers will consider the long-term impact of their work. Such a step begins to address the issue of our obligations to future generations. In 1976, Daniel Callahan, director of the Hastings Center, described what would constitute a reasonable test of this principle. Researchers, he argued, should use their "moral imagination" in anticipating all the possible adverse effects of their work.[26] Callahan observed that the very power of the new recombinant-DNA technologies suggests the magnitude of the dilemmas they are capable of generating. Some measure of the likelihood of doing long-term harm must be factored into the short-term good that we must believe is the objective of most biotechnology firms.

Almost ten years after those remarks were written, it appears as if most recombinant-DNA scientists believe that they have exercised due caution, at least in protecting against laboratory-generated harm. But now, on the eve of the release of genetically engineered organisms into the environment at large, some scientists are showing signs of impatience. Many scientists, such as Paul Berg, believe that they have paid their dues. They do not want to run the same gauntlet of public accountability again. But that is exactly what the profession needs to do if the public is to be assured of protection from major dislocations as well as of benefits. As other philosophers have pointed out, while there is no moral imperative for scientific progress, there is one for not harming.[27]

In the simplest terms, this means that the burden of proof should not be on those who oppose research, but on those who want to see it go forward where the probability of substantial harm is greater than zero. The key, of course, is how much greater? We accept as a threshold for regulatory action a risk of one cancer death in a million from chronic exposure to toxic chemicals. Comparable risk estimates for long-term irreversible effects of recombinant-DNA experimentation are harder to come by.

Callahan suggests a marginal rule for scientific research in general and rDNA research in particular: "In those cases [where] there is a high probability, i.e., greater than 50% that the harm which would result from the basic (or applied) research would be of a magnitude such as to pose serious threats to human welfare . . . the research should not go forward at all."[28] What might count as a "serious threat to human welfare"? Callahan cites the instance of permanent and irreversible injury to the general public or the environment.

While it is unlikely that lines will be drawn with great precision for the limiting cases, there is a clear and primary moral obligation to consider the secondary impacts wherever large-scale use or the release of novel engineered organisms is planned. If we can guarantee the existence of a forum for addressing just these two issues—(1) that priorities would be set in keeping with human welfare, equity, and justice, and (2) that the consequences of major recombinant-DNA projects would be carefully weighed and anticipated before implementation—it is likely that this new technology will fulfill its promise with the greatest likelihood of public good over harm.

Notes

1. Harvey Price, testimony presented before the California State Assembly Committee on Economic Development and New Technologies Hearing on "The Future of the Biotechnology Industries in California," University of California, San Francisco, June 28, 1984.

2. Cited in T. M. Powledge, "Public Says Genetic Engineers Should Proceed Cautiously," *Bio/Technology* 1 (October 1983): 645–646.

3. W. Gaylin, "The Frankenstein Factor," *New England Journal of Medicine* 297 (1977): 324–326.

4. See in particular the articles by A. Luban, "Playing God with DNA," *New Times* 8 (January 7, 1977): 48–61; and S. Budiansky, "Churches Against Germ Changes," *Nature* 303 (1983): 563.

5. Letter from Donald Fredrickson, M.D., to Ronald Cape, September 7, 1976.

6. Ibid., p. 2.

7. Letter of Donald Fredrickson dated March 2, 1978, quoted in John Lear, *Recombinant DNA, The Untold Story* (New York: Crown, 1978), p. 237.

8. S. Krimsky, "Biotechnology and Unnatural Selection: The Social Control of Genes," in *Technology and Social Change in Rural Areas,* Gene F. Summers, ed. (Boulder, Colo.: Westview Press, 1983).

9. See, for example, S. N. Cohen, "Focus on Genetic Research," *San Francisco Examiner and Chronicle* (March 13, 1977), pp. 32 et seq.

10. David Baltimore, speaking on the NOVA program, "Life—Patent Pending," transcript from WGBH, Boston (WGBH Education Foundation, 1982), p. 24.

11. Telephone interview with Don Coomb, September 6, 1984. For the prevalence of parasitic diseases in the Third World see the Report of a WHO Expert Committee on "Parasitic Zoonoses," *WHO Technical Report Series* No. 637 (WHO, Geneva, 1979).

12. See J. L. Fox, "Columbia Awarded Biotechnology Patent," *Science* 221 (1983): 933.

13. Albert Gore, "Life—Patent Pending," p. 19.

14. Gilbert, "Life—Patent Pending," p. 18.

15. Permitting rDNA generated drugs to be given "orphan drug" status by the FDA. Such designation accelerates FDA's review process and provides tax credits to the manufacturer. In early 1984, the FDA gave Cooper Biomedical, Inc., a pharmaceutical company along with Zymos (now called Zymogenetics) and an unidentified producer orphan drug status for developing the AAP product discussed above. See "Gene-Splicing Protein to Have Orphan Drug Status," *Science* 223 (March 2, 1984): 914.

16. Roy Widdus, personal communication, February 9, 1984. The document will deal with the issues and priorities for new vaccine development in the biotechnology and drug industry generally, with an emphasis on public/private sector relations.

17. Jonathan King, "Life—Patent Pending," p. 22.

18. David Martin, Jr., interview, February 8, 1984.

19. J. Leslie Glick, interview, February 10, 1984.

20. B. Zimmerman, *Biofuture* (New York: Plenum Press, 1984).

21. R. Saliwanchik, *Legal Protection for Microbiological and Genetic Engineering Inventions* (Reading, Mass.: Addison-Wesley, 1982), p. 15.

22. See Frederickson letter to Cape on Sept. 7, 1976.

23. Nicholas Wade, "Life—Patent Pending," pp. 24–25.

24. The current regulations state: "The IRB should not consider the long-range effects of applying knowledge gained in the research . . . as among those research risks that fall within the purview of its responsibility." [45 *CFR* 46 (March 8, 1983) 46. 111(a)(2)].

25. See, for example, R. P. Booth-Handford and H. Heath, "The Effect of Dietary Fructose and Diabetes on the Rat Kidney," *British Journal of Experimental Pathology* 62 (1981): 398–404; see also A. M. Cohen, A. Teitelbaum, and E. Rosenmann, "Diabetes Following a High Fructose Diet," *Metabolism* 26 (1977): 17–21.

26. D. Callahan, "Ethical Responsibility in Science in the Face of Uncertain Consequence," *Annals of the New York Academy of Sciences* 265 (1976): 1–12.

27. See M. Lappé, "Moral Obligations and the Fallacies of Genetic Control," *Theological Studies* 33 (1972): 411–427.

28. Callahan, "Ethical Responsibility," p. 10.

Appendices

Appendix A
How Recombinant DNA Works

A gene contains sequences of deoxyribonucleic acid (DNA) composed of long arrays of "bases," the fundamental building blocks of DNA.[1] Each group of three bases represents the "code word" for an amino acid. A long stretch of these groups along the DNA molecule—less some repetitive sequences that are discarded along the way—determines the positions of amino acids along the length of a protein molecule. An average sized protein consists of some 400 amino acids and hence requires about 1,200 base pairs.

The DNA of any one cell contains the entire coded material needed for producing any gene product an organism uses. Usually, only a minute portion of that information is "called up" to be transcribed ultimately into a protein or polypeptide chain needed for a specific cell function. A classic example is the ability of only one small cell population, the islets of Langerhans of the pancreas, to make insulin. Recombinant DNA permits researchers to lift out the genes for making insulin or its precursor, "proinsulin," and put them into a bacterial cell where they will function to make a protein never before constructed in bacteria.

One useful way to visualize the process by which a protein is made by such a bacterium is to think of the chromosomal material that contains this genetic information as
a master computer tape. Indeed, the analogy to computer
processing is so close that those who originally deciphered
the code wrote about the "punctuation" of the code in the
language now familiar to basic computer buffs. Genes have
their "basic language," use "stop" and "start" signals, and
can be played over and over without being used up or
destroyed. Just as users of word processing equipment
make copies of their master discs, DNA replicates by making a complementary copy of itself based on the intrinsic

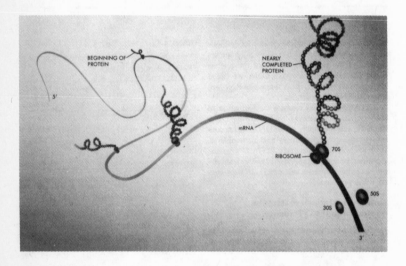

FIGURE A.1
The assembly of a protein molecule. Messenger RNA (mRNA)
carries genetic information from the DNA to the ribosomes,
where it is translated into the instructions for linking amino
acids into a polypeptide chain or protein. (*Source:* J. D. Watson,
J. Tooze, and D. T. Kurtz, *Recombinant DNA: A Short Course,*
New York: W.H. Freeman & Co., 1983. Used with permission.)

pairings of bases, adenine to thymine, guanine to cytosine.

Portions of this DNA master tape are usually brought out of the nucleus of higher organisms (and in bacteria placed directly into the cytoplasm) by a carrier molecule that is the cell's equivalent of a "working" disc. In the language of the gene, the working copy of DNA consists of another, shorter segment of nucleic acid called *messenger RNA* (mRNA).

Messenger RNA works as a template through which the cell's "software" translates the genetic instructions into a protein molecule. The three-base language of the messenger is read by individual "translator RNAs" that each carry an amino acid to special organelles in the cytoplasm called ribosomes for assembly into the protein. The stringing of amino acids into proteins is thus analogous to the assembly of chains of words into sentences. In fact, production of a final protein copy calls for the cell to "edit" out the redundant nonsense spacers in the messenger RNA, leaving the final message for translation into a protein. These steps are shown schematically in Figure A.1.

With the final molecular cues for reading the genetic code and assembling the often separate chains that make up a protein such as human insulin (see Figure A.2), the bacterial cell can be encouraged to make recombinant DNA–based proteins from almost any source.

The so-called *restriction enzymes* comprise a special group of chemicals that do the desired snipping and cutting of otherwise unwieldy lengths of DNA encountered in living organisms. (The first enzymes that would break down DNA, known as *nucleases,* lacked the ability to cleave nucleic acids at the same place each time they worked—a necessary precondition for getting consistent small fragments suitable for analysis.) We now know that each bacterial species has its own repertoire of enzymes capable of recognizing a broad spectrum of foreign DNA sequences but incapable of cleaving "self" DNA.

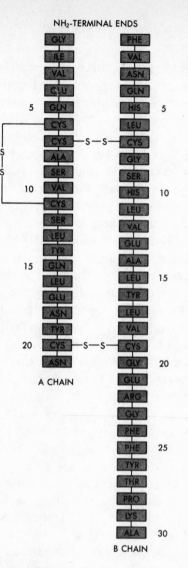

FIGURE A.2
The amino acid composition of insulin. The insulin
molecule has two amino acid chains linked by two
chemical bonds between sulfur atoms. (*Source:* J. D.
Watson, J. Tooze, and D. T. Kurtz, *Recombinant DNA:
A Short Course,* New York: W.H. Freeman & Co.,
1983. Used with permission.)

In 1970, the first restriction enzyme was isolated in the bacterium *Haemophilus influenzae* by Hamilton Smith of Johns Hopkins University. Smith and his colleagues called these enzymes "restriction" enzymes because they restricted the entry of foreign DNAs into bacterial cells. Each enzyme (and there are more than 250 now available) "recognizes" a certain sequence of four or six bases and breaks the DNA molecule at a specific point in that sequence (a representative group of these enzymes and their targeted base sequences are shown in Table A.1).

These microscopic scissors will thus reproducibly break any group of identical DNA molecules into similarly sized fragments for analysis. Conversely, where DNA chains differ in their composition at critical enzyme-recognition base sequences, the restriction enzyme will overlook that break point and produce fragments of longer length than in the other molecule.

The observation that DNA segments of different lengths can result from restriction-enzyme digestion of what were supposed to be identical DNAs sometimes gives a clue to the existence of unexpected gene mutations. Such mutations disturb the reading frame of a restriction enzyme and hence result in DNA fragments of different lengths (called restriction-fragment-length polymorphisms, or RFLPs). This abstract sounding feat is actually one of the most powerful recombinant-DNA techniques, having permitted researchers to discern the presence of the gene mutations responsible for major human diseases such as sickle-cell anemia, Huntington's chorea, and hemophilia (see Chapter 6 for a full discussion).

To make recombinant DNAs a functional reality requires the existence of a system that permits their insertion into suitable cells where the genes will operate and direct the synthesis of desired proteins. This system turned out to be based on small circular DNAs known as *plasmids* commonly occurring in parasites of bacteria. One such plasmid (known

Table A.1
Commonly Used Restriction Enzymes and the Sites of Their Cleavage Activities

Microorganism	Restriction Enzyme Abbreviation	Sequence Recognized $5' \to 3'$ / $3' \to 5'$
Bacillus amyloliquefaciens H	BamHl	G↓G A T C C C C T A G↑G
Brevibacterium albidum	Ball	T G G↓C C A A C C↑G G T
Escherichia coli RY13	EcoRI	G↓A A T T C C T T A A↑G
Haemophilus aegypticus	HaeII	Pu* G C G C↓Py* Py↑C G C G Pu
Haemophilus aegypticus	HaeIII	G G↓C C C C↑G G
Haemophilus haemolyticus	HbaI	G C G↓C C↑G C G
Haemophilus influenzae Rd	HindII	G T Py*↓Pu* A C C A Pu↑Py T G
Haemophilus influenzae Rd	HindIII	A↓A G C T T T T C G A↑A
Haemophilus parainfluenzae	HpaI	G T T↓A A C C A A↑T T G
Haemophilus parainfluenzae	HpaII	C↓C G G G G C↑C
Providencia stuartii 164	PstI	C T G C A↓G G↑A C G T C
Streptomyces albus G	SalI	G↓T C G A C C A G C T↑G
Xanthomonas oryzae	XorII	C G A T C↓G G↑C T A G C

Source: J. D. Watson, J. Tooze, and D. L. Kurtz, *Recombinant DNA: A Short Course* (New York: W.H. Freeman & Co., 1983), p. 59. Used with permission.

*Py = pyrimidine, i.e., cytosine or thymine; Pu = purine, i.e., adenine or guanine.

↓ = cleavage site.

as pSC101) was used in the first recombinant-DNA experiments by Stanley Cohen at Stanford University and Herb Boyer at UC San Francisco, which formed the basis for a patent on the basic rDNA technique. Other molecular forms of DNA, such as bacterial viruses called *phages* and *cosmids,* can also be used in recombinant-DNA work. Cosmids are specially constructed plasmids with sites that allow the insertion of longer lengths of DNA than are customarily used in naturally occurring plasmids.

A typical recombinant-DNA experiment involves five basic steps: (1) isolating or synthesizing a desired gene; (2) fusing or joining that gene with a carrier strand of DNA, usually a circular plasmid; (3) returning the "recombined" plasmid (hence the term *recombinant DNA*) to a suitable host cell; (4) putting the host cell in a controlled medium, typically in a small Petri dish, where only cells containing the "working copy" of the recombinant molecule will grow; and (5) isolating the desired protein from the medium that surrounds these cells.

In the 1970s, researchers commonly used a genetically "crippled" *E. coli* known as K12, which was unable to synthesize the essential amino acid tryptophan. The inserted plasmid, however, would carry just such a genetic capability. When the bacteria were put into a culture medium deficient in tryptophan, only those *E. coli* that carried the "genetic assist" from the tryptophan-coding plasmid would survive. The trick, of course, was to put the gene for tryptophan adjacent to the recombined gene sequence so that *both* gene products would be synthesized.

In typical *E. coli* hosts, the plasmid—and its tryptophan gene—may be replicated twenty to forty times. In conditions that encourage a plasmid to replicate, a plasmid may be duplicated up to two to three thousand times in a process known as *amplification.* As long as substantial quantities of tryptophan are required for the cells' survival, the bacterial host containing the greatest number of plasmids will preferentially survive and replicate. Once the foreign gene products are also produced, properly assembled, and released into the culture media, the researcher need only purify the desired protein from the other cell products and supporting chemicals present.

In efforts to isolate rat insulin, it was possible to force an *E. coli* host to secrete a long protein containing both a bacterial product (beta lactamase) *and* the precursor for the desired insulin molecule (rat proinsulin). Researchers then used a simple enzymatic technique to cut the protein at the appropriate junction to split off the β-lactamase from the insulin precursor, leaving a functional insulin molecule (see Figure A.3).

Yeast cells are increasingly replacing bacteria as preferred hosts. Yeasts have the advantage of not needing to be broken or "lysed" to get out desired proteins. Hence, they release fewer potential contaminants such as fever-inducing pyrogens to the external medium than do bacteria like *E. coli*. Yeasts can also withstand the higher hydrostatic pressures that may develop in large-scale reaction vessels. They also have the advantage over *E. coli* of being less likely to lose the desired gene sequence and then outgrow the cells producing the specified product. For these and related reasons, yeasts have been successfully used to produce interferon and hepatitis B vaccine proteins, substances that they readily excrete into the culture medium.

FIGURE A.3 *(opposite)*
The use of an active bacterial promotor (for the beta lactamase gene) to produce animal insulin. The resultant hybrid molecule is then enzymatically cleaved to leave the proinsulin residue. (*Source:* J. D. Watson, J. Tooze, and D. T. Kurtz, *Recombinant DNA: A Short Course*, New York: W.H. Freeman & Co., 1983. Used with permission.)

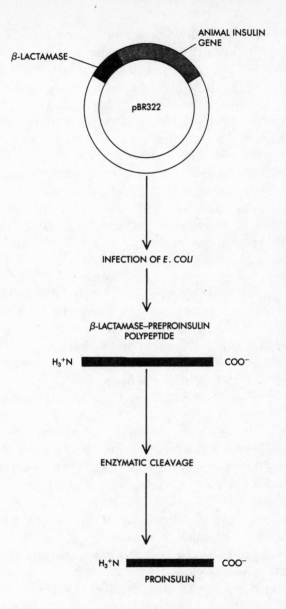

The key to getting yeasts—or any other micro-organism—to produce foreign proteins appears to reside in splicing in the proper base sequence that signals the host to start synthesizing the desired protein. This signal is called a *promotor,* or promoting sequence. In 1983, great progress was made in identifying ideal and possibly "universal" promotor signals. Promotor sequences are characteristically spliced in with other cues that induce the host cell to assemble, release, and secrete appropriate versions of foreign proteins. Some of these other cuing sequences include so-called *expression, selection,* and *maintenance* base-sequence instructions. These instructions permit a researcher to control precisely what new genetic change will be incorporated within a microorganism and to "reprogram" the organism to synthesize virtually any known biological molecule.

By knowing a specific sequence of bases along a DNA or mRNA molecule, researchers can predict what the amino acid sequence of a synthesized protein ought to look like—without necessarily having that protein in hand. Conversely, if researchers know the sequence of amino acids in a protein, they can "decode" what the original DNA molecule must have been by working backwards amino acid by amino acid and deducing from each the three-base code. Thus, if researchers wished to assemble a hypothetical protein with a particular amino acid structure, they could design and synthesize a DNA molecule "made to fit" that structure with special synthesizing kits. (These kits, along with all necessary reagents, are now widely available.)

Researchers can also work backwards from any protein preparation of reasonable purity to uncover its original genetic instructions. The trick lies in picking apart the protein's amino acid sequence one molecule at a time. Highly sophisticated machinery now permits researchers to do just that with quantities of purified proteins measured in micrograms. Once they know the sequence of amino acids, the researchers can use the genetic code in reverse to establish the actual sequence of bases that must have been used to make the protein. They can then give this sequence to a DNA synthesizer, which will construct the specific length of DNA specified by the code.

While not inexpensive (a recent brochure prices a DNA synthesizer at $29,000), the existence of this technique permits a bench scientist with an unknown protein in hand to decode it and construct the length of DNA that will make more of it. This synthetic DNA can be spliced into a length of naturally occurring DNA in any of the suitable host/vector organisms to make the desired protein molecule per cell.

Note

1. An excellent source for the science of recombinant DNA is J. D. Watson, J. Tooze, and D. T. Kurtz, *Recombinant DNA: A Short Course* (New York: W.H. Freeman & Co., 1983).

Appendix B
University/Industrial Agreements for rDNA or Related Research* 1974–1984

Date	Partners	Nature of Agreement	Size of Agreement	Conditions	Source
1. Feb. 1974	Harvard Medical School†/Monsanto	Production of TAF substance	$23 million	N.A.‡	*Science*, 2/25/77 (p. 759)
2. May 1981	Mass. General Hospital/Hoechst	R&D in rDNA; train scientists (4/yr)	$50 million (10 yrs.)	Hoechst license to use patents	*NY Times*, 5/21/81 (pp. A1, B15)
3. June 1981	Harvard Medical School†/DuPont	Basic genetics research	$6 million	Harvard has patent, licensing rights	*Boston Globe*, 6/21/81 (pp. 1, 29)
4. June 1981	University of S. Florida/Southern Biotech	Basic research	$63,600	N.A.	*Science*, 6/4/81 (p. 1080)
5. July 1981	MIT†/Whitehead Foundation	Establish institute	$125 million	N.A.	*Boston Globe*, 7/8/81 (pp. 1, 20)
6. July 1981	Michigan State University/Neogen	Develop parasite i.d. kit and related work	$455,000	Michigan to hold patent	*Comm. Biotech.* (*Commercial Biotechnology*), *OTA*, 1984 (p. 516)

	University/Company	Purpose	Amount	Rights	Source
7. Oct. 1981	Washington University/Mallinckrodt	Monoclonal antibody for cancer diagnosis	$3.88 million	Mallinckrodt has exclusive licensing rights	*Jrl. Comm.*, 10/16/81 (p. 10a)
8. Oct. 1981	Stanford University and University of Calif./Engenics	Create rDNA production procedures; process development; establish new businesses	$18 million	N.A.	*NY Times*, 10/16/81 (p. A18)
9. Jan. 1982	Mass. General Hospital/Genex	Hypertension research	N.A.	N.A.	*Bioscience*, 1/82 (p. 70)
10. Feb. 1982	Yale/Celanese	Enzyme research	$1.1 million (3 yrs.)	Celanese has exclusive patent rights	*Chem. Week*, 2/24/82 (p. 31)
11. Feb. 1982	Johns Hopkins University/Hybritech	Test antibodies made at Johns Hopkins	$1 million/yr	N.A.	*Chronicle of Higher Education*, 2/24/82, (p. 10)
12. March 1982	University College (London)/Sandoz	Create new research institute	$6 million	N.A.	*Nature*, 3/4/82 (p. 4)
13. April 1982	Imperial College/Imperial Biotech	Establish new company with venture capital	$6 million	N.A.	*Nature*, 4/1/82 (p. 384)

*Compiled with the assistance of Charles Weiner, MIT.
†Universities on record as encouraging nonexclusive licensing of patent rights (Pajaro Dunes Conference).
‡N.A. signifies "not available."

Appendix B (continued)

Date	Partners	Nature of Agreement	Size of Agreement	Conditions	Source
14. April 1982	Washington University/Monsanto	Monoclonal AB research	$23.5 million	N.A.	*Nature*, 4/1/82 (p. 384)
15. April 1982	Rockefeller Institute/Monsanto	Plant molecular biology research	$4 million	N.A.	*Science*, 4/16/82 (p. 277)
16. April 1982	University College/Endorphin	Develop and produce pancreatic endorphin	$240,000	N.A.	*Nature*, 4/15/82 (p. 595)
17. May 1982	Cold Spring Harbor/Exxon	Train scientists at Cold Spring Harbor	$7.5 million	N.A.	*Nature*, 5/20/82 (p. 175)
18. May 1982	Stanford/Syntex/ Hewlett-Packard	Consult via medical faculty	$3 million	N.A.	*Science*, 5/28/82 (p. 961)
19. May 1982	Stanford University and University of California, Berkeley/Engenics	Establish biotechnology research center	$2 million	N.A.	*Science*, 5/28/82 (p. 960)
20. June 1982	Washington University/Monsanto	Monoclonal antibody research	$1.8 million	N.A.	*Nature*, 6/17/82 (p. 529)

#	Date	Parties	Subject	Amount	Terms	Source
21.	Aug. 1982	Leicester University/British consortium of five companies	Yeast research	N.A.	N.A.	*New Science*, 8/19/82 (p. 706)
22.	July 1982	Johns Hopkins University/American Cyanimid	Treatment for lung and allergy disease	$2.5 million	N.A.	*Chemical & Engineering News*, 7/26/82 (p. 31)
23.	July 1982	University of Minnesota/Genetics International	Biotechnology research	$5 million	Genetics International to receive patent rights	*Chronicle of Higher Education*, 7/28/82 (p. 8)
24.	Aug. 1982	MIT†/W.R. Grace	Amino acid-enzyme R&D	$6–8.5 million	Grace gets all licensing rights to patents	*Chemical & Engineering News*, 8/9/82 (p. 5)
25.	Oct. 1982	Carnegie-Mellon University/PPG Industries	Product and process development	N.A.	PPG to transfer instrumentation to Carnegie-Mellon	*Chemical & Engineering News*, 10/4/82 (p. 4)
26.	Oct. 1982	Uppsala/AB Fortia	Development of industrial applications	$36 million	Use of university as industrial base permitted	*European Chemical*, 10/18/82 (p. 2)
27.	Oct. 1982	Yale/Bristol-Myers	Development of anticancer drugs	$3 million	Bristol gets exclusive marketing license	*Chronicle of Higher Education*, 10/27/82 (p. 8)

Appendix B (*continued*)

Date	Partners	Nature of Agreement	Size of Agreement	Conditions	Source
28. Nov. 1982	University of Sheffield/Plant Science	Development of plant culturing techniques	N.A.	N.A.	*Ag. Spl. Ind.,* (*Agriculture Specialties Industries*), 11/12/82 (p. 2)
29. Nov. 1982	University of Wisconsin/Cetus Madison (Agricetus)	Biotechnology R&D	$3 million	University of Wisconsin to acquire minority position in Cetus	*Biotechnology News Watch,* 11/15/82 (p. 1)
30. Jan. 10, 1983	McGill University/Allelix (Ontario)	Nitrogen-fixation studies	$2.2 million	N.A.	*Chemical Industry Report,* 1/10/83 (p. 3)
31. Sept. 19, 1983	Columbia University/Bristol-Myers	Basic research program	$2.3 million	Patents to be in Columbia's name; Columbia to own intellectual property; Bristol-Myers has first rights to patent	*Chemical Engineering,* 9/19/83 (pp. 19–20)
32. June 1, 1984	U.C. San Francisco†/Chiron	AIDS virus research	N.A.	UC may receive royalties on AIDS products; patent rights under negotiation	*San Francisco Chronicle,* 12/5/84 (pp. C-1, C-6)

Appendix C
U.S. Companies Commercializing Biotechnology and Their Product Markets*

Company and Date Founded	Commercial Application of R&D
1. Abbott Laboratories	Ph†
2. Actagen (1982)	Ph
3. Advanced Biotechnology Associates, Inc. (1981)	Ph
4. Advanced Genetic Systems, Inc. (1979)	PA
5. Advanced Genetics Research Institute (1981)	AA
6. Advanced Mineral Technologies, Inc. (1982)	Env
7. Agrigenetics Corp. (1975)	PA, SCF
8. Allied Chemical Corp.	PA
9. Alpha Therapeutic Corp.	Ph
10. Ambico, Inc. (1974)	AA
11. American Cyanamid Co.	Ph, PA, AA
12. American Diagnostics Corp. (1979)	Ph
13. American Qualex (1981)	Ph, AA
14. Amgen (1980)	Ph, PA, AA
15. Angenics (1980)	Ph
16. Animal Vaccine Research Corp. (1982)	AA
17. Antibodies, Inc. (1960)	Ph, AA
18. Applied DNA Systems, Inc. (1982)	Ph, SCF, CCE, Env
19. Applied Genetics, Inc. (1981)	AA
20. ARCO Plant Cell Research Institute	PA
21. Atlantic Antibodies (1973)	AA
22. Axonics	Ph

Source: Office of Technology Assessment (Washington D.C.: U.S. Government Printing Office), 1984.

*Does not include support firms.

†Abbreviations: *Ph:* Pharmaceuticals; *PA:* Plant Agriculture; *AA:* Animal Agriculture; *SCF:* Specialty Chemicals and Food; *CCE:* Commodity Chemicals and Energy; *Env:* Environmental (microbial-enchanced oil recovery, microbial mining, pollution control, and toxic-waste treatment); *El:* Electronics.

Appendix C *(continued)*

Company and Date Founded	Commercial Application of R&D
23. Baxter-Travenol Laboratories, Inc.	Ph
24. Becton Dickinson & Co.	Ph
25. Bethesda Research Laboratories, Inc. (1976)	Ph, AA
26. Biocell Technology Corp. (1980)	Ph
27. Biochem Technology, Inc. (1977)	Bioprocessing
28. Bio-con, Inc. (1971)	AA
29. BioGenex Laboratories (1981)	Ph
30. Biogen, Inc. (1980)	Ph, AA, C
31. Biological Energy Corp. (1981)	CCE, SC
32. Bio Response, Inc. (1972)	Mass cell culture
33. Biotech Research Laboratories, Inc. (1973)	Ph, CCE
34. Biotechnica International, Inc. (1981)	PA, CCE, SCF, Env, AA, Ph
35. Bio-technology General Corp. (1980)	PA, AA, Ph
36. Brain Research (1968)	Ph
37. Bristol-Myers Co.	Ph
38. BTC Diagnostic, Inc. (1980)	Ph
39. Calgene, Inc. (1980)	PA
40. California Biotechnology, Inc. (1982)	Ph, AA
41. Cambridge Bioscience Corp. (1982)	Ph, AA
42. Campbell Institute for Research and Technology	PA
43. Celanese Corp.	CCE
44. Cellorgan International, Inc. (1972)	Ph
45. Celtek, Inc. (1980)	Ph
46. Centaur Genetics Corp. (1981)	Ph, PA
47. Centocor (1979)	Ph
48. Cetus Corp. (1971)	Ph, AA, CCE
Madison (Agricetus) (1981)	PA
Palo Alto (1980)	Ph
Immune (1980)	Ph
49. Chiron Corp. (1981)	Ph, AA
50. Ciba-Geigy	Ph
51. Clonal Research (1970)	Ph
52. Codon (1980)	CCE
53. Collaborative Research, Inc. (1979)	Ph, SCF
54. Collagen, Inc. (1977)	Ph

Company and Date Founded	Commercial Application of R&D
55. Cooper Diagnostics, Inc.	Ph
56. Cooper-Lipotech, Inc. (1981)	Ph
57. Corning Glass Works	SCF
58. Crop Genetics International (1981)	PA
59. Cutter Laboratories, Inc.	Ph
60. Cytogen Corp. (1981)	Ph
61. Cytox Corp. (1975)	Env
62. Damon Biotech, Inc. (1981)	Ph
63. Dairyland Foods Corp.	SCF
64. Dart and Kraft, Inc.	SCF
65. Davy McKee Corp.	Bioprocessing
66. DeKalb Pfizer Genetics (1982)	AA
67. Diagnon Corp. (1981)	Ph
68. Diagnostic Technology, Inc. (1980)	Ph
69. Diamond Laboratories	AA
70. Diamond Shamrock Corp.	AA, CCE
71. DNA Plant Technology (1981)	PA
72. DNAX Corp.	Ph
73. Dow Chemical Co.	Ph, PA, CCE, SCF, AA, Env
74. Ean-tech, Inc. (1982)	El, Env, Ph
75. Eastman Kodak Co.	Ph, Env
76. Ecogen (1983)	PA
77. E.I. du Pont de Nemours & Co., Inc.	Ph, PA, CCE, SCF
78. Electro Necleonics Laboratories, Inc.	Ph
79. Eli Lilly & Co.	Ph, PA
80. EnBio, Inc. (1975)	Bioprocessing
81. Endorphin, Inc. (1982)	Ph
82. Engenics, Inc. (1981)	Bioprocessing
83. Enzo Biochem, Inc. (1976)	Ph, AA, CCE, SCF, PA
84. Enzyme Bio-systems, Ltd.	SCF
85. Enzyme Center, Inc.	SCF
86. Enzyme Technology Corp.	SCF
87. Ethyl Corp.	CCE, SCF, Env

†Abbreviations: *Ph:* Pharmaceuticals; *PA:* Plant Agriculture; *AA:* Animal Agriculture; *SCF:* Specialty Chemicals and Food; *CCE:* Commodity Chemicals and Energy; *Env:* Environmental (microbial-enhanced oil recovery, microbial mining, pollution control, and toxic-waste treatment); *El:* Electronics.

Appendix C *(continued)*

Company and Date Founded	Commercial Application of R&D
88. Exxon Research & Engineering Co.	CCE, Env, SCF
89. Fermentec Corp. (1978)	Bioprocessing
90. FMC Corp.	Ph
91. Frito-Lay, Inc.	PA
92. Fungal Genetics, Inc. (1982)	Ph, SCF
93. Genencor (1982)	SCF, CCE
94. Genentech, Inc. (1976)	Ph, AA, CCE, El
95. General Electric Co.	El, Env, Ph, SCF
96. General Foods Corp.	PA
97. General Genetics (1982)	Ph
98. General Molecular Applications (1981)	Ph
99. Genetic Diagnostics Corp. (1981)	Ph
100. Genetic Replication Technologies, Inc. (1980)	Ph, AA
101. Genetic Systems Corp. (1980)	Ph
102. Genetics Institute (1980)	Ph, PA, SCF, Env
103. Genetics International, Inc. (1980)	AA, Ph, SCF, CCE, Env, El
104. Genex Corp. (1977)	Ph, AA, SCF, Env
105. Gentronix Laboratories, Inc. (1972)	El
106. Genzyme (1981)	SCF
107. W.R. Grace & Co.	AA, SCF, Env, PA, Ph
108. Hana Biologics, Inc. (1978)	Ph
109. Hem Research (1966)	Ph, AA
110. Hoffmann-La Roche, Inc.	Ph
111. Hybridoma Sciences, Inc. (1981)	Ph
112. Hybritech, Inc. (1978)	Ph
113. Hytech Biomedical, Inc. (1981)	El, Ph
114. IBM Corp.	El
115. IGI Biotechnology, Inc. (1975)	Ph
116. Immulok, Inc. (1980)	Ph
117. Immunetech, Inc. (1981)	Ph
118. Immunex Corp. (1981)	Ph
119. Immuno Modulators Laboratories, Inc. (1982)	Ph
120. Immunogen (1981)	Ph
121. Immunotech Corp. (1980)	Ph

Company and Date Founded	Commercial Application of R&D
122. Imreg, Inc.	Ph
123. Indiana BioLab (1972)	PA, AA, SCF, CCE
124. Integrated Genetics, Inc. (1981)	Ph
125. Interferon Sciences, Inc. (1980)	Ph
126. International Genetic Engineering, Inc. (Ingene) (1980)	Ph, PA, CCE
127. International Genetic Sciences Partnership (1981)	PA, AA
128. International Minerals & Chemical Corp.	AA, PA, Env, CCE
129. International Plant Research Institute (IPR) (1978)	PA
130. Kallestad Laboratories, Inc.	Ph
131. Kennecott Copper Corp.	Env
132. Lederle Laboratories	Ph, AA
133. Liposome Co., Inc. (1981)	Ph, AA
134. Liposome Technology, Inc. (1981)	Ph, AA
135. Litton Bionetics	Ph
136. 3M Co.	Ph
137. Mallinckrodt, Inc.	Ph
138. Martin Marietta	SCF, PA
139. Meloy Laboratories, Inc.	Ph
140. Merck & Company, Inc.	Ph, AA
141. Microlife Genetics (1981)	SCF, Env
142. Miles Laboratories, Inc.	Ph, SCF, CCE, AA
143. Miller Brewing Co.	PA
144. Molecular Biosystems, Inc. (1980)	Ph
145. Molecular Diagnostics (1981)	Ph
146. Molecular Genetics, Inc. (1979)	Ph, PA, AA
147. Monoclonal Antibodies, Inc. (1979)	Ph, AA
148. Monsanto Co.	PA, AA
149. Multivac, Inc.	Ph, PA, AA, SCF
150. Nabisco, Inc.	PA
151. National Distillers & Chemical Co.	CCE
152. NPI (1973)	PA, CCE, SCF
153. Neogen Corp. (1981)	PA, AA

†Abbreviations: *Ph:* Pharmaceuticals; *PA:* Plant Agriculture; *AA:* Animal Agriculture; *SCF:* Specialty Chemicals and Food; *CCE:* Commodity Chemicals and Energy; *Env:* Environmental (microbial-enhanced oil recovery, microbial mining, pollution control, and toxic-waste treatment); *El:* Electronics.

Appendix C *(continued)*

Company and Date Founded	Commercial Application of R&D
154. New England Biolabs	Ph
155. New England Monoclonal Resources (1982)	Ph
156. New England Nuclear Corp.	Ph
157. Norden Laboratories	AA
158. Novo Laboratories, Inc.	Ph, SCF
159. Nuclear & Genetic Technology, Inc. (1980)	Ph
160. Ocean Genetics (1981)	SCF
161. Oncogen (1982)	Ph
162. Oncogene Science, Inc. (1983)	Ph
163. Organon, Inc.	Ph
164. Ortho Pharmaceutical Corp.	Ph
165. Petrogen, Inc. (1980)	Env
166. Pfizer, Inc.	Ph, PA, CCE, AA, SCF, Env
167. Phillips Petroleum Co.	Env, SCF, CCE
168. Phytogen (1980)	PA
169. Phyto-Tech Lab	PA
170. Pioneer Hybrid International Corp.	PA
171. Plant Genetics, Inc. (1981)	PA
172. Polybac Corp.	Ph, SCF, Env
173. PPG Industries	SCF
174. Purification Engineering, Inc.	Bioprocessing
175. Quidel Home (1982)	Ph
176. Replicon (1982)	Ph, SCF
177. Repligen Corp. (1981)	Ph, AA, CCE, SCF
178. Ribi Immunochem Research, Inc. (1981)	AA, Ph
179. Rohm & Haas	PA
180. Salk Institute of Biotechnology/Industrial Associates, Inc. (1981)	Ph, AA, CCE
181. Sandoz, Inc.	Ph, PA, AA
182. Schering-Plough Corp.	Ph, AA
183. SDS Biotech Corp. (1983)	AA
184. G.D. Searle & Co.	Ph, SCF
185. Serono Laboratories, Inc.	Ph
186. SmithKline Beckman	Ph, AA
187. E.R. Squibb & Sons, Inc.	Ph

Company and Date Founded	Commercial Application of R&D
188. A.E. Staley Manufacturing Co.	AA, PA, SCF
189. Standard Oil of California	Env
190. Standard Oil of Indiana	Ph, PA
191. Standard Oil of Ohio	PA
192. Stauffer Chemical Co.	PA
193. Summa Medical Corp.	Ph
194. Sungene Technologies Corp. (1981)	PA
195. Sybron Biochemical	Env
196. Synbiotex Corp. (1982)	Ph, AA
197. Syncor International	Ph
198. Synergen (1981)	AA, SCF, CCE, Env
199. Syngene Products and Research, Inc.	AA
200. Syntex Corp.	Ph, AA
201. Syntro Corp.	AA, CCE
202. Syva Co. (1966)	Ph
203. Techniclone International Corp. (1982)	Ph
204. Unigene Laboratories, Inc. (1980)	Ph, AA
205. Universal Foods Corp.	SCF, PA
206. University Genetics Co. (1980) Genetic Clinics	Ph
207. U.O.P., Inc.	SCF, CCE
208. The Upjohn Co.	Ph, AA, Pa
209. Viral Genetics (1981)	Ph
210. Wellcome Research Laboratories	Ph
211. Worne Biotechnology, Inc. (1982)	PA, CCE, Ph, AA, Env, SCF
212. Xenogen, Inc. (1981)	Ph, PA
213. Xoma Corp. (1981)	Ph
214. Zoecon Corp. (1968)	PA, AA
215. Zymed Laboratories	SCF, CCE
216. Zymos Corp. (1982)	Ph, SCF

†Abbreviations: *Ph:* Pharmaceuticals; *PA:* Plant Agriculture; *AA:* Animal Agriculture; *SCF:* Specialty Chemicals and Food; *CCE:* Commodity Chemicals and Energy; *Env:* Environmental (microbial-enhanced oil recovery, microbial mining, pollution control, and toxic-waste treatment); *El:* Electronics.

Appendix D
Some Proteins with Possible Pharmaceutical Applications Being Developed with Recombinant-DNA Technology

Class/Substance	Function	Project Sponsors	Applications
HUMAN GROWTH REGULATORS			
Growth hormone (GH)	Promotes growth	Genentech (U.S.)/Kabigen AB (Sweden)/UCSF/Eli Lilly (U.S.)	Growth promotion: healing burns, fractures, cachexia (severe weight loss)
Somatostatin	Inhibits growth-hormone secretion	UCSF/Genentech	Adjunct to insulin
Somotomedins	Mediates action of growth hormone	Chiron (U.S.)	Growth-promotion regulation
Growth-hormone-releasing factor (GRF)	Increases pituitary growth-hormone release	Salk Institute (U.S.)	Growth promotion

CALCIUM REGULATORS			
Calcitonin	Inhibits bone resorption	Genentech/Amgen (U.S.)	Bone-disease therapy
Parathyroid hormone (PTH)	Mobilizes calcium: prevents calcitonin excretion	Massachusetts General Hospital	Osteoporosis therapy, calcium metabolism
REPRODUCTIVE HORMONES			
Luteinizing hormone (LH)	Females: induces ovulation Males: stimulates androgen secretion	Integrated Genetics (U.S.)/Serono Labs (Italy)	Antifertility
Follicle-stimulating hormone (FSH)	Induces ovarian growth	Integrated Genetics/Serono Labs	Reproductive services
Human chorionic gonadotrophin (HCG)	Like LH; more potent	Integrated Genetics/Serono Labs	Pregnancy testing
Relaxin	Dilation of birth canal, relaxation of uterus	Genentech	Soften bone/connective tissue of reproductive tract; antiarthritic (?)

Appendix D (continued)

Class/Substance	Function	Project Sponsors	Applications
NEUROACTIVE PEPTIDES			
β-ENDORPHIN	ANALGESIA	AMGEN, OTHERS (U.S.)	ANALGESIA
ENKEPHALINS	ANALGESIA	AMGEN, OTHERS	ANALGESIA
PANCREATIC ENDORPHIN	UNDETERMINED	ENDORPHIN, INC.	ANALGESIA, PARTICULARLY IN CHILDBIRTH
LYMPHOKINES AND IMMUNOACTIVE PEPTIDES (OTHER THAN INTERFERONS)			
Interleukin-2	Promotes T-cell growth activity	Ajinomoto Co. (Japan) Japanese Cancer Institute Immunex (U.S.) Cetus (U.S.) Chiron (U.S.) Genex (U.S.) Biogen (U.S.) Genetics Institute (U.S.) Interferon Sciences (U.S.) Quidel (U.S.)	Maintain T-cell cultures: immunotherapy

Thymosin (fraction 5)	Promotes maturation of bone marrow cells, T-cell differentiation	George Washington University	Immunodeficiency diseases
Thymosin (alpha 1)	Promotes T-helper and T-amplifier functions	Hoffmann-La Roche (Switz.)	Systemic lupus erythmatosis; other immune disorders
Thymic hormone factor (THF)	Promotes T-helper and T-functions	N.A.	Antiviral protection in immunosuppressed patients
Thymic factor (TFX)	Restores delayed-type hypersensitivity	N.A.	Cancer treatment
Thymopoletins	Inhibits B-cell differentiation	Ortho Pharms (U.S.)	Reversing immuno-deficiencies
Macrophage inhibitory factor (MIF)	Inhibits macrophage migration	Denki Kagaku (Japan)	Immunotherapy

RESPIRATORY SYSTEM REGULATORS

Alpha-1-antitrypsin	Prevents destruction of alveolar walls by elastase	Zymos Corp. (U.S.)/Cooper Laboratories (U.S.)	Emphysema treatment

Appendix E
Basic Techniques
of Plant Genetic Engineering

The potential for genetically engineering the higher plants has come from controlling organisms that themselves have solved the problem. The key breakthrough was the discovery that plants are commonly "genetically engineered" in nature in much the same way that bacterial chromosomes can be integrated with the DNAs of viruses. In the case of plants, a common soil bacterium, *Agrobacterium tumefaciens,* inserts foreign genes that then produce proteins totally outside the genetic repertoire of the plant itself.

The history of this discovery dates to 1907, when two researchers at the U.S. Department of Agriculture—Erwin F. Smith and C. O. Townsend—discovered that a growth called a *crown gall* would occur at the site of a fresh wound that was exposed to *A. tumefaciens.* In 1947, Armin C. Braun, of the Rockefeller Institute for Medical Research, succeeded in cultivating *A. tumefaciens*-transformed plant cells in tissue culture, demonstrating their capacity for unlimited growth. The crown gall was in fact a tumor. As such, it was fascinating, because it contained within it—in embryonic form—all the possible plant tissues—leaflets, rootlets, and even miniature sex organs.

What is unique about this tumor is not that it is caused by a bacterium, but that it is caused by a piece of DNA carried outside the bacterium's own genetic material. This parasite on a parasite includes the so-called *Ti* (for tumor-inducing) plasmid. This bit of circular DNA has evolved an evolutionary strategy for survival that depends on hitchhiking with the infecting bacterium into plant cells. Once inside the plant cell, the bacterium releases the plasmid. A part of the plasmid called the *T-DNA genes* ("T" for tumor) in turn links up with the genetic material of the plant-cell nucleus. Once in association with the plant's chromosomes, the *Ti* plasmid genes somehow trigger the plant's infected cells to divide rapidly, becoming a new crown gall (See Figure E.1)

Why the bacterium should countenance the presence of the extra genes represented by a *Ti* plasmid is the key to the mystery of the hitchhiking-parasitic DNA. The *Ti* plasmid not only interlaces its own DNA with that of a plant cell, but forces the plant cell to make foodstuffs for the bacterium. These foodstuffs are novel metabolites of chemicals called *opines*.

By another evolutionary trick, the *Ti* plasmids are also geared to respond to the presence of opines by proliferating rapidly and hence infecting still more of the invading *Agrobacteria*. In provoking a tremendous proliferation of just those embryonic plant cells that the bacterium finds most amenable to infect, the plasmid ensures living room for its own survival and simultaneously creates the crown gall tumor.

Almost eighty years elapsed between the USDA's pioneering studies and the stroke of brilliant insight that signaled the beginning of a scientific revolution. For years, botanists despaired of finding a way to genetically engineer plant tissues. By introducing novel DNA sequences into a plant's DNA, this microscopic bit of infectious DNA can be said to be the first plant genetic engineer. In fact, the *Ti* plasmid is today the only successful way we know of to routinely move genes into higher plants. (While some viruses such as the caulimoviruses may offer significant promise, they are not now useful in the way that the *Ti* system is.[1])

Scientists broke the final barrier to doing plant genetic engineering by discovering how to put *additional* DNA into the *Ti* plasmid. Although the *Ti* plasmid was recognized for its ability to integrate with plant DNA in 1977, researchers were unable to grow a genetically engineered species into mature plants or to produce functional products until 1981. The reasons for this failure were traced to hormonal im-

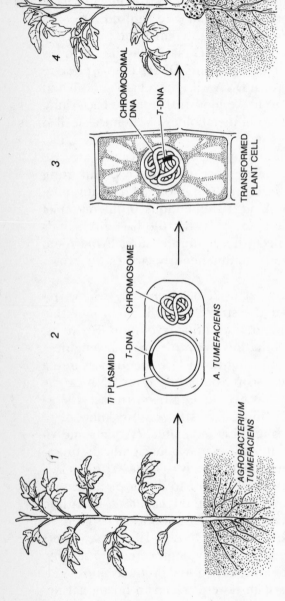

FIGURE E.1

Production of a crown gall tumor by infection with *Agrobacterium tumefaciens*. Tumor is initiated when bacteria enter a lesion, which is usually near the crown of the plant (the juncture of root and stem), and attach themselves to cells (*1*). A virulent bacterium carries, in addition to its chromosomal DNA, a *Ti* plasmid (*2*). The plasmid's *T*-DNA is introduced into a cell and becomes integrated into the cell's chromosomal DNA (*3*). Trans-

formed cells proliferate to form a crown gall tumor (*4*). The tumor cells synthesize compounds called opines, which serve as nutrients for *A. tumefaciens* cells inhabiting the gall. Two well-studied opines are octopine and nopaline. The *Ti* plasmid carried by a given strain of the bacterium induces synthesis of a given opine. (*Source:* Mary-Dell Chilton, "A Vector for Introducing New Genes into Plants," *Scientific American* 248 [1983]. Copyright W.H. Freeman & Co. Used with permission.)

balances produced when T-DNA infected a plant cell. By simply deleting the T-DNA genes responsible for this imbalance, researchers can "disarm" the *Ti* plasmid so that transformed infected cells can regenerate into whole plants.

By the end of 1982, the genes for at least three foreign proteins had been successfully introduced into plant cells, including one from a bacterium, one from a mammalian cell, and one from a plant. But only the last was successfully expressed by the *Ti*-infected host tumor cells. It was only in May 1983 that a group of British researchers reported how to use the genes in the *Ti* plasmid to direct the "promotion" of gene sequences in tobacco cells so that gene products would be fully expressed in the cells' descendants.[2]

It is now possible to use the *Ti* plasmid to introduce various forms of DNA into plant cells that can survive through the regeneration and sexual maturation of the host plant.[3] When the genetic engineering is particularly successful, the introduced DNA will be incorporated into the plants' own seeds, making it possible to propagate genetically engineered DNA. In this way, researchers can create new plant lines that stably express the chosen characteristics.

A second major approach that is less specific and more labor intensive involves the direct addition of DNA preparations to developing plant embryos at critical periods after pollination. This technique has the major advantage of permitting the selection of such polygenic traits as modulation.[4] Championed by the Chinese, the addition of exogenous DNA to cotton embryos has already permitted the selection of genetically altered and more vigorous crop lines.[5]

A third approach relies on the direct manipulation of chromosomes to induce polyploidy or parthenogenesis and thereby fix desirable traits.[6] Together, these three techniques comprise the opening moves of a still incomplete—and vital—new science of plant genetic engineering.

Notes

1. R. Hull and J. W. Davies, "Genetic Engineering with Plant Viruses and Their Potential as Vectors," *Advances in Virus Research* 28 (1983): 1–29.

2. L. Herrara-Estrella, A. Depicker, M. Von Montagu, and J. Schell, Expression of Chimeric Genes Transferred into Plant Cells Using a *Ti*-Plasmid-derived Vector," *Nature* 303 (1983): 209–213.

3. K. A. Barton and Mary-Dell Chilton, "*Agrobacterium* Ti Plasmids as Vectors for Plant Genetic Engineering," *Methods in Enzymology* 101 (1983): Part C, 527–539.

4. F. B. Holl and D. J. Olson, "The Effect of Exogenous DNA on the Nodulation of a Nonnodulating Line of *Pisum sativum L.*," *Euphytica* 32 (1983): 171–176.

5. G. Y. Zhov, J. Weng, Y. Zeng, et al., "Introduction of Exogenous DNA into Cotton Embryos," *Methods in Enzymology* 101 (1983): Part C, 433–481.

6. C. E. Purdom, "Genetic Engineering by the Manipulation of Chromosomes," *Aquaculture* 33 (1983): 287–300.

Glossary

Accession: In biotechnology, the addition of germ plasm deposits to existing germ plasm storage banks.

Amino acids: The building blocks of proteins. There are twenty common amino acids.

Amino acid sequence: The linear order of amino acids in a protein.

Amplification: In rDNA research, the process by which the production of multiple copies of a genetic sequence is encouraged in a host cell.

Antibiotic: A specific chemical substance that fights infections, usually bacterial infections, in humans or animals. Many antibiotics are produced by using microorganisms; others are produced synthetically.

Antibody: A protein called an immunoglobulin produced by animals in response to exposure to a specific antigen and characterized by specific reactivity with its complementary antigen. (See also *Monoclonal antibodies.*)

Antigen: A substance, usually a protein or carbohydrate, which, when introduced into the body of a human or higher animal, stimulates the production of an antibody that will react specifically with it.

Source: Adapted from U.S. Congress, Office of Technology Assessment, *Commercial Biotechnology* (Washington, D.C.: U.S. Government Printing Office, 1984), pp. 588–597.

Antihemophilic factor (AHF): The fraction of whole blood that contains blood-clotting agents. AHF is used to treat hemophilia, a set of hereditary disorders that prevent blood clotting.

Antimicrobial agent: See *Antibiotic.*

Applied research: Research to gain knowledge or understanding necessary for determining the means by which a recognized and specific need may be met. (This is the National Science Foundation definition.)

Attenuated vaccine: Whole pathogenic organisms that are treated with chemical, radioactive, or other means to render them incapable of producing a serious infection. Attenuated vaccines are given orally or injected into the body, which then produces protective antibodies against them to protect against disease.

Avirulent: Incapable of producing serious disease. (Syn.: Nonvirulent; see also *Virulent; Pathogenic.*)

Baccillus subtilis (B. subtilis): An aerobic bacterium used as a host in rDNA experiments.

Bacteria: Any of a large group of microscopic organisms having round, rodlike, spiral, or filamentous unicellular or noncellular bodies that are often aggregated into colonies, are enclosed by a cell wall or membrane, and lack fully differentiated nuclei. Bacteria may exist as free-living organisms in soil, water, or organic matter, or as parasites in the live bodies of plants and animals.

Bacteriophage (or phage)/bacterial virus: A virus that multiplies in bacteria. Bacteriophage lambda is commonly used as a vector in rDNA experiments.

Base: In DNA, one of the four purines and pyrimidines that make up the interior of the DNA molecule: adenine, thymine, guanine or cytosine. (See *Nucleotide base.*)

Basic research: Research to gain fuller knowledge or understanding of the fundamental aspects of phenomena and of observable facts without specific applications to processes or products in mind.

Batch processing: A method of bioprocessing in which a bioreactor is loaded with raw materials and microorganisms, and the process is run to completion, at which time products are removed. (Compare with *Continuous processing*.)

Biocatalyst: An enzyme that plays a fundamental role in living organisms or in industrial activities by activating or accelerating a chemical process.

Biochemical: Characterized by, produced by, or involving chemical reactions in living organisms.

Bioconversion: A chemical conversion using a biocatalyst.

Biodegradation: The breakdown of substances by living organisms.

Biological response modifier: The generic term for hormones, neuroactive compounds, and immunoactive compounds that act at the cellular level; many are possible targets for production with biotechnology.

Biological-warfare agents: Biological products or processes that are determined to be useful in military applications and whose export is restricted for national security reasons.

Biologics: Vaccines, therapeutic serums, toxoids, antitoxins, and analogous biological products used to induce immunity to infectious diseases or harmful substances of biological origin.

Biomass: All organic matter that grows by the photosynthetic conversion of solar energy.

Bioprocess: Any process that uses complete living cells or their components (e.g., enzymes, chloroplasts) to produce substances of commercial or scientific interest.

Bioreactor: A vessel in which a bioprocess takes place.

Biosynthesis: Production, by synthesis or degradation, of a chemical compound by a living organism.

Biotechnology: Commerical techniques that use living organisms or substances from those organisms to make or modify a product, including techniques used for the improvement of the characteristics of economically important plants and animals and for the development of microorganisms to act on the environment. Specifically, "new" biotechnology, which means the use of novel biological techniques—recombinant-DNA techniques; cell-fusion techniques, especially for the production of monoclonal antibodies; and new bioprocesses for commercial production. (This is the Office of Technology Assessment definition.)

Catalysis: A modification, especially an increase, in the rate of a chemical reaction induced by a material (e.g., an enzyme) that is chemically unchanged at the end of the reaction.

Catalyst: A substance that induces catalysis; an agent that enables a chemical reaction to proceed under milder conditions (e.g., at a lower temperature) than otherwise possible. Biological catalysts are enzymes; some nonbiological catalysts are metallic complexes, particularly platinum.

Cell: The smallest structural unit of living matter capable of functioning independently; a microscopic mass of protoplasm surrounded by a semipermeable membrane, usually containing one or more nuclei and various nonliving products. Capable of performing all the fundamental functions of life alone or in interaction with other cells.

Cell culture: The growth of cells, usually obtained from multicellular organisms, in glass or plastic containers.

Cell differentiation: The process whereby descendants of a common parental cell achieve and maintain a specialized structure and function.

Cell fusion: The formation of a single hybrid cell containing nuclei and cytoplasm from different cells.

Cell line: Cells that acquire the ability to multiply indefinitely in vitro.

Cellulase: The enzyme that digests cellulose to sugars.

Cellulose: A polymer of six-carbon sugars found in all plant matter; the most abundant biological compound on earth.

Chakrabarty decision: *Diamond* v. *Chakrabarty,* U.S. Department of Commerce, PTA, sec. 2105, 1980. A landmark case in which a majority of the U.S. Supreme Court held that the inventor of a new microorganism, whose invention otherwise met the legal requirements for obtaining a patent, could not be denied a patent solely because the invention was alive.

Chloroplasts: Cellular organelles where photosynthesis occurs.

Chromatography: A process of separating gases, liquids, or solids in a mixture or solution by adsorption as the mixture or solution flows over the absorbent medium, often in a column. The substances are separated because of their differing chemical interactions with and rates of migration through the absorbent medium.

Chromosomes: The rodlike structures of a cell's nucleus that contain genes and store and transmit genetic information. Chromosomes are composed mostly of DNA and protein and contain most of the cell's DNA. Each species has a characteristic number of chromosomes.

Clinical trial: The testing of a drug in humans as one of the final stages in the collection of data for drug approval.

Clone: A group of genetically identical cells or organisms produced asexually from a single cell that serves as a common ancestor or source of a donor nucleus.

Cloning: The amplification of particular segments of DNA, usually genes, in a suitable host organism.

Coding sequence: The region of a gene's DNA that encodes the amino acid sequence of a protein.

Commodity chemicals: Chemicals produced in large volumes that sell for less than $1 per pound (50¢ per kg). (Compare with *Specialty chemicals.*)

Complementary DNA (cDNA): DNA that is complementary to messenger RNA; used for cloning or as a probe in DNA hybridization studies.

Compulsory licensing: Laws that require the licensing of patents, presumably to ensure early application of a technology and to diffuse control over a technology.

Continuous processing: A method of bioprocessing in which raw materials are supplied and products are removed continuously, at volumetrically equal rates. (Compare with *Batch processing.*)

Corporate venture capital: Capital provided by major corporations exclusively for high-risk investments.

Culture deposits: See *Accession.*

Culture medium: Any nutrient system for the artificial cultivation of bacteria or other cells; usually a complex mixture of organic and inorganic materials.

Cytoplasm: The portion of a cell outside of and surrounding the nucleus.

Deoxyribonucleic acid (DNA): A linear polymer, made up of deoxyribonucleotide-repeating units, which is the carrier of genetic information; present in chromosomes and chromosomal material of cell organelles such as mitochondria and chloroplasts as well as some viruses. The genetic material found in all living organisms. Every inherited characteristic has its origin somewhere in the code of each individual's DNA.

Diagnostic products: Products that recognize molecules associated with disease or other biologic conditions and are used to diagnose these conditions.

Dicots (dicotyledons): Plants with two first-embryonic leaves and nonparallel veined mature leaves. Examples are soybeans and most flowering plants. (Compare with *Monocots.*)

Disclosure requirements: A patent requirement for adequate public disclosure of an invention that enables other people to build and use the invention without "undue" experimentation.

DNA: Deoxyribonucleic acid.

DNA base pair: A pair of DNA nucleotide bases. Nucleotide bases pair across the double helix in a very specific way: adenine can only pair with thymine; cytosine can only pair with guanine.

DNA probe: A sequence of DNA that is used to detect the presence of a particular nucleotide sequence.

DNA sequence: The order of nucleotide bases in the DNA helix; the DNA sequence is essential to the storage of genetic information.

DNA synthesis: The synthesis of DNA in the laboratory by the sequential addition of nucleotide bases.

Downstream processing: After bioconversion, the purification and separation of the product.

Drug: Any chemical compound that may be administered to humans or animals as an aid in the treatment of disease.

Enablement requirement: A patent requirement for adequate public disclosure of an invention, enabling others in the relevant field of technology to build and use the invention.

Enzyme: Any of a group of catalytic proteins that are produced by living cells and that mediate and promote the chemical processes of life without themselves being altered or destroyed.

Equity investment: An investment made in a company in exchange for a part ownership in that company.

Escherichia coli (E. coli): A species of bacteria that inhabits the intestinal tract of most vertebrates. Some strains are pathogenic to humans and animals. Many non-pathogenic strains are used experimentally as hosts for rDNA.

Eukaryote: A cell or organism with membrane-bound, structurally discrete nuclei and well-developed cell organelles. Eukaryotes include all organisms except viruses, bacteria, and blue-green algae. (Compare with *Prokaryote.*)

Fatty acids: Organic acids with long carbon chains. Fatty acids are abundant in cell membranes and are widely used as industrial emulsifiers.

Feedstocks: Raw materials used for the production of chemicals.

Fermentation: An anaerobic bioprocess is used in various industrial processes for the manufacture of products such as alcohols, acids, and cheese by the action of yeasts, molds, and bacteria.

Fibrinolytic agents: Blood-borne compounds that activate fibrin to dissolve blood clots.

Food additive (or food ingredient): A substance that becomes a component of food or affects the characteristics of food and, as such, is regulated by the U.S. Food and Drug Administration.

Foot-and-mouth disease: A highly contagious virus disease of cattle, pigs, sheep, and goats characterized by fever, salivation, and formation of vesicles in the mouth and pharynx and on the feet; it is transmissible to humans. (Syn.: Hoof-and-mouth disease.)

Fractionation (of blood): Separation of blood by centrifugation, resulting in components sold as plasma, serum albumin, antihemophilic factor, and other products.

Free-living organisms: Organisms that do not depend on other organisms for survival.

Fungus: Any of a major group of saprophytic and parasitic plants that lack chlorophyll, including molds, rusts, mildews, smuts, and mushrooms.

Gamete: The male or female haploid cell, e.g., the egg or sperm.

Gametocyte: The cell of the gamete stage of the life cycle of a parasite, e.g., *Plasmodium vivax*.

Gamma globulin (GG): A protein component of blood that contains antibodies and confers passive immunity.

Gene: The basic unit of heredity; an ordered sequence of nucleotide bases composing a segment of DNA. A gene contains the sequence of DNA that encodes one polypeptide chain (via RNA).

Gene amplification: In biotechnology, an increase in gene number for a certain protein permitting the protein to be produced at elevated levels.

Gene expression: The mechanism whereby the genetic directions in any particular cell are decoded and processed into the final functioning product, usually a protein. (See also *Transcription* and *Translation*.)

Gene transfer: The use of genetic or physical manipulation to introduce foreign genes into host cells to achieve desired characteristics in progeny.

Genome: The genetic endowment of an organism or individual.

Genus: A taxonomic category that includes groups of closely related species.

Germ cell: The male and female reproductive cells—egg and sperm. (See *Gamete.*)

Germ plasm: The total genetic variability available to a species.

Glucose: A six-carbon sugar molecule used as a basic energy source by the cells of most organisms.

Glycoproteins: Proteins with attached sugar groups.

Growth hormone (GH): A group of peptides involved in regulating growth in higher animals.

Helminth: A parasitic worm.

Herbicide: An agent (e.g., a chemical) used to destroy or inhibit plant growth; specifically, a selective weed killer that is not injurious to crop plants.

Hormone: A chemical messenger found in the circulation of higher organisms that transmits regulatory messages to cells.

Host: A cell whose metabolism is used for growth and reproduction of a virus, plasmid, or other form of foreign DNa.

Host/vector system: Compatible combinations of host (e.g., bacterium) and vector (e.g., plasmid) that allow stable introduction of foreign DNA into cells.

Human chorionic gonadotropin (HCG): A hormone produced by human placenta, indicating pregnancy; widespread target of MAb developers to diagnose pregnancy at an early stage.

Human Growth Hormone (HGH): A hormone produced by the pituitary gland that stimulates growth.

Human Insulin: A hormone that stimulates cell growth via glucose uptake by cells. Insulin deficiency leads to diabetes.

Human Serum Albumin (HSA): An abundant protein in human blood; as a product, used mostly in medicine, primarily in burn, trauma, and shock patients.

Hybrid: The offspring of genetically dissimilar parents (e.g., a new variety of plant or animal that results from the cross-breeding of two different existing varieties, or a cell derived from two different cultured cell lines that have fused).

Hybridization: The act or process of producing hybrids.

Hybridoma: The product of fusion between a myeloma cell (which divides continuously in culture and is "immortal") and a specifically primed lymphocyte (antibody-producing cell); the resulting cell grows in culture and produces monoclonal antibodies.

Hybridoma technology: See *Monoclonal antibody technology.*

Immune response: The reaction of an organism to invasion by a foreign substance. Immune responses are often complex, and may involve the production of antibodies from special cells (lymphocytes or plasma cells), as well as the removal of the foreign substance by other cells.

Immunoassay: The use of antibodies to identify and quantify substances being measured; often followed by tracers such as radioisotopes.

Immunogenic: Capable of causing an immune response. (See also *Antigen.*)

Immunotoxin: A molecule attached to an antibody capable of killing cells that display the antigen to which the antibody binds.

Interferons: A class of glycoproteins (proteins with sugar groups attached at specific locations) important in immune function and thought to inhibit viral infections.

In vitro: Literally, "in glass"; pertaining to a biological reaction taking place in an artificial apparatus. Sometimes refers to the growth of cells from multicellular organisms under cell-culture conditions. In vitro diagnostic products are products used to diagnose disease outside of the body after a sample has been taken from the body.

In vivo: Literally, "in life"; pertaining to a biological reaction taking place in a living cell or organism. In vivo products are used within the body.

Joint venture: A form of association of separate business entities that falls short of a formal merger but unites certain agreed on resources of each entity for a limited purpose; in practice most joint ventures are partnerships.

Leaching: The removal of a soluble compound such as an ore from a solid mixture by washing or percolating.

Lignin: A major component of wood.

Lignocellulose: The composition of woody biomass, including lignin and cellulose.

Lipids: A large, varied class of water-insoluble organic molecules; includes steroids, fatty acids, prostaglandins, terpenes, and waxes.

Liposome transfer: The process of enclosing biological compounds inside a lipid membrane and allowing the complex to be taken up by a cell.

Lymphocytes: Specialized white blood cells involved in the immune response; B lymphocytes produce antibodies.

Lymphokines: Proteins that mediate interactions among lymphocytes and are vital to proper immune function.

MAb: Abbreviation for monoclonal antibody.

Medical devices: Instruments or apparatuses (including in vitro reagents such as MAbs) intended for use in the diagnosis or treatment of a disease or other condition and that do not achieve their intended purposes through chemical action within or on the body.

Merozoite: The stage in the life cycle of the malaria parasite when it divides and is released from red blood cells.

Messenger RNA (mRNA): RNA that serves as the template for protein synthesis; it carries the transcribed genetic code from the DNA to the protein-synthesizing complex to direct protein synthesis.

Metabolism: The physical and chemical processes by which foodstuffs are synthesized into complex elements, complex substances are transformed into simple ones, and energy is made available for use by an organism.

Metabolite: A product of metabolism.

Metallothioneins: Proteins, found in higher organisms, which have a high affinity for heavy metals.

Methanogens: Bacteria that produce methane as a metabolic product.

Microencapsulation: The process of surrounding cells with a permeable membrane.

Microorganisms: Microscopic living entities; microorganisms can be viruses, prokaryotes (e.g., bacteria), or eukaryotes (e.g., fungi).

Mixed culture: Culture containing two or more types of microorganisms.

Molecule: A group of atoms held together by chemical forces; the smallest unit of matter that can exist by itself and retain its chemical identity.

Monoclonal antibodies (MAbs): Homogeneous antibodies derived from single clones of cells; MAbs recognize only one chemical structure. MAbs are useful in a variety of industrial and medical capacities since they are easily produced in large quantities and have remarkable specificity.

Monoclonal antibody technology: The use of hybridomas that produce monoclonal antibodies for a variety of purposes. Hybridomas are maintained in cell culture or, on a larger scale, as tumors (ascites) in mice or ruminants (cows).

Monocots (monocotyledons): Plants with single first-embryonic leaves, parallel-veined leaves, and simple stems and roots. Examples are cereal grains such as corn, wheat, rye, barley, and rice.

Multigenic: A trait specified by several genes. (Syn.: Polygenic.)

Mutagen: An agent that causes mutation.

Mutagenesis: The induction of mutation in the genetic material of an organism; researchers may use physical or chemical means to cause mutations that improve the production of capabilities of organisms.

Mutant: An organism with one or more DNA mutations, making its genetic function or structure different from that of a corresponding wild-type organism.

Mutation: A change in a DNA sequence usually at the level of a nucleotide base.

Myeloma: An antibody-producing tumor.

Myeloma cell line: Myeloma cells established in culture.

Neurotransmitters: Small molecules found at nerve junctions that transmit signals across those junctions.

New biotechnology firms (NBFs): Companies formed after 1976 whose functions are research, development, and production using biotechnological means.

NIH Guidelines: Guidelines established by the U.S. National Institutes of Health to regulate the safety of NIH-funded research involving recombinant DNA.

Nitrate: A compound characterized by an NO_3 group. Sodium nitrate and potassium nitrate are used as fertilizers.

Nitrogen fixation: The conversion of atmospheric nitrogen gas to a chemically combined form, ammonia (NH_3), which is essential to growth. Only a limited number of microorganisms can fix nitrogen.

Nodule: The anatomical part of a plant root in which nitrogen-fixing bacteria are maintained in a symbiotic relationship with the plant.

Nucleic acids: Macromolecules composed of sequences of nucleotide bases. There are two kinds of nucleic acids: DNA, which contains the sugar deoxyribose, and RNA, which contains the sugar ribose.

Nucleotide base: A structural unit of nucleic acid. The bases present in DNA are adenine, cytosine, guanine, and thymine. In RNA, uracil substitutes for thymine.

Nucleus: A relatively large spherical body inside a cell that contains the chromosomes.

Oligonucleotides: Short segments of DNA or RNA.

Organelle: A specialized part of a cell that conducts certain functions. Examples are nuclei, chloroplasts, and mitochrondria, which contain most of the genetic material, conduct photosynthesis, and provide energy, respectively.

Organic compounds: Molecules that contain carbon.

Organic micropollutants: Low-molecular-weight organic compounds considered hazardous to humans or the environment.

Passive immunity: Disease resistance in a person or animal due to the injection of antibodies from another person or animal. Passive immunity is usually short-lasting.

Patent: A limited property right granted to inventors by government allowing the inventor of a new invention the right to exclude all others from making, using, or selling the invention unless specifically approved by the inventor, for a specified time period in return for full disclosure by the inventor about the invention.

Pathogen: A disease-producing agent, usually restricted to a living agent such as a bacterium or virus.

Pathogenic: Capable of producing disease.

Peptide: A linear polymer of amino acids. A polymer of numerous amino acids is called a polypeptide. Polypeptides may be grouped by function—for example, "neuroactive" polypeptides.

pH: A measure of the acidity or basicity of a solution on a scale of 0 (acidic) to 14 (basic). For example, lemon juice has a pH of 2.2 (acidic), water has a pH of 7.0 (neutral), and a solution of baking soda has a pH of 8.5 (basic).

Pharmaceuticals: Products intended for use in humans, as well as in vitro applications to humans, including drugs, vaccines, diagnostics, and biological-response modifiers.

Photosynthesis: The reaction carried out by plants whereby carbon dioxide from the atmosphere is fixed into sugars in the presence of sunlight; the transformation of solar energy into biological energy.

Plant Patent Act of 1930 (35 U.S.C. §5161-164): Confers exclusive license for seventeen years on the developer of new and distinct asexually produced varieties other than tuber-propagated plants.

Plant Variety Protection Act of 1970 (7 U.S.C. §2321): Provides patentlike protection to new plants reproduced sexually.

Plasma: The liquid (noncellular) fraction of blood. In vertebrates, contains many important proteins (e.g., fibrinogen, responsible for clotting).

Plasmid: An extrachromosomal, self-replicating, circular segment of DNA; plasmids (and some viruses) are used as "vectors" for cloning DNA in bacterial "host" cells.

Polymer: A linear or branched molecule of repeating subunits.

Polypeptide: A long peptide consisting of amino acids.

Polysaccharide: A polymer of sugars.

Probe: See *DNA probe*.

Proinsulin: A precursor protein of insulin that yields insulin when enzymatically or chemically shortened.

Prokaryote: A cell or organism lacking membrane-bound, structurally discrete nuclei and organelles. Prokaryotes include bacteria and the blue-green algae. (Compare with *Eukaryote*.)

Promoter: A DNA sequence in front of a gene that controls the initiation of transcription (see below).

Propagation: The development of a whole plant in vitro from a small aggregate of cells.

Prophylaxis: Disease prevention.

Protease: Protein-digesting enzyme.

Protein: A polypeptide consisting of amino acids. In their biologically active states, proteins function as catalysts in metabolism and, to some extent, as structural elements of cells and tissues.

Protoplast fusion: The joining of two cells in the laboratory to achieve desired results, such as increased viability of antibiotic-producing cells.

Protozoa: A diverse phylum of eukaryotic microorganisms; structure varies from simple single cells to colonial forms; nutrition may be phagotrophic or autotrophic; some protozoa are pathogenic.

Public offering: The Securities and Exchange Commission approved sale of company stock to the public.

Pyrogenicity: The tendency for some bacterial cells or parts of cells to cause inflammatory reactions in the body, which may detract from their usefulness as pharmaceutical products. A pyrogen elevates the host's basal temperature.

Reagent: A substance that takes part in a chemical reaction.

Recombinant DNA (rDNA): The hybrid DNA produced by joining pieces of DNA from different organisms together in vitro.

Recombinant-DNA technology: The use of recombinant DNA for a specific purpose, such as the formation of a product or the study of a gene.

Recombination: Formation of a new association of genes or DNA sequences from different parental origins.

Regeneration: The laboratory process of growing a whole plant from a single cell or small clump of cells. (See *Propagation*.)

Regulatory sequence: A DNA sequence involved in regulating the expression of a gene.

Replication: The synthesis of new DNA from existing DNA and the formation of new cells by cell division.

Resistance gene: A gene that provides resistance to an environmental stress such as an antibiotic, herbicide or other chemical compound.

Restriction enzymes: Bacterial enzymes that cut DNA at specific DNA sequences.

RNA: Ribonucleic acid. (See also *Messenger RNA*.)

Scale-up: The transition of a process from an experimental scale to an industrial scale.

Selection: A laboratory process by which cells or organisms are chosen for specific characteristics.

Single-cell protein: Cells or protein extracts from microorganisms grown in large quantities for use as human or animal protein supplements.

Slimes: Aggregations of microbial cells that pose environmental and industrial problems; may be amenable to biologic control.

Sludge: Precipitated solid matter produced by water and sewage treatment or industrial problems; may be amenable to biologic control.

Specialty chemicals: Chemicals, usually produced in small volumes, which sell for more than $1 per pound (50¢ per kg). (Compare with *Commodity chemicals.*)

Species: A taxonomic subdivision of a genus. A group of closely related, morphologically similar individuals that actually or potentially interbreed.

Sporozoite: The stage in the life cycle of the malarial parasite when it leaves the mosquito's intestinal tract and enters its saliva.

Starch: A polymer of glucose molecules used by some organisms as a means of energy storage; starch is broken down by enzymes (amylases) to yield glucose, which can be used as a feedstock for chemical or energy production.

Steroid: A group of organic compounds, some of which act as hormones to stimulate cell growth in higher animals and humans.

Storage protein genes: Genes coding for the major proteins found in plant seeds.

Strain: A group of organisms of the same species having distinctive characteristics but not usually considered a separate breed or variety. A genetically homogenous population of organisms at a subspecies level that can be differentiated by a biochemical, pathogenic, or other taxonomic feature.

Substrate: A substance acted upon, for example, by an enzyme.

Subunit vaccine: A vaccine that contains only portions of a surface molecule of a pathogen. Subunit vaccines can be prepared by using rDNA technology to produce all or part of the surface protein molecule or by artificial (chemical) synthesis of short peptides. (See *Vaccine.*)

Symbiont: An organism living in symbiosis, usually the smaller member of a symbiotic pair of dissimilar size.

Symbiosis: The living together of two dissimilar organisms in a mutually beneficial relationship.

T-DNA: Transfer DNA; that part of the *Ti* plasmid that is transferred to the plant chromosome.

Technology transfer: The movement of technical information and/or materials from one sector to another to produce a product or process; most often refers to the flow of information between public and private sectors or between countries.

Therapeutics: Pharmaceutical products used in the treatment of disease.

Thermophilic: Heat loving. Usually refers to microorganisms that are capable of surviving at elevated temperatures, a capability that may make them compatible with industrial biotechnology schemes.

Thrombolytic enzymes: Enzymes such as streptokinase and urokinase that initiate the dissolution of blood clots.

Thrombosis: The blockage of blood vessels.

Ti **plasmid:** A plasmid from *Agrobacterium tumefaciens* used as a plant vector.

Totipotency: The capacity of a higher-organism cell to differentiate into an entire organism. A totipotent cell contains all the genetic information necessary for complete development.

Toxicity: The ability of a substance to produce a harmful effect on an organism by physical contact, ingestion, or inhalation.

Toxin: A subtance, in some cases produced by disease-causing microorganisms, that is toxic to other living organisms.

Toxoid: A detoxified toxin with its antigenic properties intact.

Trade secret: An invention used continuously by its holder in his or her business to maintain a competitive edge over competitors who do not know or use it. Trade secrets are often used instead of patents to protect production information.

Transcription: The synthesis of messenger RNA on a DNA template; the resulting RNA sequence is complementary to the DNA sequence. This is the first step in gene expression. (See also *Translation.*)

Transformation: The introduction into a cell of new genetic information via naked DNA.

Translation: The process in which the genetic code contained in the nucleotide base sequence of messenger RNA directs the synthesis of a specific order of amino acids to produce a protein. This is the second step in gene expression. (See also *Transcription.*)

Transposable element: A segment of DNA that moves from one location to another among or within chromosomes in what is possibly a predetermined fashion, causing genetic change; may be useful as a vector for manipulating DNA.

Trihalomethanes (THMs): Organic micropollutants and potential carcinogens consisting of three halide elements attached to a single carbon atom; they may be biologically destroyed during water purification. THMs include chloro- and bromoforms.

Turbid: Thick or opaque with matter in suspension.

Vaccine: A suspension of attenuated or killed bacteria or viruses, or portions thereof, injected to produce active immunity. (See also *Subunit vaccine.*)

Vector: A DNA molecule used to introduce foreign DNA into host cells. Vectors include plasmids, bacteriophages (viruses), and other forms of DNA. A vector must be capable of replicating autonomously and must have cloning sites for the introduction of foreign DNA.

Venture capital (venture capital funds): Money invested in companies associated with a high level of risk.

Virulent: A condition of a virus or bacterium capable of producing serious illness or death when introduced into an organism.

Virus: Any of a large group of submicroscopic agents infecting plants, animals, and bacteria and unable to reproduce outside the tissues of the host. A fully formed virus consists of nucleic acid (DNA or RNA) surrounded by a protein or protein and lipid coat.

Volatile organic compounds (VOCs): A group of toxic compounds found in ground water that pose environmental hazards; biologically destructible during water purification.

Wild-type: The most frequently encountered phenotype in natural breeding populations.

Yeast: A fungus of the family Saccharomycetacea used especially in the making of alcoholic liquors and as leavening in baking. Yeasts are also commonly used in bioprocesses.

Index